Judgment, Rhetoric, and the
Problem of Incommensurability

Studies in Rhetoric/Communication
Thomas W. Benson, Series Editor

Judgment, Rhetoric, and the Problem of Incommensurability

RECALLING PRACTICAL WISDOM

Nola J. Heidlebaugh

University of South Carolina Press

UNIVERSITY OF SOUTH CAROLINA *BICENTENNIAL*

© 2001 University of South Carolina

Published in Columbia, South Carolina, by the
University of South Carolina Press

Manufactured in the United States of America

05 04 03 02 01   5 4 3 2 1

Library of Congress Cataloging-in-Publication Data

Heidlebaugh, Nola J., 1949–
  Judgment, rhetoric, and the problem of incommensurability : recalling practical wisdom /
Nola J. Heidlebaugh.
    p. cm. — (Studies in rhetoric/communication)
  Includes bibliographical references and index.
  ISBN 1-57003-400-1 (alk. paper)
  1. Reasoning. 2. Judgment (Logic) 3. Rhetoric—Philosophy. 4. Comparison (Philosophy)
I. Title. II. Series.
BC181 .H45 2001
160—dc21   2001000371

For my daughter Katy
and in memory of my sister Kathryn

Contents

Series Editor's Preface

In *Judgment, Rhetoric, and the Problem of Incommensurability,* Professor Nola Heidlebaugh asks how, in an age dubious of religious or rational authority, it might be possible to discuss the issues about which we disagree most fundamentally. We disagree, writes Heidlebaugh, not only about the issues but also about the rules of argument that might compel us to agree about how to judge the debate. Heidlebaugh suggests that at least part of the answer might be found in early Greek rhetoric, which described forms of judgment that are directed to the production of novel ideas. For, she writes, the mode of judgment adopted by a person who assumes the obligation to participate in the argument differs from the judgment likely to be exercised by the mere spectator, who sits in critical and detached safety. Heidlebaugh proposes a method of "active, artistic judgment" as a response to contemporary anxieties about uncertainty and incommensurability in practical and moral argument.

Heidlebaugh engages the history of incommensurability as a concept in the work of Thomas Kuhn, Richard Rorty, Alasdair MacIntyre, and others, and then traces incommensurability into the practice of contemporary public argument. This conception shows modern public debate to be wrecked on its most rational aspirations. Seeking to practice a rhetoric based on common standards of judgment, we totalize our own frames of reference and try to demand that others agree with them. Seeking to clarify, correct, and represent, we leave no room for genuine disagreement. Seeking to achieve moral certainty, we arrive at intolerance. If my argument is rational and you reject it, how am I to regard you? Or you me? Faced with incommensurable argumentative positions, both of which meet normal descriptions of rational argument, but which disagree on fundamental premises, are we left only with power, diatribe, silence, or the hope of utter conversion as the only modes of response? There certainly is plenty of evidence in contemporary public debate to justify such a gloomy view.

Heidlebaugh offers a vision of rhetoric as an inventional practice, a mode of discovering pragmatic novelty in moments of communicative crisis, through the practice of active, artistic judgment. Heidlebaugh recognizes that all these terms are problematic, because they envision rhetoric in a way that is contrary to the quasi-scientific, spectatorial conception we are likely to take for granted. The search for clues about how it might be possible to develop a technique for the artistic creation of rhetorical arguments that can meet the problem of incommensurability takes Heidlebaugh and the reader back to early Greek rhetoric and poetry, where Heidlebaugh discloses how the sophistic concepts of *apatê* and *kairos* might usefully offer a new view of rhetoric.

Judgment, Rhetoric, and Incommensurability is a rich, inventive, and balanced work of scholarship, full of scholarly treasures, pragmatic optimism, and common sense. It is a welcome addition to the University of South Carolina Press's series in Rhetoric/Communication.

THOMAS W. BENSON

Preface

The major problem approached in this study is this: In an age of diversity and pluralism, how can we talk productively about those issues that most divide us? Two of the subquestions I encountered have given this work its particular shape. One is this: At a time when standards for what counts as "reasonable" vary profoundly, how do we reason together in order to make good decisions? The second is similar: When standards for what counts as "good" are shifting, how can we know how to produce "good" rhetoric? Each of these two questions is compounded by the problems implicit in the other: Without consensus on standards of reason, how can we have good public argument? And without the eloquence and enriched conversation of good public argument, how can we reason together in order to reach consensus on the issues before us?

Eventually, I recognized that both of these questions focused on the problem of judging the *outcomes* of rhetorical invention: Are there grounds for consensus on whether the invented arguments are reasonable or unreasonable, good or weak? I began to ask what would happen if, instead of focusing on judgment of the outcomes, we were to focus on the process of judgment that must be undertaken by the inventor who must produce arguments. If we were to articulate productive judgment better, could we also learn something about how we might make useful talk?

Trying to locate productive judgment led me to look at the inventional *technai* of the early sophists and their intellectual ancestors, the Greek epic poets. The sophists faced problems of teaching speaking before standards of knowledge, reason, and rhetoric became fixed. Their challenges suggested a similarity to our own times that was relevant to my questions and that has encouraged a revival of other scholarly interest in the sophists. The key to articulating the productive form of judgment was in examining the methods of the poets as conditioned by the constraints of oral performance. Some sense of the oral and improvisational seemed necessary to judging for the purpose of inventing. The value of that focus led me to my final key questions: What would other ancient forms of inventional judgment and method look like if they were all regarded as conditioned, in some way, by circumstances of oral performance? And what could we take today from these forms of judgment and method that would carry forward as helpful suggestions? All these are questions I respond to in this book.

I have received the help and encouragement of many people since I first undertook this project. All my teachers at Penn State influenced my thinking, but two have had a direct impact on this project. The first is Jerry Hauser, friend and advisor for many years now. It was Jerry who encouraged me to look to the methods of the oral epic poets in order to better understand the compositional methods of the sophists. He directed the dissertation that first reflected my thinking on the matter. He will find little of that dissertation in the present work, but one reason for that is that along with solid direction he also gave me much room to continue exploring. The second is Carroll C. Arnold, who in early seminars impressed upon us a distinction I was not to forget: that Aristotle had written a treatise on *doing* rhetoric, not on criticizing it. Arnold's essay "Oral Rhetoric, Rhetoric and Literature" provided me with another set of distinctions that are deep background to this study.

Professor Arnold also provided me with the gift of his expert editorship on most of the chapters of this book. His detailed readings of these chapters and his suggestions for them have enriched them greatly. I have been privileged to have had the assistance of a second University of South Carolina Press series editor, Tom Benson, whose help, persistence, and consistent high standards also have been invaluable. Others have assisted directly with this manuscript: Christopher L. Johnstone provided important assistance with Greek translations; Peter Hertz-Ohmes listened attentively and critically to my readings of Gadamer and Heidegger as they related to this topic; and two anonymous reviewers provided me with their individual perspectives, thorough readings, and detailed and helpful comments. The involvement of all these people has made this a better piece of work, but the flaws in it are, of course, entirely my responsibility.

A grant from the National Endowment for the Humanities allowed me to participate in a summer seminar in the Classics Department at Princeton University, in which the participants engaged in lively discussions about many of the matters I explore here. It was also during these seminars that the relevance of the concept of *kairos* was brought to my attention. My thanks to the seminar leaders Elaine Fantham, M. M. Mackenzie, and, particularly, Andrew Ford; without his encouragement this book literally would not be.

I also received valuable financial assistance from the State University of New York College at Oswego in the form of a summer Faculty Enhancement Grant and a leave. Without this assistance I would not have been able to complete this work.

Friends and colleagues have provided help of many kinds. Judith Martin contributed encouragement in every sense of the word, along with helpful readings. Marcia C. Moore leant me support and skill as the patient proofreader of the entire manuscript. Bill Nothstine provided me with friendship, comic relief, and a helpful early reading of the chapter on Aristotle. Robert A. Rubinstein provided me with information about the Public Conversations Project. Chris Ulanowski and Jane Kelly were effective liaisons with National Public Radio.

Others provided me with support and opportunities. Alan Brinton's encouragement some years ago to continue thinking about this topic is still greatly appreciated. Joan Loveridge-Sanbonmatsu, John K. Smith, and Sara Varhus were sources of discussion and patient support. A number of colleagues provided ways for me to become involved in formal and informal discussions on a variety of topics relevant to the questions I pose here.

Katy Messere contributed years of patience and the light of her presence.

Last but never least, Fritz Messere provided me with everything else: readings, proofreadings, frequent computer assistance, cheerleading, patience, the willingness to defer his own dreams, sandwiches-at-the-desk, and much more.

Judgment, Rhetoric, and the
Problem of Incommensurability

Rhetoric and the Problem of Rationality

One version of the question that has motivated this study is this: When absolute knowledge of what is right and what is wrong seems impossible in an age of skepticism and uncertainty such as ours, how are we to act? How can we take a position? How can we say something worthwhile? In other words, how can we exercise judgment with respect to the various difficult issues that confront us?

These are ancient questions that recur particularly when our ability to know how to make things has become disconnected from our ability to know how to act. Our technology thrusts new questions about our actions upon us daily. We can harvest fetal tissue for other use, but should we? We can identify the chromosome that marks an individual for fatal disease, but should we?

Technology, however, is only one force driving the recurrence of dilemmas of action. These questions piggyback on less technologically based ones that also involve difficult human action. We may pass laws guaranteeing "freedom of expression," but can we do so without compromising the rights of some citizens to be free of harassment? By the same token, we may enforce laws against harassment, but can we do so without compromising free speech? These questions apparently turn on issues of interpretation of formal and informal law and custom: Whom must the law protect? What rights are the more fundamental, requiring more protection? When values or standards compete, which ones transcend the others in our presumed hierarchy? Which ones are seen as unassailable and thus absolute, and hence demand more allegiance?

A major reason that we cannot find fully satisfactory responses to those questions is that they presume the need for some level of consensus on values and standards. But at this historical juncture, we rarely agree on what values are absolute. And instead of falling into an agreed-upon hierarchy, values that we might call upon to guide our decision making compete for primacy. Although moral philosophy may have struggled for some time to find ultimate standards on which beliefs and actions might be grounded, today we face the abandonment—in the face of an abundance of experience—of the entire notion of ultimacy, of grounding beliefs, and of hierarchy. So important has this lost sense of ultimacy become that to some it signals the ousting of the great legitimizing narrative of the Enlightenment, which dominated Western thought to the point of its own invisibility.[1] Speaking in less sweeping terms, and, significantly, still from the position of Enlightenment subject, Richard J. Bernstein laments "the growing sense that there may be nothing—not God, Philosophy, Science, or Poetry—that satisfies our longing for ultimate foundations, for a fixed Archimedean point upon which we can secure our thought and action" (230).

Whether couched as a crisis in legitimation (Jürgen Habermas), rationality, or (as for French post-structuralists) representation (Fredric Jameson), the revolutionary shift in Western thought brings with it a crisis in practical judgment. Ronald Beiner, describing reasons for his own concern about political judgment, quotes Norman Jacobson: "The sapping of authority has inevitably been accompanied by a crisis in judgment, for centuries thought somehow linked to 'common sense.' But what today may be regarded as 'common' amongst men, even those occupying the same boundaries and subject to the same laws and regulations? As for 'sense,' the doubts cast by science upon what was once believed to 'make sense' have eroded the confidence of individuals and publics still further. Consequently, many of us cringe back from the precipice of judgment, for fear either of error or of fatal involvement in what we cannot even dimly comprehend" (Beiner, *Political Judgment,* 3–4).[2]

Bernstein's and Jacobson's statements aptly capture, both in tone and content, the sentiment prevalent in contemporary Anglo-American thought about judgment. Even as awareness emerges that there are no fixed Archimedean standards, that awareness is expressed as anxiety, even fearfulness. And a nostalgia, even a longing, remains for some form of rationally arrived-at standards, at least in matters of practical judgment.

As has happened at similar historical moments of uncertainty, some have turned away from the rational-deductive methods thought to underwrite certainty and have instead embraced, substituted, or at least suggested paying attention to the arts or sciences of communication. The best-known historical example is Vico, who, in responding to the limitations to rationality and knowledge imposed by Cartesianism, called for a return to education in rhetorical topics. More recently, attention to communication—sometimes given systematically and sometimes in passing—as a response to problems of judgment and choice has come from likely sources, like speech communication, and from less likely sources, like the philosophies of science and social science.[3]

Despite the enormous productivity and promise generated by these efforts, and the broadening of our understanding of choice making, an anxiety about judgment and the place for right-thinking human action remains. I will take up some of the difficulties of approaching a crisis of judgment with communication theories that are themselves haunted by that crisis in more detail later. But some preliminary observations about judgment and communication are in order. We need to accompany a turn to communication with a vision of judgment that replaces the normative conception of judgment with which we are most familiar. The groundbreaking work of Richard Rorty on philosophy and the crisis in rationality, and the criticism his claims have invited illustrate this need.

Western Anxiety and the Turn to Conversation

Much of Rorty's work, particularly in *Philosophy and the Mirror of Nature* (1979), may be regarded as an effort to rescue philosophy from a scheme of authority in which rationality, philosophy, and epistemology are identified. This scheme, arguably, is also assumed to determine in Western thought what may be called good judgment.

The history of post-Enlightenment philosophy related in *Philosophy and the Mirror of Nature*[4] describes the dominance of the identification of rationality, philosophy, and epistemology. After the Middle Ages, philosophers became regarded as the "guardians of rationality" (317), dedicated to discovering ways in which knowledge claims could be grounded by some rational means, rather than based on the authority of church or tradition. During the eighteenth century, the search for a way of grounding knowledge claims transmuted into a concern for determining the nature and foundation of knowledge itself; it became "difficult to imagine what philosophy without epistemology could be" (357). As it became a commonplace of philosophical discourse that the search for an authoritative foundation for knowledge was fruitless, the crisis in rationality presented itself, and confidence in the judging self began to erode.

Much Western philosophy began to search out a way to think of philosophy without identifying it with the futile effort to establish the foundations of knowledge. Rorty's own controversial turn to "edifying" philosophical talk as a means of reviving philosophy and restoring self-confidence is an example of the way in which philosophy has been drawn to consider solutions within non-normative discursive practices. In a position he has defended and expanded upon since 1979, Rorty suggests that philosophers must turn away from analytic philosophy, the goal of which had become establishing the foundations upon which knowledge and judgment could be based. In a controversial suggestion, he recommended instead a hermeneutic turn to discovery through good discussion, which would produce "edifying" rather than grounded statements (*PMN*, 265–379). Philosophers, he claimed, would fruitfully abandon the goal of finalizing discussion in end points of knowledge claims in favor of participating in the "ongoing conversation" that results from provocative discourse. Edification is usually a result of "abnormal" discourse rather than the normal, systematic discourse of philosophy. "Normal discourse is that which is conducted within an agreed-upon set of conventions about what counts as a relevant contribution, what counts as answering a question, what counts as having a good argument for that answer or a good criticism of it. Abnormal discourse is what happens when someone joins in the discourse who is ignorant of these conventions or who sets them aside" (320).

However, Rorty's turn away from epistemological grounding and toward edifying conversation does not by itself restore confidence in judgment. The turn away from grounding claims and toward discovering ideas through provocative conversation is not enough to overcome the longing for standards. In fact, while Rorty's own argument for hermeneutics has itself succeeded at provoking much discussion (and is therefore, perhaps, successful on Rorty's terms) some of that discussion simply invites recourse to traditional standards of philosophical judgment. Anthony M. Matteo, for instance, worries about setting aside evaluative standards of philosophical judgment and turning over the creation of knowledge to meandering conversation. Without standards, he says, we cannot know if our conversation is taking us anywhere; we are unable to distinguish "meaningful conversation from mad and incoherent ravings" (242–43). While such concerns may not trouble Rorty or his more sympathetic readers very much, they seem destined eventually to present themselves during the course of philosophical conversation.

But there are other questions about standards that challenge the turn to conversation. Even the most sympathetic readers must admit that implicit in Rorty's own descriptions is a paradox involving normative or evaluative standards: once we cite the belief that we should improve our talk by aiming for edification or by valuing abnormal discourse, we also seem to be reinscribing normalization of discourse, despite the fact that any such normalization is counterproductive to abnormal discourse. Rorty himself is aware of various versions of this paradox[5] and there are many. For instance, in *Philosophy and the Mirror of Nature* when he establishes Kierkegaard, Nietzsche, and others as exemplars of edifying philosophers and tells us even offhandedly that they are "reactive and offer satires, parodies, aphorisms" (369), he invites hosts of questions about meaningful standards: What counts as satire and parody? How do I recognize it? Is there some good satire as opposed to unsatisfactory satire, and if so, how do I tell the difference? The locale for these questions may have shifted from philosophy to literary criticism, but the questions remain. What also remain are the apparently allied (and far more insidious) questions of method: How do I produce abnormal discourse? How can I become a Rortian "philosopher"? Perhaps we should not even pose these questions, because they are impossible to pose meaningfully within the constraints Rorty suggests: it is inconsistent—

even incoherent—to suggest we should want a system to produce abnormal discourse. But herein lies the problem: as soon as we have produced injunctions *not* to say something, we have *stopped* conversation rather than allowing it to be ongoing. And conversation stoppers can be insidious and subtle: ignoring a contribution because we don't know how to respond to it or we cannot find a context in which it seems worthwhile is only one way in which conversation becomes self-limiting. Jean-François Lyotard points out that "countless scientists have seen their 'move' repressed, sometimes for decades, because it too abruptly destabilized the accepted positions . . . in the problematic" (*Postmodern Condition*, 63). Once we declare some questions to be out of bounds or, literally, out of order for discussion, we have normalized abnormal discourse, established standards and rules for it.

This apparent exegesis on Rorty is really intended to raise some questions about the turn in philosophy to communication as a way to recoup rationality without resorting to epistemological models. The insistent anxiousness to reinstate standards for judgment even where Rorty insists we should do without them opens his suggestions to the accusation that he has merely reinscribed the same problems onto a new model. In short, faced with dilemmas presented by philosophy or by practical life, a so-called radical turn like Rorty's to conversation (or to rhetoric or poetry for that matter) does not by itself make the task of decision making any easier; judgment remains encased in the same epistemological model. We may still feel compelled to institute standards for our communication, to locate ways of knowing if we are "doing it right," even though to do so means trying to normalize abnormal discourse. The inconsistency inherent in this desire is paradoxical: we want what we cannot want.

Turning to Rhetorical Invention

Desire, however, does not respect the rules of propositional logic: we can want two contradictory things. The urge to satisfy such desire is where abnormal discourse should begin, as a discourse of the impossible. It is out of such contradictions that new ideas may be generated. Furthermore, within such moments of contradiction, especially between desire and accepted practice, inheres a less well-recognized form of judgment that is not based on the application of standards but on a particular kind of *need:* the need to respond with something novel. This sort of judgment is not so susceptible to erosion with the collapse of epistemology and should enhance the production of creative, divergent discourse.

The balance of this volume will elaborate the form of judgment involved in generating novel ideas, a form that I see as deriving from the improvisational methods of early Greek rhetoric. A significant change takes place in the locale of judgment when the focus is on the judgment exercised by the producer or inventor of ideas. The locus of judgment becomes the speaker, caught in an impossible situation to which he[6] must respond with speech, rather than the consumer or spectator, who weighs ideas already before him against some standard. The judgment of the actor comes into play in trying to fashion a response. The judgment of the spectator—which comes into play, for instance, in judging the value of ideas that have been produced already—is the kind I have been alluding to as being currently beset by crisis.

Methods that allow us to produce "good" discourse do not necessarily derive from methods by which we understand, judge, or critique discourse as good. To put the point in simple but very traditional terms, we think differently when we are pressed to come up with something to say than we do when we are sitting back trying to determine the value of something that has already been said. In the latter situation, we can afford to have rules for judgment that allow us to throw some things out and retain others. In the former setting, however, we must exercise judgment in such a way as to come up with ideas to satisfy the needs of the moment. This form of judgment is not susceptible to the imposition of rules, largely because we are driven to respond out of the novelty of the moment.

These two forms of judgment may be contrasted with respect to the dilemmas of choice cited earlier. The consumer or spectator responds by evaluating the alternatives with an eye toward choosing among them. With no clear grounds for choice, the spectator is without resources. For the inventor or actor, however, the material for her creativity is the substance of the dilemma. Her judgment is engaged in those moments that seem impossible for her to respond to, but to which she nonetheless must respond. Her effort is to develop ideas or alternatives that are not already before her, that seem to be impossible. These species of "abnormal discourse" arise from needs to speak at moments when normal discourse will not do.

Rorty points out that novelty cannot be produced or studied methodically or systematically: "There is no discipline which describes it, any more than there is a discipline devoted to the study of the unpredictable, or 'creativity'" (*PMN*, 320). Abnormal discourse must resist normalization by method, but the notion that method must be normalizing may not be the obvious truth that it seems. The idea that method must be normalizing is an epistemological bias that has caused controversy for rhetoric, one of the ancient arts of discourse, in its past. The effort to articulate rhetorical invention was in part, in its ancient history, the effort to systematize the unpredictable. The Sophists initiated the effort to systematize, at least sufficiently to make it teachable, what could not so plainly be submitted to method. Their efforts unfolded in a struggle with Plato, himself representative of an epistemological bias about method. Later, after Aristotle's description of rhetoric as an art of invention and his association of art with method, rhetoric held the promise of its contradiction: the promise of the existence of a method—and a form of judgment—that could result in creativity.

I explore this form of judgment, which I call 'active artistic judgment,' and its methods in two major moves in this book. First, I elaborate the problems posed by the postmodern anxiety about judgment. I trace that anxiety from its manifestation in the problem of incommensurability introduced by Thomas S. Kuhn and Paul Feyerabend. The apparent intractability of incommensurate frames, particularly when the scene shifts from questions of scientific knowledge to moral and practical questions, suggests the need to explore a different form of judgment.

In the second move, I locate this judgment in the improvisational forms of the oral epic poets who were among the intellectual ancestors of ancient Greek rhetoric. The epic poets linked together unrelated, even contradictory elements into new relationships by pulling those elements into common places. This "commonplacing" is at the heart of active artistic judgment. When the oral nature of rhetoric and the commonplacing nature of invention are foregrounded, judgment may be found to meet ever more pressing moral and practical challenges in the inventional methods of the Sophists, Aristotle, and even Cicero. An important turning point may be found in Aristotle, who articulated clearly the virtues of practical wisdom that must be present in rhetorical commonplacing.

I use the Sophists to link these two major moves. The Sophists' early attempts to theorize invention emphasize the key point presented earlier: moments are vitalized when they present themselves to us as impossible moments. The Sophists' teachings responded to the urge to make speech possible at impossible moments. The paradox that reflects the anxiety of much Western philosophy—wanting what we cannot want—presents such an impossible moment. For sophistic rhetoric, the violence done to one form of judgment by the presence of incommensurability does not imply defeat but signals an opportunity for the generation of new forms.

The problem-solving approach of my inquiry supports a historiography of "contemporary appropriation" rather than a "historical reconstruction." These two categories, introduced by Edward Schiappa and Omar Swartz and adapted from Rorty (in his 1984 article, "Historiography of Philosophy") distinguish two goals in the reading of ancient texts. Whereas rhetorical scholars engaged in historical reconstruction examine ancient theories in order "to understand the cultural context in which these theories originally appear" (Schiappa and Swartz, xi), scholars engaged in contemporary appropriation study historical texts "in order to shed insight on rhetorical concerns as they are manifested in today's environment" (xi). While contemporary appropriation does not justify playing fast and loose with facts or with accepted interpretations, it does demand "less rigidity and more creativity in the process of interpreting how dead authors through their texts speak to live, contemporary audiences" (Schiappa, *Protagoras*, 66).

My own contemporary appropriations may be considered "pragmatic" in the sense that I begin with a contemporary problem and draw on ancient texts in order to determine a response to it. This approach justifies certain exclusions and inclusions in the telling. For the most part I exclude such controversies as whether the Sophists can be treated as a group and whether the transition from orality to literacy was gradual or revolutionary. These are, of course, important questions that should continue to influence our thinking about ancient history, but for the reasons I have already explained, I am justified in bracketing them while in pursuit of answers to my own questions. On the other hand, I look widely for hints in a variety of places about where and how orality may be fore-grounded as conditioning rhetoric during early literacy. Consequently, my work relies equally on classical texts and their twentieth-century interpreters. For example, my discussion of Aristotle offers an original account of how his system of rhetorical *topoi* might work, but my discussion of Ciceronian *stasis* is intended to extend and recontextualize Otto Loeb Dieter's and Michael J. Buckley's interpretations.

Additionally, in many cases throughout this work I have drawn ideas into relationship with one another with less regard for any consistency in their intellectual pedigrees than for their capacities to illuminate a particu-lar problem; these capacities, partly a product of my own treatment, may be the only "unity" some of the ideas herein may show. This, I hope, is consis-tent with my own understanding of practical wisdom as it may be drawn from Western rhetorical tradition and with active artistic judgment.

The arguments in this book will not please everyone. In seeking to recapture the potential of classical rhetoric for contemporary performance, I have given short shrift to the importance of some positions that seem to me not compatible with my goal. For instance, some readers may feel I have unfairly ignored or criticized some resistant discourses like diatribe and other forms of political protest. I have included these forms in the category of "emotive" discourse, which, I suggest, devalues the inventive work that accompanies more traditional rhetorical practice. I think this categorization is necessary for capturing the character of these traditional rhetorics.

For similar reasons, I have assumed the availability of a great deal of individual freedom of expression and not dealt here with the material forces that limit or homogenize those apparent freedoms. I have no wish to dupli-cate the active and good work already going on in those directions, and I have concerned myself instead with the problems that accompany "giving up" on practical discourse and the ways in which we can overcome the temptation to do so.

My scholarly methods are speculative and theoretical rather than criti-cal or interpretive. Looking at the textual evidences of the discourse prac-tices of others, including the ancients about whom I write here, could have been one way to approach the issues I have raised. Some of the reasons for my resistance to that approach are articulated fully in this book, I believe, as the difference between relying on spectator judgment and engaging in active judgment; these two forms of judgment correspond, respectively, to criticism/interpretation and performance. My belief is that in speech communication, our interest in rhetorical criticism has in recent years been livelier than our interest in theorizing about how to perform and invent rhetorically. My goal here—to help people talk better together about novel and difficult matters—means thinking about ways they may find responses when responses seem impossible. I hope to adopt the prospective point of view of the speaker and to ask what factors may permit and encourage possibilities for inventive responding. Throughout, where I have introduced specific pieces of discourse, I have done so primarily to clarify statements about invention and performance, rather than to engage in retrospective critical judgments about the discourse.[7]

Judgment, Rationality, and Rhetoric

The contemporary challenge to judgment seems to lie in our loss of faith in common standards and in agreement on what makes sense. However, Jacobson's apt expression of concern, that "many of us cringe back from the precipice of judgment, for fear either of error or of fatal involvement" (Beiner, *Political Judgment,* 4) is particularly applicable to only one sort of judgment: spectator judgment, which has, unfortunately, become synonymous with all judgment. Spectator judgment, as I will argue here, is more open than active judgment to doubts like those voiced by Jacobson about the ideals of agreement and common standards. These doubts have challenged the possibility of judgment in very specific ways that have led to a similar loss of faith in rhetoric. Spectator judgment, it may be granted, seems to rest naturally on the existence of a community of agreement on standards, which in turn seems to rest on a capacity for "seeing things the same way." If that capacity is eroded, however, we may not need to lose faith in rhetoric or in the active judgment to which it is related.

A good starting place for examining the limitations of spectator judgment is with the philosophy of science. In attributing the loss of faith in part to the findings of science, Jacobson joins those philosophers of the late twentieth century who cast the crisis in judgment in terms of agreement, or "commensurability," on what is rational. For these philosophers the threat to the very possibility of commensurability parallels and conditions the threat to community. The same threat also offers an appropriate starting place for observing the role discourse may play in judgment.

Agreement and Incommensurability

Commensurability consists of agreement on a rules-based way of making and legitimizing judgments. Rorty's definition is provocative: "By 'commensurable' I mean able to be brought under a set of rules which will tell us how rational agreement can be reached on what would settle the issue on every point where statements conflict. . . . The dominating notion of epistemology is that to be rational, to be fully human, to do what we ought, we need to be able to find agreement with other human beings" (*PMN*, 316).

The observation by Kuhn, in *The Structure of Scientific Revolutions*, that the scientific method itself, considered to be a model of rationality, did not assure commensurability in the examination of data, threatened the prevalent conceptions of rationality and of ourselves as rational beings. If scientific rationality did not consist of adherence to a method using law-like rules for evaluating data, then what did it consist of? Could the scientific method be considered a model of rational choice making at all, and if not, could such a model be found?

Kuhn's version of the so-called incommensurability thesis, which derived from his examination of the growth of scientific knowledge, makes the point that major paradigm shifts in science (for instance, the shift from an Aristotelian to a Gallilean astrophysics) seem not to be the result of systematic data collection that proceeds until the errors of old conclusions are eradicated and more accurate explanations are formalized into theory. Instead, Kuhn observed, "normal" data collection contributes only to the advancement of knowledge that is consistent with the paradigm or scientific worldview current at the time. The reason that normal data collection cannot result in radical paradigm shifts is that the conceptual "view finder" for those data is determined to a large extent by the current paradigm itself. Kuhn's descriptions suggest that what is apparent in the data generated from within a new paradigm is not perceptible from within the old one. Consequently, the move from one paradigm to another is "revolutionary," a "transformation of vision" (*Structure*, 120) rather than the result of anything describable in terms of traditional scientific method. Moreover, two paradigms are "incommensurable"; that is, neither can be accepted or rejected in terms of the other. The "rules of logic" for each are different. As Kuhn was to put the point later in his career, normal science might, in fact, proceed algorithmically, but the algorithms employed by different scientists might to some extent be "individual" in nature rather than inherent in the scientific method (*Essential Tension*, 329).

Kuhn would argue throughout his career that he had not intended to suggest that scientific choice was less than rational but rather that the scientific method did not render choice "unproblematic" (*Essential Tension*, 328). The history of science as Kuhn read it indicated that choice was not algorithmically determined but required elements of what other philosophers insisted on calling subjectivity. Despite Kuhn's insistence that his arguments could be seen to enlarge rather than diminish the realm of rationality, Kuhn's critics protested that the process he described reduced science to an irrational activity.[1]

The nature and vehemence of the criticisms demonstrate, among other things, the strength of the identification of commensurability and rationality, at least among philosophers of science. The incommensurability thesis has threatened the conception of rational selves held by modern scientists and philosophers of science. This threat is perceivable even to those who have questioned the validity of the thesis. N. L. Porus states that "behind the ill-formulated problem of 'incommensurability' hides an important and non-imaginary problem of scientific rationality, best to be grasped in the form of a question: Can the process of development of scientific knowledge undergo 'rational reconstruction,' and if it can, what sense can we make of the concept of 'rational' within the given context?" (376).

Interestingly, the incommensurability thesis, as it was originally described by Kuhn, has been problematic in part because it conflates two ways by which we might be said to gain knowledge about the world: the visual and the linguistic. I would argue, in fact, that the incommensurability thesis collapses linguistic understanding into visual.

This becomes apparent when we return to a metaphor, used early by Kuhn, that has by turns enriched and inhibited understanding of incommensurability: the metaphor of gestalt "illusions"[2] —pictures constructed so as to make it equally possible for a viewer to find Image A in the picture as to find Image B. One such "illusion" cited by Kuhn allows a viewer to see either a duck or a rabbit in the figure. Whichever image is perceived will make use of all the data—that is, each line or point in the drawing. Consequently, in either view, some elements will stand out as figure, while others will recede to become background. The duck and the rabbit picture will "foreground" or "background" different details. Consequently, with one image firmly in view, the perceiver will find it impossible to see the other image *at the same time*, or even to see how the elements of the drawing might compose the other image. A gestalt shift—a shift to the perception of the other image—happens suddenly and totally rather than gradually through the discovery of one bit of "data" after another.

In *The Structure of Scientific Revolutions*, Kuhn made the point that scientific paradigms are, essentially, accepted or assumed views of the world that determine for scientists what data they will see, that is, what will stand out as figure. Paradigms are tacitly assumed, according to Kuhn; for instance, students immersed in a particular paradigm may be taught to use instrument X to look for datum Y, although such behaviors will not be articulated as an expectation for acting rationally. Paradigms consisting of more than specifically articulated behaviors are world views (Kuhn's expression) outside of which a scientist cannot step (during the course of normal scientific work) in order to observe that there is a paradigm, that it is only one view, and that the way of collecting data suggested by that paradigm is only one way. He cannot find such a standpoint anymore than I, fixed on seeing a duck, can tell you to be sure to look at the duck rather than the rabbit, or to look for the bill rather than the ear: as far as I am concerned, there is no rabbit, and there is no ear.

Consequently, paradigms act as visual models to induce a community of scientists to see some things rather than others. The dominant paradigm of a community, Kuhn argued, constrains the vision of scientists so that they see some experiments as worth performing (*Structure*, 18), and they see certain facts rather than others as worth reporting (25). Overall, a paradigm does not so much limit the scientific enterprise as define it: a paradigm provides tacit guides for models by which science is taught, sanctions procedures and rules, and authorizes the generation of predictions. Kuhn supposed, in fact, that experimental results reported during normal science are compared with predictions drawn from the dominant paradigm (26) rather than with nature. Nature itself, as it is defined and discussed, is not unmediated by the scientific paradigm through which it is observed.

It is in part because of the gestalt-like nature of scientific paradigms that Kuhn believed paradigm switches took place through radical transformations of vision. More important to issues of judgment and choice, however, are two other concerns. If a view (whether we use the term loosely or more technically) is relative to framework and expectation, then we are invited to conclude that there is no logical way of stepping outside to compare different frameworks for acceptance or rejection: we are always drawing standards for comparison from some framework. Moreover, even if there were such a logic, there is no neutral standpoint for seeing reality outside our own framework, no final arbitrating standard for deciding between paradigms or frames. Rather than saying that "Priestley and Lavoisier both saw oxygen, but they interpreted their observations differently," we are compelled, essentially, to say that they saw different things (*Structure*, 120), much as I saw an ear where you saw a bill. For those subscribing to the idea of incommensurability, the impact on judgment was great: if there were no objective, nonarbitrary standards guiding decisions in science, how then could there be any standards against which we should weigh any claims to our belief? Feyerabend, for instance, pointed out that, with respect to the task of interpreting and critiquing different styles in painting and drawing, "there are no 'neutral' objects which can be represented in any style, and which can be used as objective arbiters between radically different styles" (*Against Method*, 230).

In developing his conception of paradigms in predominantly visual terms, Kuhn did two things: he accepted a norm of science, which is the importance to knowledge of evaluating and measuring observations. And he remained, himself, within a dominant paradigm of philosophical metaphor, the visual.[3] Kuhn admitted that some of the ensuing confusion over the incommensurability thesis was a result of his conflation of the visual and conceptual: "I, for example, made much use of the double sense, visual and conceptual, of the verb 'to see,' and I repeatedly likened theory-changes to Gestalt switches" ("Commensurability," 669).

In doing both of these things, he participated in inscribing upon questions of judgment a visual character and in mixing other metaphors as well. Visually, a paradigm is totalizing, and having standards of comparison implies having a way to judge how data ought to fit into the total picture of nature—as part of figure or ground, as significant or insignificant.[4] As visual as the idea of paradigms seems to be, Kuhn's own definitions emphasize the linguistic: "The claim that two theories are incommensurable is then the claim that there is no language, neutral or otherwise, into which both theories, conceived as sets of sentences, can be translated without residue or loss" ("Commensurability," 670).[5] While the contingency of scientific paradigms may be most colorfully apparent in references to gestalts and gestalt shifts, contingency is also apparent from Kuhn's illustrations drawn from scientific language.

In Kuhn's original description of the incommensurability thesis, the capacity to see something as data is relative not only to a perceptual scheme but also to the entire categorical or conceptual scheme that a viewer brings to the enterprise of perceiving, and there is no neutral observation language or "language of pure precepts" (*Structure*, 127) allowing escape from some sort of conceptual determinism. Kuhn persisted with this reference to conceptual contingency. Scientific languages, Kuhn argued, are learned holistically, "in clusters" ("Rationality and Theory Choice," 566). For example, a student cannot learn to use the terms *force* and *mass* without learning both simultaneously; each term makes meaningful reference to nature only by reference to the other and to an entire conceptual "frame" in which both are constituted. Once a scientific language is acquired, "the member terms of an interrelated set [of terms] can be used to formulate infinitely many new generalizations, all of them contingent" (566). Just as importantly, terms like *force* and *mass* function as meaningful terms—that is, as standards—only within a certain conceptual universe: "only in a world in which Newton's Second Law holds" (566).

The contention that scientific terms derive meaning at least as much from one another in language "worlds," "sets," or "clusters" as they do from reference to objects in nature makes it easier to accept a companion contention of relativism about the social world. The value-laden language in which social issues are couched rarely is assumed to have even the same objectivity as scientific language; therefore (the thinking goes), it must provide little capacity for stating the grounds for judgment objectively. In addition, as we talk about social, practical, or even moral issues, where we are admittedly talking about differences among people rather than among conceptions of nature, the influence of different worldviews or language communities gains still greater importance. The generalization of incommensurability is discussed especially by Alasdair MacIntyre, whose arguments I shall take up shortly.

At the same time that relativism presents itself, the conceptual determinism that seems implicit in the incommensurability thesis invites an identification of the three activities of seeing, understanding, and agreeing. In common parlance, if we can see things the same way, if we can understand one another's viewpoints, we can also determine how our differences should be settled. Conversely, if we cannot see things the same way, we cannot determine how our differences should be settled. Ultimately, agreement rests on understanding, and understanding rests on clarity. Understanding is necessary and sufficient for agreement.

There is little in the efforts either to rebut or to defend the incommensurability thesis that denies this identification of seeing, understanding, and agreement. Major efforts to rebut the incommensurability thesis (or to weaken its apparent effects on rationality) often bracket that assumption and choose instead to attack the arguments that seem to imply determinism. Evidently, so central to incommensurability does the argument for conceptual contingency seem to be, that some philosophers have assumed that if it can be overturned, the entire thesis will fall, and with it problems of judgment.

Examples are Hillary Putnam's and Donald Davidson's attempts at rebutting incommensurability. Both framed incommensurability as a problem of "translation" from one language or conceptual scheme to another. Davidson said, in fact, that " 'incommensurable' is, of course, Kuhn and Feyerabend's word for 'not intertranslatable'" ("Conceptual Scheme," 73). Both Putnam and Davidson more or less disposed of the incommensurability thesis, at least as a problem of intertranslatability. Putnam, drawing on empirical evidence and common sense, concluded that of course translation is possible; we translate often from one natural language to some other, despite the fact that each may structure experience differently. Davidson disputed the authority of conceptual schemes altogether, arguing that discussions like Kuhn's and Feyerabend's mistakenly substituted a new duality for the Cartesian one, a duality of experience and "something" (a conceptual scheme) that organizes experiences in a uniquely meaningful way. Davidson pointed out that our intellectual history tells us that this duality must be false: if conceptual schemes truly provided organizations of experience that made the meanings of those experiences comprehensible only to those sharing those schemes, transitions from, say, a Newtonian to an Einsteinian physics would be impossible. He concluded that we need to give up all such dualities: language alone does not serve as a medium of understanding. Understanding, according to Davidson, is achieved with the help of an "attitude" toward people rather than toward sentences ("Conceptual Scheme," 77). We gain access to the theories (or meaningful concepts) held by others if we concede to them that the sentences they accept as true are, in fact, true to them. At the point at which we achieve such understanding, we may be enabled to understand any larger scheme in which such a sentence is meaningful. The searching after truth is itself conditional on our making such an effort.[6]

Kuhn's own efforts to defend incommensurability against analyses like Putnam's and Davidson's are attempts to cast doubt on their equating of translation with interpretation in order to show that, while translation between paradigmatic "languages" is not possible, interpretation of one by the other—and consequently comparison—is *not* impossible ("Commensurability"). He does not challenge their assumption with respect to understanding, however. In fact, in a frequently quoted maxim, he affirms the centrality of attitude and understanding: "When reading the works of an important thinker, look first for the apparent absurdities in the text and ask yourself how a sensible person could have written them. When you find an answer . . . then you may find that more central passages, ones you previously thought you understood, have changed their meaning" (*Essential Tension*, xii).

Whether or not our percepts are translatable, however, understanding is an inadequate guarantee for achieving agreement on standards; it may be necessary, but it is not sufficient. With respect to scientific judgment, for instance, Rorty observes that "the results of looking can always be phrased in terms acceptable to both sides ('the fluid looked darker,' 'the needle veered to the right . . .'). Kuhn should have been content to show that the availability of such an innocuous language is of no help whatever in bringing decision between theories under an algorithm" (*PMN*, 324).

In moral and practical matters, the ability to make sense of someone else's choices does not by itself facilitate good judgment. Getting someone else's world fully in view, even if and when that is possible, does not mean either that we become willing to adopt it or that we can locate standards of agreement satisfactory to both worlds. Conceding that someone's statements make sense to him and are rational within his scheme of rationality does not help us discover ways to act in concert with that person. However, decisions that are made on some other basis besides agreement on a rational standard appear less than rational. Our moral and practical talk today shows vividly that incommensurability exists as a *presumed* barrier to serious discourse largely because we accept a modern dilemma: the notion that judgment consists in and only in applying unassailable standards, but that we can never have them.

Incommensurability and Practical Discourse

In his discussion of moral or practical talk, Alasdair MacIntyre shows clearly how reasoning with one another becomes impossible when we count on shared standards to undergird rational talk but believe that we have lost them. Citing such controversies as abortion, socialized medicine, and the morality of war, he demonstrates the apparent "conceptual incommensurability of the rival arguments in each of the three debates. Every one of the arguments is logically valid or can be easily expanded so as to be made so; the conclusions do, indeed, follow from the premises. But the rival premises are such that we possess no rational way of weighing the claims of one against another. For each premise employs some quite different normative or evaluative concept from the others. . . . It is precisely because there is in our society no established way of deciding between these claims that moral argument appears to be necessarily interminable" (8).

MacIntyre expands his observation with descriptions that make clear that in much moral and practical argument the central concepts invoked by each side are incommensurate, and that incommensurability consists of differing measures or standards inherent in those concepts (ch. 17). His central example is a hypothetical version of actual political disputes in which liberal B squares off against the more conservative A on any of a number of possible issues involving justice and fairness. A, who opposes raising taxes as unjust, "claims to have a right to what he has earned and that nobody else has a right to take away what he acquired legitimately and to which he has a just title" (244). B "is impressed with the arbitrariness of the inequalities in the distribution of wealth" and "the inability of the poor and the deprived to do very much about their own condition as a result of inequalities in the distribution of power" (245). B concludes that "redistributive taxation which will finance welfare and the social services is what justice demands" (245).

What is impressive to MacIntyre about these two positions is that they are not only logically incompatible but also incommensurable (245). The incommensurability lies, not in the fact that the two concepts of justice differ, but in the *way* in which they differ: "The type of concept in terms of which each frames his claim is so different from that of the other that the question of how and whether the dispute between them may be rationally settled begins to pose difficulties. . . . Our pluralist culture possesses no method of weighing, no rational criterion for deciding between claims based on legitimate entitlement against claims based on need. Thus these two types of claim are indeed, as I suggested, incommensurable, and the metaphor of 'weighing' moral claims is not just inappropriate but misleading" (246). MacIntyre goes on to show a similar incommensurability between formally argued positions on justice advanced by philosophers Rawls and Nozick.

The significance of these descriptions is in showing how heavily our choices and our talk about choices rely on methods of weighing and measuring: "A aspires to ground the notion of justice in some account of what and how a given person is entitled to in virtue of what he has acquired and earned; B aspires to ground the notion of justice in some account of the equality of the claims of each person in respect of basic needs and of the means to meet such needs" (246). Consequently, each can and will argue that certain measures, opposed by the other, are "just." The problem is not simply that each is using the term *justice* differently; the problem is that in each case the concept provides different valences to the issue before them.

Perhaps more to the point, each one's conception of justice provides different, noncomparable, and incompatible units of measurement for use in judgment. Understanding the way these terms are used, even from the perspective of the other, does not guarantee adoption of the other's usage, or agreement, or even a willingness to weigh relevant issues according to the same measure. Moreover, each party is concerned, in his talk, with establishing the validity of his claim according to his own conception. Neither moral philosophy nor the commonly practiced rhetoric of today offers ways to bridge the gap.

MacIntyre's use of the term *incommensurability* here is apt in a number of ways. It validly expresses how talk is frustrated by our discovery that we are employing standards that seem to have no validity outside our own conceptual frames. Most of us have felt ourselves rendered mute with the discovery that we cannot find common ground with others in order to discuss concerns. And the use of the term *incommensurability* emphasizes as well that we accept metaphors that contribute to that frustration. A and B both assume standards of comparison to be conceptually determined; that is, like other data of experience, standards are meaningful only within the terministic array that makes up the conceptual universe of each. Without a conversion experience (the moral equivalent of the gestalt switch), they cannot find a common language sufficiently meaningful to provide common standards; and without common standards for grounding argument, there can be no conversion.

Rhetorical critics have documented how fruitless and damaging to debate is a rhetoric obsessed only with grounding our own arguments, particularly in times of pluralism and incommensurability. For instance, W. Barnett Pearce, Alison Alexander, and Stephen W. Littlejohn, in "The New Christian Right and the Humanist Response: Reciprocated Diatribe," trace an ongoing ideological conflict between the New Christian Right (then identified as a loosely structured political party known as the Moral Majority) and the so-called secular humanists. Their analysis not only describes the way incommensurability is manifested in moral debate but also illustrates MacIntyre's observation that rhetorical theories at present offer more in the way of developing logical argument than of bridging differences.

A logical component to the incommensurability of the "Christian-Humanistic" argument is apparent from the outset. Each side argues from fundamental concepts that rule out the fundamental concepts of the other. The "monistic" worldview of the Moral Majority militates against compromise as well as against changes from a doctrinaire Christian commitment even for pragmatic purposes. By contrast, a "secular humanist" worldview (detectable despite the fact that those who hold it might, in fact, deny holding a worldview) is pragmatic and pluralistic. As Pearce and his colleagues put the point, "Pluralism is a way of thinking which presupposes the existence of incommensurate groups within society and thus makes tolerance and means of communication more important virtues than faith and evangelical zeal" ("The New Christian Right," 184). Secular humanists "honor those with sufficient courage to throw away previously acceptable standards in favor of the new information" of shifting foundations of moral certainty (185).[7]

These mutually exclusive grounding concepts affect the standards for decision making held by each side. Argumentative standards, which include what must be permitted as acceptable grounds for argument, differ, for instance. Given the pragmatic/pluralistic assumptions of secular humanism, virtually any issue or any commitment can and should be regarded as grist for discussion and critical examination *except* the assumption that undergirds that particular standard: the toleration for incommensurate groups and the envisioning of a perfected open form of communication as a means of managing pluralism. Confronted by intolerance for openness in communication—especially intolerance that grows from an ideological frame—the humanist (like other relativists) is left without a response because she is left without her accepted *logical grounds* for response. Members of the New Christian Right, for their part, argue from the existence of objectively verifiable standards, usually those found in Christian interpretations of the New Testament. They often operate under the assumption that tolerance and openness of communication are incompatible with their monism and theism (although this incompatibility does not apply to some constitutional protections of free speech).

These differences in argumentative standards lead to unbridgeable differences in perceptual standards. When either side does not meet the argumentative standards of the other, each is perceived as falling outside the paradigm of rationality that is thought by the other to underwrite argumentation; that is, one side is inevitably seen by the other as irrational and intransigent. Moreover, the discourse of the other side is interpreted in such a way as to confirm negative expectations. Pearce et al. (1987) find that the secular humanists, instead of trying to adopt the worldview of the New Christian Right, "treat the New Christian Right as if they were managing issues within the secular framework and doing so poorly" (187). For their part, the Moral Majority see in their version of the other's worldview the anticipated interactional limitations of the humanists: "The mythology of 'secular humanism' has been so deeply entrenched in the contemporary social and political institutions that the liberals no longer see it as a 'perspective.' The content of liberalism is 'tolerance' and 'pluralism' and this, ironically, makes liberals particularly blind to the possibility of a view which does not celebrate tolerance and pluralism. As a result, the New Christian Right accuses the liberals either of arguing in 'bad faith' or of being deluded by their own ideology" (188). In the view of the New Christian Right, the unclear epistemic and ontological foundations of secular humanism offer no grounds for consistent argument and lead humanists either to bad faith or to irrationality.

Despite their differences, the two groups exhibit a key similarity in their communication theories. A covert assumption the two seem to share is that the purpose of communication is conversion and that conversion happens through *showing*, that is, through displaying the logic of a claim. Secular humanists promote the proliferation of a variety of views, and New Christian Right advocates oppose it out of this same underlying belief. However, the shared assumption that the sheer exposure to views is powerful does not lead to improved communication between the two groups; in fact, it seems to undermine it.

This assumption, that rhetoric functions by revealing viewpoints with effectiveness, does little to help two disparate groups with incommensurate belief systems deal with one another. Pluralism and tolerance, while perhaps necessary preconditions to good discussion, by themselves merely assure that different views will be allowed to "sprout up" together like different species of flowers in the same field. However, there is no developed method for getting them together into any sort of relationship, even the temporary relationship required for genuine debate. MacIntyre says, "It is not just that we live too much by a variety and multiplicity of fragmented concepts, it is that these are used at one and the same time to express rival and incompatible social ideals and policies and to furnish us with a pluralistic political rhetoric whose function is to conceal the depth of our conflicts" (253). Consequently, even the live-and-let-live worldview of secular humanists, for instance, cannot make for productive, genuine communication between groups.

Incommensurability and "Normal" Rhetoric

Communication fails, in part, because we have adapted postmodern assumptions about science to the subject of communication and because we have limited methods of rhetoric to something analogous to what Kuhn calls "normal" science. First, we assume that discussion cannot succeed without common standards of judgment preceding it. Second, those standards are assumed to be part of entire totalizing frames by which the elements of our worlds gain meaning to us. And third, we also assume that the purpose of talk is clarification and correction: we hope that the material of our discussions (the data) will be rearrayed within an existing framework into a better representation of the world. Confronted with evidence of different frameworks, we often cannot find ways to talk productively about significant differences.

Ong observed that Descartes's successful "campaigning" for "clarity and distinctness registered an intensification of vision in the human sensorium" (*Orality and Literacy,* 72). Since Descartes's time, Western rhetoric has adopted the same pattern of thought as normal science. In other words, rhetoric has been seen as functioning to find ways of *showing*. At its most rational, rhetoric would show how conclusions are valid *in terms of* some master concept; clarity of argument was thought to be identifiable with correctness of thought. This is precisely the rhetoric MacIntyre sees being currently practiced: it allows logical cases to be made for each side, following from the first principles of each; but it offers few resources for discussing issues generated by incommensurate first principles.

The results of post-Cartesian rhetorics are documentable. They include public address that draws its eloquence from either the fiery vilification of opposition or from the carefully crafted logical argument in defense of one's own position.[8] As assurance in a single logic declined, however, a gradual degradation of rhetoric resulted. In fact, post-Cartesian rhetorics led to a threat to rationality in public talk similar to that which science experienced but more dramatic. Some rhetorical efforts slid gradually into a form of display, a logical extension of the showing function that rhetoric had taken on.

These efforts might have their origin in the assumption that ideal talk was to represent clear and distinct thought. In this view, the facts, discovered before any rhetorical exchange, should "add up" to one "picture" of a situation if properly presented. The eighteenth-century rhetoric of George Campbell is one example. By creating "vivacity" or liveliness in the facts, a speaker could, according to Campbell, develop a "moral certainty" in the listener. In the midst of eighteenth-and nineteenth-century modernism, confidence in a rationality defined by the epistemological project was high, and of course voices that did not share that confidence were generally muted.[9] At that time it seemed possible to claim that if the facts were laid out with sufficient power or clarity before someone but she did not "get the picture," she was not rational: she was stupid, obdurate, or at worst psychologically unfit to see what was there. The only alternative explanation, one dear to such early-twentieth-century writers as I. A. Richards, was that the communication itself needed to be revised: the speaker was not being as clear as he thought he was being; otherwise, conversion would result. Problems arose as the foundations of rationality were challenged and as alternative voices gained strength. We were left with little faith in the necessity of facts to add up to a single clear picture and with few models of rhetoric that could do anything *but* rely on the proper presentation of facts.

The predictable result was a loss of confidence in rhetoric as a rational enterprise. After the flourishing in the 1950s of a rhetoric that relied heavily on the shared belief in the importance of facts, modern rhetorics made their first collision with postmodern doubt in the 1960s. Wayne C. Booth documented this collision in his *Modern Dogma and the Rhetoric of Assent*. During student protests of the 1960s, Booth observed the dominance of various kinds of speech, verbal and nonverbal, which manifested a complete disregard for the importance of facts or reason giving. Booth also made note of the prevalence of "demonstrations" as a means of attempting to produce conviction in an audience. Demonstrations also manifested disregard for fact and argument but nevertheless invoked a variation of fact-based rhetoric: rather than making the facts speak (vividly) for themselves, demonstrators presented evidence of strong feelings (shown either by numbers of people involved or by loudness of expression, both vocal and visual) with the expectation that strength of feeling would speak for itself. The fact-based rhetorics of the 1950s mutated into an expressive rhetoric in the 1960s, a rhetoric that has continued into the 1990s.[10]

Demonstrations and their various progeny are curious communicative instances of what MacIntyre tags "emotivism." Emotivism reflects a belief in the loss of rationality and "is the doctrine that all evaluative judgments and more specifically all moral judgments are *nothing but* expressions of preference, expressions of attitude or feeling, insofar as they are moral or evaluative in character" (12). MacIntyre frames the distinctiveness of emotivism in terms of judgment: "The moral element in such judgment is to be sharply distinguished from the factual. Factual judgments are true or false; and in the realm of fact there are rational criteria by means of which we may secure agreement as to what is true and what is false. But moral judgments, being expressions of attitude or feeling, are neither true nor false; and agreement in moral judgment is not to be secured by any rational method, for there are none. It is to be secured, if at all, by producing non-rational effects on the emotions or attitudes of those who disagree with one. We use moral judgments not only to express our own feelings and attitudes, but also precisely to produce such effects in others" (13–14).

MacIntyre suggests that, for the emotivist, there no longer exists any form of judgment to underwrite moral positions for which we might argue and hence no form of judgment to underwrite argument. If I am an emotivist, I might say, "If reason is neither final nor convincing, and if my own moral choices are not the result of reason, then the most I may do is display my thoughts, feelings, and attitudes to you with the hope that they may find analogs in you."

No matter how the outcomes have varied, none of these post-Cartesian rhetorics includes a place for judgment or a discovery of truths within the rhetorical transaction itself. In other words, rhetoric has been thought to begin with judgments made previous to any thought of giving them voice. The point of the rhetoric that follows the judgments is to defend, present, promote, or at least effectively display them. Discovery of truths is to be made by some means prior to and external to presentation; the only discovery or judgment left to these rhetorics has to do with determining the ways in which these truths might be presented effectively. However, we seem to have lost confidence in the judgments made prior to their promotion in rhetoric and in the methods by which those judgments have been made.

Once lost, that confidence cannot be restored by models of discourse that derive from the same conception of rationality from which those methods of judgment themselves came.

Rhetorical Judgment and Rhetorical Invention

The kind of judgment urged by philosophers since the eighteenth century to determine both moral decisions about political remedies and scientific decisions about theory choice has been a form of judgment grounded in the epistemological standard of agreement: we assume that political judgment ought to emerge from consensus on moral principles and scientific judgment, from consensus on scientific method. However, political remedies often do not follow as a result of "normal discourse" any more than scientific revolutions follow from normal science.

In MacIntyre's view, revolutionary political remedies emerge from conflict rather than from consensus. MacIntyre takes issue with Ronald Dworkin on this point. According to MacIntyre, Dworkin would like "to see the Supreme Court's function as that of invoking a set of consistent principles" that have been codified into law (253). Judgment by the Court, as Dworkin sees it, should consist in the application of those principles. In actuality, MacIntyre points out, the Supreme Court, during times of the most profound conflict, may instead act creatively to craft decisions that somehow draw from both sides. Rather than simply adjudicating, MacIntyre argues, the Court sometimes performs a peacemaking role. Such was the case in Bakke v. California, in which the Court "forbade precise ethnic quotas for admission to colleges and universities, but allowed discrimination in favor of previously deprived minority groups" (253). There is no "set of consistent principles behind such a decision" and there are no consistent sets of principles to invoke and apply in our society, according to MacIntyre (253). The Court did not perform "by invoking our shared moral first principles" but rather by finding a means of "negotiating its way through an impasse of conflict" (253).

Three points (at least) are observable in this example. First, as MacIntyre points out, the Court was moved to act out of the existence of conflict, not consensus. Moreover, what motivated the conflict was a specific incident rather than an academic challenge to a principle. Second, the Court acted, at least in MacIntyre's explanation, not by finding consistent grounds for uniting the two sides (there are no such grounds, according to MacIntyre), but rather by finding a way to keep peace between the two sides. The two sides are united only in the Supreme Court decision. Third, the Court's decision realigned the relationship between the two rival positions, changing the way the two sides had to operate toward one another.

In this example, MacIntyre effectively offers a way to contrast two kinds of judgment, the first of which, following observations by Hannah Arendt in "The Crisis in Culture" (*Between Past and Future*, 219), I label "spectator judgment"; and the second, "active artistic judgment." The first is the type of judgment we have typically associated with rationality, both in rhetoric and in decision making. In fact, this is the way we think of judgment in general: as associated with finding and invoking fixed standards that undergird the making of a particular decision.

Generally, for instance, we assume that judgments about right or wrong (or efficient or inefficient, fair or unfair, just or unjust) precede matters of decision. Beiner, who finds our reliance on such an assumption provocative, points out that grammatically our expressions of judgment of all kinds tend to be propositional and that the grammar "leads us to think of judgment as something that *follows* the object of judgment, like a verdict" (*Political Judgment*, 7). In fact, the Port Royal logic, an influential eighteenth-century logic, defined judgment as an affirmation or denial. The label "spectator judgment" affirms the activity of scrutinizing something that was created at some earlier time; Arendt used the term in "The Crisis in Culture" to refer to the refined scrutiny of the cultured citizen appreciating art.

Arendt's designation of "spectator judgment" suggests the possibility of some other, alternative sort of judgment, the judgment of the actor; in fact, the idea of "active judgment" was given relevance by Arendt herself.[11] Arendt likened aesthetic judgment, especially as considered by the ancient Greeks, to an activity: "To 'love beautiful things' is no less an activity than to make them" (214). She went on to associate with aesthetic judgment, following Pericles on love of art, a virtue we might associate with an activity like archery: "accuracy of aim," which she saw as "the virtue of the man who knows how to act" (214). Excellence in judgment was to embody accuracy. No less important was her insistence that politics was to be considered "in terms of virtuosity or performance" (Beiner, *Political Judgment*, 16). However, Arendt pointedly classified judgment of both kinds as belonging to the spectator; her concern was actually with showing spectator judgment to be active. "Accuracy of aim" was presumably an accuracy informed by knowledge of the standpoint of another, which was informed, in turn, by active experience of and with the other. Enlarged mentality is achieved, in other words, out of experiencing the other and out of actively imagining the responses from the standpoint of the other (Beiner, *Political Judgment*, 17–18). Although Arendt spoke persuasively about the active nature of spectator judgment, she did not think the judgment of the actor relevant or distinct, although she showed a keen awareness of the different kind of thinking that went into actually producing those things that were to be judged (*Between Past and Future*, 216).

Beiner, however, is sensitive to the opening suggested by Arendt for locating and understanding the distinct form of judgment exercised by the actor. He points out that judgment itself has become identified exclusively as spectator judgment, leaving little room for the judgment of "the actor" who "judges just as much as the spectator does." The spectator model has likewise squeezed out what Beiner considers the truly practical judgment that is "prospective" rather then "retrospective" (*Political Judgment,* 7). He claims that the two types of judgment are distinct and not reducible one to the other (107), and he provides a working definition contrasting the two: "The spectator discerns the meaning of a political event, and thereby bestows dignity on those involved. Through the search for meaning, the judging spectator rescues the actor from the flux of time. The critical distance which the spectator establishes between himself and the events judged enables him to perform this dignity-bestowing function. The standpoint of the spectator, then, is governed by the principle of dignity. The standpoint of the agent, by contrast, is governed by the principle of wisdom in the pursuit of substantive purposes" (107). For instance, it is one thing to act on the Bakke case, another to provide a later critique of the decision.

Active judgment, as I intend it here, follows in part from Beiner's observations. Active judgment differs from spectator judgment in two important ways. First, our ability to judge actively is engaged when we are acting—and particularly when circumstances force us to act—rather than when we are scrutinizing. Second, active judgment cannot be reduced to the application of standards, rules, principles, or procedures for knowing; on the contrary, we engage in active judgment when we perceive there to be no method dictating our decision making about how to act. Active judgment may be characterized as the concentrated engagement we experience when we must act but there is no method dictating how.

Active judgment, unlike spectator judgment, requires what MacIntyre would call know-how. Know-how, more than knowledge of principle, is required to captain a ship in a storm or to act as a peacekeeping body. MacIntyre would also insist that know-how is an element of some kinds of virtuous behavior. He describes moral judgment to be less "the knowledge of a set of generalizations or maxims which may provide our practical inferences with major premises" and more "knowing how to select among the relevant stack of maxims and how to apply them in particular situations" (223). Virtuous behavior may involve more than know-how, but know-how is the element that has most clearly become lost to our sense of virtue today. In fact, virtue has become so completely detached from the idea of know-how, according to MacIntyre, that a reliable sense of virtue itself has been lost: "Since a virtue is now generally understood as a disposition or sentiment which will produce in us obedience to certain rules, agreement on what the relevant rules are to be is always a prerequisite for agreement upon the nature and content of a particular virtue" (244).

Hence virtue, thought of as determined by rules that derive from a specific moral center, becomes part of the problem of incommensurability, since we no longer agree on a body of rules. Exercising spectator judgment may require, at least in part, reference to agreed upon rules. To judge the elegance of, say, a football pass, will require my knowledge of, and reference to, some standard of excellence. We may argue over what the standard should be, but our argument rests on the assumption that we require standards allowing us to pronounce the pass elegant or inelegant. However, knowing that standard will not *by itself* help me throw the pass, given all the unforeseeable contingencies of the specific game, as much as will knowing how to perform and being able to perform well—with virtuosity.

Artistic judgment is also different from, and complementary to, spectator judgment. The contrast between *artistic* judgment and spectator judgment provides an emphasis different from the contrast between *active* judgment and spectator judgment. Artistic judgment is prospective. Artistry may be described, in part, as the way we act when we have an end in mind. In essence, the artist recognizes that what is already before us in the world may not be all there can be. A new theory, a Supreme Court decision, a solution to a problem, are all fashioned. The artist looks creatively at what is before her with an eye toward fashioning something new in the world. Unlike the vision of the spectator, which is directed backward to what is already there, the vision of the artist is directed outward and forward. In fact, this difference in direction is one way of characterizing the classical distinction between contemplative reason and artistic reason. In writing of Aristotle's distinction between art and science, Richard McKeon notes that while science reasons back to nature, art reasons "outward to the action in which the power is actualized in external effects" (213). Just as a form of judgment appropriate to producing outward effects is inappropriate to judging what has already been produced, the reverse is also true. Kantian forms of judgment are ill suited to producing new ideas. New ideas are more the product of the artist engaged in the concentrated task of inventing. Something novel may develop from a dynamic interaction of material, artist, and the point at which the artist happens to be at a particular intellectual moment.

We may adapt Arendt's notion of "accuracy of aim" to help contrast the activities of the artist and the scientist. To the scientific mind, "accuracy" implies the correct, unadorned description of nature; "precision" means that the measure applied to that view introduces a minimum of distortion. On the other hand, for the artist actively engaged in making art, accuracy and precision come together to indicate a drive to embody a vision in such a way that it fulfills its purpose perfectly. Kenneth Burke describes this goal as "the sense of the work as entelechial actualization" (416). An artist is concerned with developing, not just any new thing, but a new thing that embodies his or her vision of what may be potential in the material.

Moreover, behaving as an inventor or maker puts the artist squarely in the camp of the actor. Whereas the spectator chooses by applying a principle that is already existent, the artist is aware that not all her alternatives are already before her. The development of the potentially novel requires a form of judgment that allows the artist to perceive and invent alternatives at the same time that she chooses among them: where and how and if a chisel should be placed, how and whether and what color (an old or a new one) might be applied. In acting artistically, therefore, the artist engages in active judgment.

The distinction between the artist and the aesthete who judges the art is an important one, therefore. When we focus on the activity of the artist who is engaged in making art, we are speaking of a drive toward an uncertain end, because despite the aim toward perfection, the artist, as she is acting, cannot be sure that that perfection will be fulfilled. In fact, an artist whose eye is only on the end product, on how it will be and how it will look to others, may lose sight of what she must do to respond actively to the material at the moment. Once engaged in art, the artist is not asking herself if the artistic product will be, in fact, novel or in some other way good; these are the kinds of criteria applied afterward by judging spectators. We can expect the artist to embody different intellectual virtues as well as a different form of judgment. Rather than being good at applying established criteria based on sets of values, the virtuous artist must possess the kinds of know-how or wisdom necessary to invent criteria as she goes along. In addition, the artist must be able and willing to appreciate what is before her for its malleable quality, as though it is material for creating.

Rhetoric, as an art, is concerned particularly with developing ideas and forms that meet the demands of a publicly constituted moment. When recognized not as *persuasion* (to be evaluated by its success, its effects, its formal qualities, or the ethics of its ends) but as an art of *discovering* the available means of persuasion in the given case, rhetoric may be viewed as a particular kind of art, involving a particular form of active artistic judgment. Unlike some other arts, rhetoric is always concerned with communication. As an art, rhetoric is concerned with finding and developing the best idea and form *for a particular purpose in a particular place and time.* If the art is being practiced to its fullest, that purpose is always infused by a desire that could be called "pragmatic novelty": the rhetorical artist hopes, always with some external purpose in mind, to discover heretofore unrecognized dimensions in issues and ideas so as to get others to see them in a new light. Because a rhetor seeks a response to a specific, practical community problem, rhetorical judgment realizes itself to be time-bound. Hence, anyone acting rhetorically should be, *at that time,* committed to the malleability of ideas and their time-boundedness.[12]

The time-boundedness of rhetorical judgment and the malleability of the materials of rhetoric have been at the center of some traditional disputes between rhetoric and philosophy. Plato opened the door for a condemnation of rhetoric that has been made periodically since fifth-century Greece, based on the claim that rhetoric deals with the shifting grounds of appearance rather than the stable, permanent ground of reality. The virtues connected with art and craft, which were concerned with doing things with the plastic or malleable rather than discovering what was permanent, were likewise less nurtured after the fifth century in Greece, with Plato's influence being only one of many.[13]

With a devaluing of the virtues connected with art, there also developed a disparaging of the very idea of *technê*, or artistic method, itself. Typical of a contemporary devaluing are the remarks of Arendt as she sought to place political judgment with the spectator. Arendt pointed out that the Greeks had and appreciated great art but that, paradoxically, they mistrusted artists. "Fabrication," for instance, was persistently excluded from political activity. The reason was that artists and artisans were of necessity seen as guilty of the philistinism that came from thinking constantly in terms of means and ends: "Fabricators cannot help regarding all things as means to their ends or, as the case may be, judging all things by their specific utility" (216). Moreover, this artistic deficiency was promoted by *technê:* the deficiency was most likely to occur in those who had mastered the techniques of an art (216).

Arendt's objections, however, are a statement of her interest in specifying the conditions for sound spectator judgment and of her post-Platonic assumption that artistic thinking was narrow. However, the art of rhetoric, as it developed before and concurrently with Plato's thought, was infused by elements of craft virtue that allow focused rather than narrow thinking about material. The first of these virtues is *kairos*, or timely acting, which, in translation, relates (not coincidentally) to the opportune moment for an archer to take aim (White, 13). The second is *apatê*, which very loosely relates to artful acting.[14] The skills of timely and artful acting, as they apply to rhetoric, have roots in the performing habits of preliterate bards like Homer. When the inventive *technai* that developed after Homeric Greece— the *technai* of commonplaces, topics, and *stasis*—are seen as conditioned by the factors of performance presented in an oral culture, they may be viewed as providing methods of active artistic judgment.

Those methods will be specified in what follows, after which I will draw some conclusions about the ways in which the judgment of a rhetor may be developed and used appropriately at those times at which a spectator's judgment is not appropriate. Relating rhetorical *technai* to the problems of incommensurability permits us to look beyond the effort to find *grounds* for bringing together incommensurate points of view and to talk instead about finding *ways* to bring them together. Ancient conceptions of rhetorical invention offer such forms of "know-how."

Sophistic Invention
Apatê *and* Kairos

Faced as we are with a discourse inadequate to discussing incommensurate problems, we need a perspective I have labeled active artistic judgment. Instead of grounding our discourse in spectator judgment, we require an alternative perspective in order to make use of contradictions as sources of invention and to generate new categories of thought. Rhetorical invention, as I have suggested, can be viewed in such a way as to offer a method for active artistic judgment. This chapter will describe the ironies that exist and have existed in efforts to methodize the rhetorical art, and the way the sophistic notions of *apatê* and *kairos* may usefully change our conceptions of rhetorical method.

Associated as rhetoric has become with spectator judgment, however, it is hard to imagine such a method. The idea of an active form of judgment guiding the invention of ideas diverges from our conventional sense. Histories of rhetoric typically separate judgment of ideas from their invention. In some accounts, in fact, the tasks of invention and of judgment are assigned to different people: the rhetor invents arguments; and the judge, sitting very much as a spectator, judges them. Even when a task of judgment is accorded to the rhetor himself, that action is separated in time from the task of invention: "disposition" in rhetoric is a concern with the arrangement or strategic use of arguments, and it generally follows invention.[1]

The idea of active *artistic* judgment, in rhetoric or anything else, is even more difficult to conceive. The doubt remains, expressed eloquently though ironically by Rorty, that the artist can be considered to be acting rationally: "We think of poets and painters as using some faculty other than 'reason' in their work because, by their own confession, they are not sure of what they want to do before they have done it" ("Science as Solidarity," 39). The implication is that if the artist makes decisions, they seem to grow from the moment and cannot be articulated in advance or reduced to rational principles; hence, some would argue that what I have been calling artistic judgment is not a real form of judgment. Moreover, by further implication, judgments that cannot be articulated in advance or reduced to rational principles are not real judgments.

It was from just this sense of randomness that Aristotle sought to rescue rhetoric. Seeking to defend the artistic status of rhetoric on grounds established by Plato, Aristotle defined it in terms of method or system: "Ordinary people do this [discussion] either at random or through practice and from acquired habit. Both ways being possible, the subject can plainly be handled systematically. . . . And every one will agree that such an inquiry [into the reasons for success or failure] is the function of an art" (*Rhetoric*, 1354a, 4–11).[2] Aristotle's implication, following Plato's challenges, was this: what can be systematized is rational, and what is rational can be systematized; that is, reasons for decisions can be articulated in advance. In seeking to establish the rationality of art, and particularly of rhetoric, on Plato's terms, Aristotle virtually eliminated from study those forms of activity in which the actor was fully—that is, actively—engaged in making judgments as he or she went along.[3]

In the twentieth century, some philosophers claim that we have handed over much of our decision making to method as it has been defined in such post-Platonic terms. The result has been that we have sacrificed the personal involvement in decisions that makes for the practical wisdom, what the Greeks called *phronêsis*, necessary to taking action. Some late-twentieth-century philosophers have made the same observation. Martin Heidegger, Hannah Arendt, and Hans-Georg Gadamer, for example, have pointed out ways in which scientific consciousness has encroached upon the process of practical decision making. Scientific thinking, they suggest, sought to regularize human conduct under verifiable methods for making valid decisions in much the same way that the scientific method underwrote the production of scientific knowledge. Method, science, and *epistêmê* have become identified in our age.

Method, which was inherently objectifying (in our tradition), taught us to remove ourselves from the subject matters of decision making, including communities of tradition of which we were a part. As Joel C. Weinsheimer says of Gadamer's stance on method, "Method derives from this sense of living among objects to which one no longer belongs" (4). Gadamer, like Heidegger and Arendt, tended to characterize the problem in terms of a technological consciousness by which "many forms of our daily life are technologically organized so that they no longer require personal decision" ("Hermeneutics and Social Science," 312–14). Richard Bernstein summarizes their thought in terms specific to what I have been calling active judgment: "While technical activity does not require that the means that allow it to arrive at an end be weighed anew on each occasion, this is precisely what is required in ethical know-how. In ethical know-how there can be no prior knowledge of the right means by which we realize the end in a particular situation" (147). *Technê*, once disconnected from practical wisdom, as Gadamer believed it to have been, leaves us with no resources at times when ends or means are unclear.

While I make no attempt here to exhaustively examine Gadamer's,

Arendt's, and Heidegger's thoughts on this matter,[4] I do mean to point out how much of the problem that they see with method stems from our "thinking that the subjective-objective distinction is a fundamental one" (Bernstein, 46). Thinking exclusively of ourselves as separate from the materials of our work and from the objects we produce makes active judgment impossible. The novelist Robert Pirsig gives this idea flesh-and-blood application in *Zen and the Art of Motorcycle Maintenance.* Pirsig decries reliance on the advice of repair manuals, which are written well in advance of the motorcycle mechanic's encounter with a problem. Problem solving, Pirsig says, is situation bound; it takes place in the here and now. Thus, judgment cannot stem from rules set down in advance. Pirsig's sense of this is acute, and it is behind his contention that the caring worker does not presume that his decisions have been made for him in the past and have taken form in the instruction manual (160). Furthermore, his decisions cannot be made by any a priori principles or rules; they must be made on the basis of the problem as it is faced in the present. Pirsig, in a sense, sees real decision making as possible only when the split between the working subject and the objective of his work is eliminated. The mechanic and the motorcycle change and develop as one: "The material and his thoughts are changing together in a progression of changes until his mind's at rest at the same time the material's right" (161). Therefore, the worker makes judgments by being alert and responsive as he works, not by relying on a repair manual.

The same commonality of spirit may also be applied to invention and creativity, although the idea is often overlooked.[5] Innovation may not grow from a separation of subject and object accompanied by a willful mastery over material; it grows, rather, from losing oneself in the task and material. A sculptor, relying on her own judgment, may move back and forth between a view of the particular piece of marble she is working on and a vision of the final piece. Rather than judgment working linearly—and blindly—to achieve a prediscovered end, judgment works productively and responsively to adjust the specific piece of marble to the end product, and the end product to the peculiarities of the individual piece of marble. Rather than rightness—or good—being determined by the subject, rightness and good develop in interaction between caring subject and object. This dialectic is an act of imagination that requires active judgment.

Although active judgment cannot be reduced to proper method, the idea of method need not be seen as foreign to producing active judgment. The craftsperson, for instance, would willingly use those *technai* that are validated through her experience as helpful in freeing her imagination and releasing her ability to judge actively. In fact, rhetorical *technai* do provide methods of actively and rationally judging so as to develop new ideas and approaches. However, these *technai* cannot perform this function if they are defined in the terms set by Plato, terms that reveal familiar expectations about knowledge and method. We may productively disabuse ourselves of some Platonic habits of thought about rhetoric and look instead at rhetorical *technai* through lenses provided by some of the Sophists, especially Gorgias.[6] The Sophists' pretheoretical notions of *apatê* and *kairos* provide a structure for appreciating in rhetorical *technai*, not specific linear methods for knowing and making, but habits of inventiveness.

Judgment and Method in Fifth-Century Greece: Plato's Objections to the Sophists

Method, Knowledge, and Judgment

The notions that a *technê* should be developed from a body of principles established in advance and that the result of its application should be a product arose as Platonic notions. Moreover, these assumptions about method related directly to assumptions about judgment. According to these views, principles for making artistic judgments should be drawn from criteria for an acceptable end product. These criteria constitute principles for the judging spectator. A method drawn from these principles should, ideally, result in a final created product that stands up to the scrutiny of a judge using those same principles. Shipbuilding *technai*, for instance, should be productive of an excellent ship. Common principles and a method drawn from them were assumed to create a sort of isomorphy between artist and judge. The irony, of course, is that if an artistic moment is truly novel, there can be no body of principles guiding the artist's response to it.

This problem of principle and method was at the heart of one challenge issued by Plato to the ideas introduced by the Sophists, who claimed that rhetoric was an art usable in varied situations. In the fifth century BCE, a number of Sophists had claimed that what they taught was a *technê*, an art informed in some way by principles.[7] Earlier, speechmaking had been assumed to be a random activity with much left to chance; the claim of a *technê* may have been revolutionary. In any case, the claim and its popularization subsequently invited the Sophists' philosophical undoing at Plato's hand.[8]

Plato saw the connection of *technê* with product as implying that a specific subject matter was connected with a given method; for example, the subject matter associated with the teaching of shipbuilding was shipbuilding. However, the proper subject matter of the *technê* being taught by the Sophists was unclear. In several of his dialogues, but notably the *Gorgias* and the *Phaedrus*, Plato challenged Sophists' claims to have a genuine, principled method. The grounds were several, but two are important to the present discussion. First, rhetoric was intended for situations in which persuasion was required, and these situations were so varied that it was impossible for a single art to have a coherent set of principles that could meet every novel moment. The Sophists simply could not have the knowledge to teach what they claimed to be teaching, if that was, in fact, a method for being persuasive in all circumstances. This was the primary objection to rhetoric that Aristotle sought to meet in his *Rhetoric*.

Second, Plato's diatribe against rhetoric rested in part on his belief that it should not be taught. For Plato, the Sophists' claim that they had a *technê* was not merely annoying but morally reprehensible. The problem here lay in what Plato saw as the proper relationship among language, knowing, and virtue. In his scheme, knowledge and the good were identified; acting virtuously was a matter of knowledge—a matter of knowing the good. As Terence Irwin points out in his introduction to the *Gorgias*, virtue and *technê* were not unrelated in Plato's thought. Because knowledge of what was right or good provided the foundation for knowledge of the proper *technê*, having the proper *technê* was necessary and sufficient to do something well or right (2–3). The claim that rhetoric had a method was false to Plato because the activity of rhetoric did not rest on knowledge of the good. Suggestions to the contrary could only mislead its practitioners into believing that they were able to produce virtue.

In the *Gorgias* and the *Protagoras*, the Sophists of each dialogue were made to claim that the subject matters of their teaching included justice and virtue. Plato's demonstration that their so-called *technai* could not lead to either one showed rhetoric as falsely promising to teach virtue or justice. By yoking together the attainment of virtue and the knowledge of principle, Plato made moral decision making dependent upon knowledge: the only genuine *technê* had to rest on knowledge of some principle.

Sophistic rhetoric was a particular target for Plato because it was a linguistic art and as such competed with the only art that could really lead to knowledge of the invariable and good: Plato's dialectic, which, he believed, used language properly to attain knowledge of the good. Rhetoric used language to produce pleasure (*terpsis*), which was not a virtue (Irwin, 8). At best, such pleasure was a distraction from the attainment of knowledge; at worst, pleasure deceived listeners into believing they had knowledge when they had only its appearance. Rhetoric was associated with the changing and unreliable shadows of reality; dialectic was seen to lead above the deceptive world of sensation to that of the Forms. As the only permanent entities, the Forms could be the only true objects of knowledge.

Agreement, Disagreement, and Methods of Rhetoric

For Plato, sound agreement had to be based on certain knowledge; to him, agreement derived from sophistic rhetoric was based only on illusion, emotion, and choice. The belief held by many of the Sophists that all reality was shifting and that nothing was certain was, to Plato, a confusion of sense appearances with reality, and of the impermanence of things with the permanence of the Forms. Moreover, when students of the Sophists transferred this confusion to beliefs about the functioning of language, they were misled into believing that genuine knowledge could not be sought and were seduced into believing that nothing final could be said about anything: "Opposing contrary but apparently equally supported views . . . lead to the conclusion that the world itself, in line with the arguments that reflect it, lacks a stable nature" (Nehamas, 12). W. K. C. Guthrie summarizes Plato's concerns: "The worst offenders are the men who deal in contradictions . . . and think it is the height of cleverness to have discerned that there is no soundness or certainty in anything or any argument" (*Sophists*, 177).[9] Plato and his followers suggested that discourse, properly undertaken, should, in fact, lead to end points of knowledge. The effect of discourse was to be agreement. Plato's own dialectic, of course, serves as an example of the way in which he believed discourse should be conducted. However, an equally good example, especially with respect to the purpose of agreement, may be the rhetoric promoted by Aristotle.[10]

Aristotle was the first theorist to recognize that different sorts of disputes—scientific, political, forensic—call for different genres of discourse. His efforts to improve the quality of deliberation in each type of dispute amounted to borrowing from logic to do so. The obvious evidence of this is that, like Plato, Aristotle saw contradictories as arising from weaknesses of thought, and he sought to correct those weaknesses. But more importantly, Aristotle's efforts to standardize the reasoning for each genre of discourse meant reducing each to a particular language game. The assumption was, of course, that even if there could be different forms of reasoning appropriate to different forms of dispute, everyone in a particular dispute should engage in the same form of reasoning: despite some similarities between them, forensic reasoning called for a particular type of reasoning, legislative for another. In seeking to perfect these forms of reasoning, Aristotle, too, tried to eliminate the ambiguities from language, as he made clear by identifying and cataloguing false enthymemes. There is no provision in Aristotle's rhetoric for creating discourse that can reach across discursive universes; more importantly, there is no value placed on trying to do so. Sound deliberation and agreement rested on consensus on what constituted a logical case within a genre.

Aristotle's rhetoric was not as limited as I have painted it. However, if we do adopt this portrait of Aristotelian rhetoric, we come to believe that the primary function of rhetoric in disputation is to develop a logical case on each side. Successful education in just such a philosophy of rhetoric, it may be argued, has helped produce the situation lamented by MacIntyre in which either side can develop a tightly logical defense and which actually disallows productive discussion. It is therefore worth exploring the idea that rhetoric in the Platonic-Aristotelian tradition may have had its part in creating moral and practical incommensurability. It is equally worth exploring what is offered by a sophistic rhetoric that begins by embracing contradictories as potential means of generating discursive worlds.

Recovering Sophistic Methods of Inventive Judgment

Sophistic rhetorics did, indeed, deal in contradictions, but whether or not the Sophists were the relativists Plato thought them to be is open to question.[11] What does seem clear is the likelihood that sophistic rhetorics, especially Gorgianic rhetoric, saw inventiveness as having an important place with respect to agreement. Contradictions were not to be eliminated but to be valued as providing opportunities for creativity.

The Sophists were by no means the only thinkers of their day concerned with contradictions, contraries, oppositions. In fact, concern with the evidence of competing and opposing realities dominated serious Greek thought before Socrates. The inventive methods of the Sophists may be understood against the backdrop of the cosmology of their day, including that of the pre-Socratic philosophers, who in some cases instructed the Sophists. Although the Sophists were not usually philosophers, they did in some cases participate in various philosophical "schools" of the time.[12]

As early philosophers sought to understand the origins of the universe and the way in which it maintained itself, they were confronted by evidence of oppositions in nature, especially the realities of change and permanence. Birth and death, for instance, were different, even opposed; but because they repeated cyclically, they seemed to be guided by a single principle of harmony and order. The question of which was fundamental—the many, sometimes opposing moments, or the singular order or rhythm behind them—generated attempts at reconciling seemingly contradictory evidence: that on the one hand the single and the permanent were fundamental, and on the other hand that change and the many were fundamental.

Out of the debates over the one and the many arose debates about the presence of opposition in the cosmos. Heraclitus and Empedocles were among those pre-Socratic philosophers who attempted to resolve the dilemma of opposition by introducing *activity* as a force in the universe. They saw polarization as "strife" and the universe as consisting in the striving of opposites toward one another. For Heraclitus, the universe was not itself contradictory, but was a unimodality that came together out of the strife of a plurality of elements. Heidegger appreciatively finds the notion of strife, or *polemos*, fundamental to Heraclitean thought (*Metaphysics*).

The apparent presence of opposition seemed to act as a heuristic to the Greek imagination, and fascination with oppositions persisted into the Socratic period. Philosophical attention shifted somewhat from the nature of the universe to the nature of knowledge (Copleston, vol. 1, pt. 1: 95–96), and with this shift the ideas of paradox and strife became central in a different way. While cosmological strife between the one and the many persisted as a subject of thought, it was eventually incorporated into considerations of the epistemological strife between truth and falsity. In fact, the apparent knowledge of contradictory truths shaped, in terms of knowledge, what Mario Untersteiner calls the "master antithesis" of the age (111). The coexistence of truth and falsity was the important paradox to which thinkers began to respond.

The Sophists found their own voice within these debates. While they are individual in much of their thought, the Sophists constituted a discernible group partly because of their interest in the practical affairs of human beings. Their work was in politics rather than in what we might today classify as philosophy, and they were teachers of rhetoric, among other things. Consequently, their responses to the paradoxes suggested by the pre-Socratics tended to be neither cosmological nor epistemological; they were practical, especially to the teaching of civics and speech.

The Sophists found the existence of contraries to be *at least* compounded by the presence of speech. For Sophists like Protagoras and Gorgias, the apparent existence of contraries was thought to drive speech, but perhaps less than the existence of speech drives contraries. Many of the assertions they made about contraries were made in the context of teaching speaking. Protagoras frequently began with the assumption that what *is* is what can be argued; and what can be argued consisted in a multiplicity of things, including contradictions: for instance, blame and praise could be produced for the same thing (Guthrie, *Sophists,* 181–82). His reported insistence on teaching students to speak on both sides of any case suggests a sophistic goal that built on Heraclitus's observations about strife: through speech, to recreate conditions for *polemos* by bringing together ideas not usually thought to belong together, especially ideas thought to be in opposition.

But the sophistic relationship between contraries and speech is most dramatically presented in Gorgias's "On the Nonexistent" (also referred to as "On Not-Being" and "On Nature"), where he asserted "first and foremost, that nothing exists; second, that even if it exists it is inapprehensible to man; third, that even if it is apprehensible, still it is without a doubt incapable of being expressed or explained to the next man" (Sextus, 65).[13] The first two premises are the key points in considering contradiction.

The treatise has been submitted to a great deal of interpretation, some of it about the purpose of the piece.[14] Schiappa categorizes two opposing interpretations of the piece as either "'pure' rhetoric" or "'pure' philosophy" ("Interpreting Gorgias's 'Being'," 16). The pure rhetoric group, citing the playfulness of the argument and the apparent absurdity of its first premise, imply that the treatise, "devoid of philosophical significance," is designed to "dazzle and delight" (16). The pure philosophy group often cite the likely relationship of Gorgias's treatise to the absorbing controversy, initiated by Parmenides (and taken up in a later generation by Zeno and Melissus, and eventually Plato) about the nature and existence of Being.[15] Parmenides' influential philosophical poem is also about inquiry and the journey away from misapprehension and toward knowledge of Being.

The relevant point in Parmenides' poem may be summarized as the claim for the clear absurdity of accepting contradictions to Being. Being, as eternal and immutable, exists prior to our knowing, and we cannot gain knowledge of what is not. Guthrie translates: "Thou couldst not know what is not—that is impossible—nor declare it" (*History of Greek Philosophy*, 2:14), and Jonathan Barnes paraphrases: "Whatever we inquire into exists, and cannot not exist" (qtd. in Schiappa, "Interpreting Gorgias's 'Being',"24).[16]

For Parmenides, as Guthrie paraphrases, "What is, is, and cannot not-be" (*History of Greek Philosophy*, 2:16), and furthermore, only what is can be known. Just as significantly, Parmenides, arguably, identified knowing with speaking; not only can we not know what is not, but we also cannot declare it. After reviewing several translations, Guthrie concludes that "in saying something *is*, Parmenides undoubtedly had in mind what can be talked and thought about, since he explicitly identifies the two" (Guthrie, *Presocratic Tradition*, 15). In fact, according to one translation, Parmenides is saying that "what can be spoken and thought about must be" (J. Burnet, qtd. in Guthrie, *History of Greek Philosophy*, 2:14). The proper role of speech and thought is, in some respects, to counteract the evidence of the senses that things come and go, pass into and out of existence, and that there is no prior form of Being for us to know. He claims that, as Being can be predicated, it is and cannot not be. In this way, Parmenides pioneered the identification of concerns about knowing with concerns about predication as correct saying (Kerferd, 95). Although problems of correct predication might remain, it seems apparent that we cannot, sensibly, say both that "x is y" and "x is not y."

Read as a concern about inquiry and predication, Parmenides' poem is a cautionary tale. The path to knowledge of Being can be taken when one grasps what can be spoken of and then does not deny it by uttering its contradiction. Schiappa paraphrases the point in this way: "The sense of the sentence is that once one predicates being, one cannot predicate not-being of the same 'thing'" ("Interpreting Georgias's 'Being'," 18). Suggesting that we can think about what does not exist (or take the wrong path of inquiry, as the Goddess of the poem puts it) leads nowhere but to confusion, helplessness, and eventually to absurdity (19). Significantly, the danger of the wrong path (the path of contradiction) is so great that the Goddess guiding Parmenides on his journey enjoins him from taking it: once having said something, one cannot say its opposite without falling into the traps of uttering nonsense (Guthrie, *Presocratic Tradition*, 13–22).

The consequence of Parmenedes' poem was to put at stake the relationships among saying, knowing, and being. Parmenides implies a singularity not only of Being but of meaning. The proper function of language is to represent correct meanings faithfully so as to lead us along the path toward recognition of real Being. To say both "x is" and "x is not" is to fall into confusion. Parmenides may be seen to begin the work of Plato and then Aristotle in stripping language down to representation of essences. Speech that does more than that will lead to confusion. In a sense, the work of Parmenides begins to caution against *too much* speech.

Whether a serious response or a clever take, when read as a treatise on what can and should be predicated in speech, "On the Nonexistent" counters Parmenides in such a way as to serve effectively the needs of the Sophist as a teacher of speaking. Parmenides says, in essence, that what can be thought or spoken must be, and that we are therefore barred from then uttering or thinking the opposite of what we have already thought or spoken. Whatever else Gorgias attempts, simply *developing* "On the Nonexistent" performed a rebuttal to the notion that saying one thing bars the saying of its opposite. In claiming that "nothing exists," he asserted the contradiction to Parmenides' claim that Being exists. If the treatise was designed to dazzle, it flies in the face of the presumed function of language in Parmenides' poem, which was to be toward Being and away from confusion. Demonstrably, for Gorgias saying one thing does not bar saying its opposite. The Sophist shifted the discussion away from the injunctions of Parmenides' Goddess and toward something else: rather than worry about the way language should or should not be used, Gorgias demonstrated how it *can* be used.

Gorgias went much farther, of course. By argument as well as performance, he took on Parmenides' assumptions about the proper functioning of language and was not above issuing, through demonstration, injunctions of his own. Beginning with the notion of premising rather than with Being, Gorgias recast the relationships among language, being, and knowing so as to promote rather than decry contradiction. Contrary to Parmenides' claim, Gorgias claimed that nothing exists, neither existence nor nonexistence. The case about nonexistence rests upon what can be premised of it, whether it can be thought to exist or not: "If the nonexistent exists, it will both exist and not exist at the same time, for insofar as it is understood as nonexistent, it will not exist, but insofar as it *is* nonexistent it will, on the other hand, exist" (Sextus, 67). While acknowledging the absurdity of concluding that nonexistence both can and cannot exist, Gorgias nonetheless demonstrated that nonexistence *does* both exist and not exist. As Eric Charles White paraphrases, "Insofar as Not-Being *is* nonexistent, it *is*." And furthermore, Not-Being exists because we can speak of the existence of Being: "It [Not-Being] *is* as the diacritical contrary whose presence (or existence) is necessary if the contrastive meaning 'Being' is to emerge" (33). Contrary to Parmenides, for existence or Being to be thought of or predicated, it is dependent on its opposite, nonexistence, or Not-Being. Gorgias argued that "if the nonexistent exists, the existent will not exist, for these are opposites to each other, and if existence is an attribute of the nonexistent, nonexistence will be an attribute of the existent" (Sextus, 67). The existent, or Being, is dependent on its opposite being conceivable; to say something exists requires conceiving of its nonexistence.

White regards the treatise as an effort to overturn the ontology described in Parmenides' poem by overturning the doctrine of an eternal and immutable Being. By asserting that Not-Being both is and is not, "Gorgias seeks to establish the fundamental ambivalence and ambiguity of reality" (32). Such ontological interpretations are reasonable, given the groundwork set by Parmenides. It seems equally apparent, however, that Gorgias makes a case for the inventive potential of language as its true function. In suggesting that Being or Not-Being depends for its genesis on its opposite, Gorgias freed meaning, predication, and reference from the self-limiting function Parmenides placed on them. White points out that "if thought can posit the existence of eternal immutable Being only by making a contrast with Not-Being . . . then "Being" can claim no mirroring correspondence with ultimate reality" (33). Meaning is not conferred in mirroring reality but emerges through contrast with other meaning. Whether or not Gorgias opposes an eternal, immutable, and ultimate Being in favor of more fleeting and ambiguous realities, as White supposes (32), he does counterpose representation with invention.

Demonstrably, for Gorgias, saying one thing not only does not bar saying the opposite; in fact, the saying of one thing is what makes possible the emergence of its opposite. In a sense (although Gorgias is unlikely ever to have stated this as principle) the ability to articulate one term (in this case, Being) makes possible the articulation of its opposite. In this way, contradictories emerge as means of generation in Gorgias's thought.

Some scholars remark that in his treatise Gorgias undercuts the philosophical importance of truth, hence Guthrie's conclusion that Gorgias is showing that "it is as easy to prove 'it is not' as 'it is'" (*Sophists*, 194). But in developing the argument against Being as he does, Gorgias did more than undermine the possibility of knowledge. At the same time that the act of proving anything (at least, with finality) was being undermined, the act of *asserting* was being salvaged—through proof. His "On the Nonexistent," far from indicating that Gorgias had given up on finding truth or settled for a weakened sense of truth, indicates his capacity for celebrating the possibilities of invention through speech. In beginning to assert the possibility of many truths through speech, Gorgias could concentrate on invention of what was articulable as truth without fearing the invention of a countervailing truth. Indeed, the fact that "On the Nonexistent" is refutable does little to undermine the fact that it raises possibilities for discussion. That countervailing truth might be articulated by Gorgias himself at another time, because the discovery of opposition made such assertion possible. Gorgias's

effort may as well be interpreted as directed toward finding ways of generating assertions rather than finding ways of establishing air-tight proofs. The
existence of contraries meant that truths generated through speech should
be multiple. All that can be predicated should be.

Gorgian Apatê as Artistic Acting

Gorgias's sense of the relationship of truth to speech was part of his fairly thor-
ough-going consideration of language. Gorgias, remembered by Aristotle and
others for poetic excess, regarded the strength of language to be its capacity to
distort and enliven rather than to represent essences as nearly as possible. The
virtue of language in its poetic power is most apparent in the conception of
apatê, particularly as *apatê* stands in contrast to more mimetic theories of language. Gorgias suggested a sharp contrast to Plato on the subject of agreement.

The Greek word *apatê* suggests a melding of ideas that come together
only uneasily in English. The word may be translated as "trick, fraud,
deceit," according to the Liddell-Scott-Jones lexicon, and there are also
undercurrents of an intent to beguile. The notion that the role of speech is
to deceive appears in some form in all of Gorgias's extant and reported
works, but Gorgias seemed also to have in mind a sort of justice to the
beguilement offered by speech. Speech, he says in the "Encomium to
Helen," is a powerful and deceptive master (8), and if Helen fell under the
spell of persuasive *logos,* her deeds need to be excused. But in a writing pre-
served by Plutarch, Gorgias observed that the one who uses deception is
more just than the one who does not: "He plays the literary game more cor-
rectly than the one who does not" (Rosenmeyer, 227). Art involving *logos* is
more just when it deceives.

Some of this attitude toward deception stems from a consideration of
the function of art. As Thomas Shearer Duncan points out, Gorgias was
speaking of the tragic poets when he likened just behavior to deceitful
behavior (408). Gorgias seemed to suggest that beguiling and distortion
have their place on the stage, and in that setting our own willingness to be
deceived is itself noble; we should be willing to accept and be aroused by
the staged fire we might see during a play. Being fooled is more just than
not being fooled. But to Gorgias the influence of *logos* was similar in other
settings. Gorgias admitted to no essential difference between the beguiling
meters of poetry and the disturbing effects of prose on the psyche. Helen's
case was not unique; she was fooled because all persuasion proceeds "by
molding a false argument" ("Helen," 11). Speech is not capable of reproducing reality; the capacity of speech is to produce effects on the soul, much
as drugs produce effects on the body ("Helen," 14).

In "On the Nonexistent," Gorgias suggested that "speech and reality are
not commensurable" (Rosenmeyer, 232); that is, word does not act as sign
of thing. In "On the Nonexistent," Gorgias accounted for the inability of

words to communicate by the fact that words are entities separate from things and thus can reveal only themselves: "That by which we reveal is *logos* but *logos* is not substances and existing things. Therefore we do not reveal existing things to our neighbors, but *logos*, which is something other than substances" (Sextus, 84). Consequently, according to Charles P. Segal, there could be "no such thing as a purely objective transmission of reality" (109). This might seem a curious conclusion, but rather than defeating the possibility of a valid utterance as it might to the Platonist, to Gorgias it "frees the *logos* from any ontological implications" (110). Hence, autonomous from the world of things, the *logos* is as "free from the exigencies of mimetic adherence to physical reality . . . as from an instrumental function in a philosophical schematization of a metaphysical reality" (110).

To Gorgias, words do not represent or transmit reality; in fact, to him their natural function is to distort reality. This conclusion may derive, for Gorgias, from the unstable nature of the corporeal universe. Because of the flux of entities in the universe, words simply cannot stand in any sort of one-to-one relationship with entities.[17] Each time a word serves to try to represent something, the entities to which it seems to refer have already changed. Thus, *logoi* are "by nature *apatêloi*" (Rosenmeyer, 232) or distortive. The proper function of language, therefore, is to employ distortion to work magic on the soul in the same way that drugs work their magic on the body, as Gorgias indicated in the "Encomium to Helen."[18] Because language functions properly to create illusions and excite the listener, the "deceiver" is more noble than the nondeceiver.

There was a further reason that the distortive power of *logos* needed to be exploited fully. Human opinion, or *doxa*, is notoriously unstable, as is apparent from the varieties of opinion held on opposing metaphysical interpretations. *Doxa* is easily deceived and is therefore itself deceiving. Strong opinions, stated persuasively, impress our psyches just the way certainty would. Segal analyzed Gorgias's works incisively on this point: Gorgias saw *doxa* as "deceptive and unstable . . . but the human psyche has no better guide" (111). Because the human psyche needs guidance in order to interpret things and make decisions, persuasion is necessary. And because the psyche, under the spell of opinions, is constantly in danger of coming to a conclusion about the timeless nature of Being without full appreciation for the uniqueness of a moment, all persuasion rests on the potential deceptiveness of speech. The deception that Gorgias sees as inherent to persuasion is to him "a necessary and practical corollary to his conception of the normal state of the human psyche . . . *man's bent is toward error and not, as ultimately in the Platonic view, toward truth*" (112, emphasis mine). Error may be corrected only by persuasion to some other error, received (deceived) opinion only with new received opinion. Gorgias spoke, for instance, of "the words of the astronomers who, substituting opinion for opinion, taking away one but creating another, make what is incredible and unclear seem true to the eyes of opinion" ("Helen," 13). Appearances are not to be replaced by higher truths but only by more appearances.

The Gorgian assumptions about language and its role highlight two values regarding method and truth that are different from Platonic values. First, to reemphasize a point made earlier, the Sophists did not concern themselves primarily with weighing, evaluating, and choosing among truths. They engaged themselves instead in the proliferation of truths. Their challenges lay in finding means for inventing rather than principles for validating.

A second value concerns the usefulness of contradictories. Plato found the Sophists' trafficking in contradictories to discourage speech; the Sophists (at least Gorgias) saw contradictories as something close to a principle of invention. When I use "principle" here, I do not mean that they saw the existence of contradictories as validating their decisions about how to invent or about what should be invented. There is little evidence to suggest that the Sophists sought philosophical validation. I mean that they sought a way to fulfill the potential of speech to generate truths from other truths; furthermore, that "way" may have originated in a relationship between contradictories (like paradoxes) and speech.

It is worthwhile for us, though, to consider what *apatê* and the sophistic attitude toward contradictories might validate, even if the Sophists did not so treat the matter. One point that seems indicated is that contradictories can and do exist side by side in language, in paradoxes. In a brief analysis of a sophistic paradox, Lyotard illustrates how, in its generation, the semantic category in which winning and not winning cannot coexist *is not* absolute. Opposites do exist together—in paradoxes, as paradoxes exist in speech.

Lyotard's telling of the paradox further illustrates certain differences between what has been framed here as spectator judgment and what I have called active artistic judgment. These differences imply the distinctive ways in which establishing agreement would be achieved by each type of judgment. Lyotard repeats the legendary story of Protagoras's demanding payment from his student Euathlus, who has refused to pay him on the ground that he, Euathlus, has not yet won a case with the techniques taught him by the Sophist.[19] Protagoras replies that if he, Protagoras, were to win his case against Euathlus, Protagoras would win payment; and if Protagoras were to lose his case, Protagoras must still win payment since Euathlus would have won the case. Lyotard condenses the paradox as follows: "If Euathlus has won at least once, he must pay. If he never won, he still won at least once [against Protagoras, by proving that he, Euathlus, had never won], and must pay" (*Differend*, 6).

Without complaining of it, Lyotard indicates that such a form can exist only by virtue of a "category error." Russell's theory of types demonstrates that "a proposition (here, the verdict in the litigation between master and pupil) that refers to a totality of propositions (here, the set of prior verdicts) cannot be a part of that totality" (6). As Lyotard says, "The paradox rests on the faculty a phrase has to take itself as a referent" (6).

If we accept Russell's logic, then we ought to accept *uncritically* his conclusions about such forms as Protagoras's paradox and eliminate them from our discourse. If we do so, then in this case the dilemma evaporates: agreement with one side (Euathlus's) is clearly indicated. What if, however, the privileging of Russell's logic as the sole ground for such judgment is not assumed (as it might not be in the latter half of the twentieth century)? If we eliminate this privilege, then we may see, along with Lyotard, that the Sophist is doing something that the logician does not suspect: "The logician has nothing but scorn for the sophist who ignores this principle; but the sophist doesn't ignore it, he unveils it" (6–7).

The value of this unveiling may be unclear until we explore the function it may serve. Where the logician seeks to eliminate the ambiguities of language, the Sophist seeks to exploit them in practice. So the logician and the Sophist demonstrate a difference in their aims: the logician's efforts are directed toward teaching us what we *cannot* say, while the Sophist's efforts are directing us toward *saying*.

The concern with criteria for evaluating phrases, as opposed to the concern with the capacity for producing "interesting" or "provocative" phrases, distinguishes spectator judgment from the active artistic judgment that comes about from the sophistic placing of oppositions next to one another in, for instance, Protagoras's paradox.

Hence, sophistic thought teaches us that speech can create the conditions in which opposites are brought together while the integrity of the opposition is maintained. Neither side need be reduced to the terms of the other (as in, for instance, a gestalt picture), nor need we seek, fruitlessly, a subsumptive conceptual category that eliminates the opposition between sides. Incommensurability need not exist when circumstances demand that grounds for discussion be found. In Platonic terms, incommensurability between some positions or universes of discourse is unassailable. In sophistic terms, a condition of incommensurability is one possible appearance shaped by the resources of language.

Gorgian Kairos as Timely Acting

The second sophistic notion to enrich our understanding of active artistic judgment is the notion of *kairos*, understandable to us roughly as a principle of the "opportune moment" (Poulakos, "Sophistic Definition," 36). The idea that the rhetor must locate the opportune moment for speaking seemed to be held by several of the Sophists (Schiappa, 73–74; Poulakos, "Sophistic Definition," 40). It was Gorgias, however, who may have produced a treatise on the matter, now lost,[20] and from whose writing a fully considered concept has been fleshed out by contemporary writers like Eric Charles White and Bernard A. Miller. The Gorgian sense of the opportune moment and its importance derives, in part, from the sensed flux of the universe and the autonomy of the *logos* from the corporeal universe. In this respect the notion of *kairos* seems to be related in sophistic thought to *apatê*. However, the Gorgian *kairos* also incorporates a concern for the press of time and novelty on decision making. *Kairos*, therefore, speaks to one of the paradoxes that exist with respect to discovering methods of active artistic judgment: what sort of method is possible for addressing situations acknowledged to be completely novel?

According to White, *kairos* emerged for Gorgias as "a principle of spontaneity and risk" (20) from two entwined concerns: the tragic recognition of the inevitable struggle of polar opposites and the inability of the *logos* "to contain all the possible meanings of the world" (31). The freedom in which the *logos* may do its work arises out of the relationship of speech to the oppositions and strife in the universe. In the world of human affairs, the nature of antithesis dictates that oppositions cannot be overcome by application of any external principle of justice. This deep-seated sense of opposition is the basis for the tragic vision shared by Gorgias and the Greek tragedians. Untersteiner, in a well-known passage, presents this tragic view as an "irrationalist" one because it is irresolvable through rational methods: "Knowledge of the power possessed by the irrational constitutes the victory of the tragic. Man cannot escape the antitheses. His thought discovers only the opposite poles in all propositions which try to explain reality philosophically" (159).

For Gorgias, the dilemma of inaction in the face of tragic antithesis may be overcome, not by the rational will at all, but rather by allowing the moment to force itself upon us. The idea presents itself most vividly in Gorgias's "Funeral Address," in the context of a battle. As Untersteiner describes it, the battle requires a moment of decision for the soldiers, in which they must decide between two competing, equally valued goods: respecting the sanctity of life or preserving the *polis* (177). This situation is the ultimate example of the tragic circumstances in which the universe presents itself to us. We are faced frequently with dilemmas that cannot be intellectually resolved, and yet we need to act; but in the battle the dilemma is exacerbated by the need to act immediately.

Kairos thus has to do in part with the way in which the dilemma itself must shape our action. We may act only by allowing the moment, in all its novelty, to wash over us, to dictate to us. So novel is the moment that old patterns of thought must be abandoned so that we may be open to the novelty. For the Pythagoreans, the mastery accorded to the wise man included mastery of the strife of opposition (Untersteiner, 82), and such mastery was achieved with knowledge of the "right thing at the right moment" ("Funeral

Address").[21] For Gorgias, the need to decide immediately, as in battle, reversed the customary relationship of justice and cognition. Untersteiner says that "the act of cognition capable of being transformed into action cannot come from a rigorously logical law but from the persuasive force of the *logos* which is released in the instant of the decision . . . which has as its object . . . 'the right thing at the right moment'" (177). In other words, cognition does not "release" or give birth to the appropriate decision, which in turn permits the choice of the appropriate word; rather, the forcefulness of the moment releases the word, which, through its impact, "persuades" cognition into existence. In turn, a different sense of justice results: "A decision cannot come from 'the arrogance of positive right . . . but from the kindness of true justice'" (Untersteiner, 177, quoting from the "Funeral Address").

In addition, though, the dilemma itself shapes the moment, vitalizes it, breaks everyday sequences of time, and shatters old habits of thought. A moment of dilemma forces a realization of utter newness on the human being: what once seemed clear and uninvolving no longer seems so, and established principles for handling the moment are no longer meaningful. Meaning itself has to be reinvented in terms offered up by the moment. As for the embattled soldiers, "The basis of the tragedy was, in effect, a disrupted time sequence. The predictable, expected and familiar were shattered; the chaos beneath an otherwise well ordered world surfaced, imminent in the decision" (Miller, 176). The immediacy of the dilemma, in creating a time out of time, opens possibilities for new meanings. This is a second outcome of the *kairotic:* disruption of the old and radical reinvention.

From this understanding of timeliness, we may conclude that Gorgias endorsed improvisation as the beginning place of inventiveness.[22] Much more, however, is evident in Gorgias's commitment to *kairos.* He implies not only that we can or should invent through improvisation but also that true decision making may occur only by losing oneself in the moment; it is only through opening ourselves to the moment that its meaningfulness may be realized through us in our action. Hence, for action to take place on the basis of any sort of truth, the present must ever be reinvented (White, 15) by a sort of "radical principle of occasionality" (14).

The need for this reinvention is bolstered further by the inadequacy of the *logos* to represent the cosmos without distortion. Distortion occurs for many reasons, as we saw when we examined *apatê.* John Poulakos, for instance, comments that, for the Sophist, all speech encloses as much as it discloses, silences as much as it speaks ("Rhetoric, the Sophists, and the Possible"). A reason for this inadequacy is, again, the sophistic embracing of antithesis: the antithesis itself invalidates any actualization of reality codified in speech, because once an idea is spoken, a falsifying opposite immediately presents itself, begging for actualization. "Being" begs for its own falsification in "Not-being," so both are equally false, equally true. In discussing the

Gorgian *kairos*, White comments in similar terms on "the inability of any dogmatic scheme to contain all the possible meanings of the world" (31), an inability Gorgias addresses in "On the Nonexistent."

Again, two conclusions follow. First, all commentary is temporary and provisional, so speakers and listeners alike must be prepared to disconnect from what has been said before and abandon "a repetition of tradition" (White, 31) as a guide to decision. They must be prepared and enabled to reinvent meaning as the occasion demands, despite the lure of tradition and habit. Secondly, reinvention can be assisted rather than hampered by the *logos*. The *logos* can, indeed, fool us into a false belief in a stable reality; however, *logos* can also actualize the antithetical over and over and in concrete form. Paradoxes, we saw, were one such actualization, pulling oppositions into relationships that were unexpected, disjoined from our habitual way of thinking of them, essentially making possible the impossible. The antithetical nature of *logos* also serves *kairos* well, revealing previously unconsidered possibilities in (and for) the concrete terms offered by the specific occasion.

This radical occasionality, suggested both in dilemma and in *logos*, holds implications for both rhetoric and rhetor. First, rhetoric must function, in part, to induce a readiness for sharp discontinuities from the habitual, tired thinking that makes immersion in the moment and its meanings impossible. Along these lines, White, like Thomas G. Rosenmeyer and others, notes the similarity between Gorgias and the tragedians. White points out that "tragedy *induces* in its audience a state of cognitive dissonance, an unresolved tension between opposite or contrary forces" (15, emphasis mine). This, in some respects, is the opposite of argument based in logical models, which seeks to clarify or remove dissonance in order to convince.[23] *Logos*, with its powers to seduce and overwhelm the senses, has the power to induce a tragic set of mind, a readiness for improvisation that would not otherwise exist in everyday life. The treatise "On the Nonexistent," similarly, may be less important for establishing a logical case for the incapacity to know or speak of Being than for inducing a skepticism in the conventional wisdom: "The skeptical *ataraxia* ideally produced by the treatise 'On Not-Being' would result, then, in a mental attitude resistant to dogmatic self enclosure, abiding neither in Being nor in Not being" (White, 35).

The portrait above, however, should not suggest an audience being bent to the will of a speaker or of a speaker "taking charge" of a situation. The speaker himself must be enabled to surrender to the will of the occasion and to the *logos:* "That is, in order to achieve success, the orator as seducer must be 'seduced' in turn by the occasion of speech. Persuasion depends on self-effacement, on acceding to the terms laid down by the circumstances confronting the speaker. . . . Lacking a fixed identity, the orator's self would thus become identical with its present performance" (White, 38). In other, more

pragmatic terms, an openness to improvisation requires, first, the willingness of the rhetor to become absorbed in the work of the moment. To an
extent, the orator seeks to induce or at least replicate in himself the anxiety
or sensed crisis of a battle. Perhaps for this reason, Gorgias entertained by
offering programs of extemporaneous oratory during which a listener would
suggest a topic and the Sophist would compose on the spot, "trusting to the
fortune of the moment to produce an utterance that truly answers to its
occasion" (White, 16).

Second, the rhetor must find what to say by surrendering himself to the
conditions of the *logos* offered up by the moment. He must engage in the
constant dynamic of antithesis, of moving back and forth between the possible and the impossible, the actual and the not yet actualized, the conventional and the novel. An illustration of this back-and-forth movement lies in
the sophistic uses of historical narrative, as Susan C. Jarratt sees it. In her
feminist reading of the Sophists, Jarratt describes the sophistic goal of
appropriating historic incidents to new purposes. Using Gorgias's "Helen"
to illustrate, Jarratt points out how Gorgias employs a variation on the story
of Helen in order to draw consideration to a series of themes not usually
connected with the story. In the encomium, contentions about the *logos* and
about "Helen" bounce off one another imaginatively, each contention giving
rise to others. In order to establish and explore those relationships, Gorgias
sets aside concerns about establishing historic truth as it might exist outside
his own developing narrative. He also sets aside the habit of thinking of history as linear cause and effect, a habit that may blind us to the vitality of particular moments of history. The plausibility of the relationships among
elements and events is validated within the speech itself, not necessarily
within traditional historic narrative. Jarratt comments that "The opportunities for speculation provided by the narrative situation [in "Helen" and in
"Protagoras"] . . . supersedes [*sic*] the establishment of the 'factual' status of
the materials themselves as a goal for the discourse" (16). No historical truth
is permitted to remain stable.

Implications for *Technê*

The concepts of *apatê* and *kairos* point us toward what we should expect of any
technê that is to promote rather than undermine active artistic judgment. In
attempting to teach rhetoric, the Sophists, especially Gorgias, suggested a
technê in which subject and object merge in response to the dictates of a powerful moment. The power and novelty of the moment are such that habitual
thinking like that in the methods useful to everyday craftsmanship are inadequate for meeting the moment. A *technê* grounded in "radical occasionality"
must assist in disrupting the methods of routine production, in muting or con-
cealing the habitual, and thus allow the craftsperson to respond directly to the
moment, to see it freshly.

The *technê* of the Sophists began from exploiting the natural contradictoriness in language, particularly the language of real, concrete events. Although they made use of speculation, the Sophists did so to a practical end, which in some cases was the projection of new insight into situations. Language had little mimetic use in a shifting reality but had great usefulness in creating illusions, new realities generated from the oppositions and contradictions of old linguistically known realities.

How would such a *technê* be actualized? The likely response to this question is to examine the *technê* based on "commonplaces" and often associated with the Sophists. We need to be careful about the implications of the commonplace method for the radical inventiveness of the Sophists. It is a thesis of this book that in the twentieth century the so-called commonplace method is not adequately understood as reflective of *apatê* and *kairos*. In fact, the method of commonplaces should have the opportunity of being viewed without the distorting veil of Aristotelian rhetoric. *Apatê* and *kairos* are first evident in the practices of oral performance among preliterate bards and subsequently in the newly found literacy of the fourth century.

Commonplacing
Composition as Inventing and Judging

The sacred and magic character of style is interwoven with the rigidity of logic
in such a way that the tragic consequences of the latter are nullified by the persuasive and deceptive force of particular formal expressions. In this interaction
of exacerbated logic and magical formulae, which recur with confusing
rhythm, there is formed the germ of something new which, though connected
with the forms of poetry very differently felt and used, is prose, the "artistic
prose" expressing the delight of reason which insists, desperately insists, on
ideas of triumphant novelty breaking in upon the consciousness of man.

Mario Untersteiner, *The Sophists*

If we are looking for an example of active artistic judgment in the rhetorical art
and thought of the Sophists, the obvious place to begin looking is in their methods of prose invention, and specifically the so-called method of commonplaces.
We would hope to find a pretheoretical *technê* based in *kairos* and *apatê*. The
rhetor would need to use judgment in order to be constantly responsive to the
moment and to produce something to say about it. Moreover, there is a need
for an artistic *technê* to enhance responsiveness and make meaningful con-
cealing and revealing possible. The method of commonplaces, often regarded
as an unsophisticated precursor to more analytic topical systems, is generally
acknowledged as a hallmark of sophistic method.[1]

The method of commonplaces does, in fact, provide a seminal example
of such a *technê*. But this conclusion seems to fly in the face of some com-
mentaries on sophistic method, which find commonplaces better directed to
reproducing than producing and not generative of any kind of judgment. My
contention is that the commonplace provides a method for judgment when
thought of as a verb form: *commonplacing*. In order for this idea to be clear,
we need first to see more typical uses of the term 'commonplace,' contrast
them to my notion of 'commonplacing,' and move on to seeing how commonplacing typifies the oral methods of the epic singers and the Sophists.

Commonplaces and Commonplacing

Typical of definitions of the commonplace is George A. Kennedy's. Commonplaces, he tells us, are "the topics, the traditional examples, the maxims which
the orator had heard and used before" (5). Walter J. Ong, in *The Presence of*

the Word, similarly defines "cumulative commonplace" as "a pre-fabricated passage for an oration or other composition" (81). Commonplaces, therefore, are "cullings from what has been said about a subject before" (262), or "purple patches on set themes such as treachery, loyalty, honesty of character, decadence" (56).

According to such standard interpretations, commonplaces were neither capable of producing anything original, nor were they applied or chosen with much judgment. Compositions for similar occasions could be developed with relative ease because commonplaces were presumably gathered on a variety of topics and used again and again. Once commonplaces were memorized, speeches could be developed to any desired length since "commonplaces or specimens of oratory were like building blocks from which a speech could be constructed" (Kennedy, 53). The repetition of blocks of discourse in different speeches and the existence of arguments apparently drawn from the same cultural maxims made ancient orators and Sophists remarkable to the modern mind mainly for their lack of originality. These characteristics would also make the commonplace method a poor method of active artistic judgment.

The notion that the so-called method of commonplaces contributed to a lack of originality ill suited to the needs of rhetoric is by no means a conclusion reached only in modernity but was an indictment offered up by, for instance, Isocrates. Thomas Cole, while agreeing that sophistic commonplaces contributed to a lack of originality, cites the awkwardness of the transition from oral to written teaching and composing as a cause. The Sophists, he says, rather than producing theoretical *technai* like Aristotle's, taught more in the way of the epic poets, through imitation and example. Whereas the poets (as we shall see) learned the epic stories and the techniques of singing through concentrated listening to oral performances, the Sophists produced written models and lists of commonplaces for their students to learn and perhaps memorize. These seemed to be inadequate to the task of meeting novel situations with fresh argument. Cole quotes Isocrates' complaint: "'Anyone can see that whatever has to do with writing is rigid and unchangeable and that with speech just the reverse is true. What has been said by someone else can never be useful to a later speaker to the same degree: those considered the most skillful speakers are those whose remarks are original as well as to the point'" (81).

Hence, the developing art of rhetoric was caught up in a complex web of expectations pulled in from an oral age of myth and oral composition. Isocrates' complaint about writing, echoed in a variety of ways among the ancients, as Cole shows, only implies the difficulties of transition from the conservative medium of myth, which was to be repeated, to the less conservative medium of rhetoric, which had to observe the novelty of different occasions. Even if the change from orality to literacy had not played a direct role in the Sophists' teaching, the reliance on methods like those useful for reproducing myth would meet with distress or at least criticism as awareness of occasionality grew (and, of course, as awareness of occasionality grew, so did Plato's pointed observation that there could probably be no method for rhetoric).

However, the accusations against commonplaces as leading to unoriginal composing may have been misplaced. Commonplaces, as used by the Sophists, must have been controversial. Far from being unwilling to meet the needs of novel occasions, Sophists like Protagoras and Gorgias found the "radical occasionality" of rhetoric to be of key importance, as we have seen. The importance of *kairos* to some Sophists does not square perfectly with the criticisms we have observed.

Moreover, many ancients (and more sympathetic twentieth-century commentators) found the Sophists anything but unoriginal. The Sophists were credited by their contemporaries with some remarkable achievements related to their compositional art. Ancients who came after Protagoras, including even his detractors, reported that Protagoras was the first "to expound the importance of the right moment" (Diogenes Laertius, 9.52), as well as to concern himself—for better or worse—with correct meanings of words in oratory (Diogenes Laertius, 9.52), and to develop "eristic arguments" (Heschius, *Onomatologus*) based on the notion that there were two *logoi* to every argument.[2] Gorgias was credited by Philostratus with founding sophistry and beginning "extemporaneous oratory" (*Lives of the Sophists*, 2). His use of rhythmic figures and antithesis, although eventually becoming so popularized as to seem "tiresome" and "contrived," was at first considered innovative (Diodorus Siculus, 12.53.1).

Perhaps especially telling is Plato's endorsement of sophistic thought along one important line. Plato's telling in the *Protagoras* of the Sophist's famous myth of the origin of human civilization reveals Plato's implicit suggestion that Protagorean thought represented a break from mythic thought (Untersteiner, 58–59). In poetic and tragic forms, myth (in a way truly despised and feared by Plato) had provided both form and substance of thought. The mythology had been collectively internalized in the telling and retelling and had disallowed speculation about history and the universe. Protagoras, to the extent that Plato's telling of the myth is attributable to him,[3] was using myth representatively, as external representation of individual thought and as support for a claim. Individuation of thought and the burgeoning use of claims and supports were innovations over poetic that were encouraged by Plato.

Protagoras's myth is reminiscent of another significant evolution linked to the development of prose composition from poetic: the development of historical prose. Charles Rowan Beye reports that the first prose was historical, a nonmetered telling of the stories previously told in poetic myth (198).

Like Protagoras's myth, and unlike the old poetic reportage, a "point" of the new history as told by Herodotus, for instance, was its relevance to present time. Richard Leo Enos, in fact, emphasizes the highly "rhetorical intent" to Herodotus's work, "his effort to present history as a sort of argumentative proof" (29). Such writing of history was to lead gradually to history as we know it, with the questioning of reports and interpretations that we find, eventually, in Aristotle. A hint of what was to come, though, was in Protagoras's dramatic—and original—questioning of the existence of the gods in his "On the Gods." Gorgias's argument against existence was probably considered equally original and almost as irreverent. Indeed, as the previous chapter suggested, an urge to produce oppositional discourse may have underwritten Gorgias's and Protagoras's methods.

Protagoras and Gorgias were at the center of yet another significant development in fifth-century thought. Protagoras's concern with the correct interpretation of words led him to pioneer a conception of Greek myth as an object of study. Schiappa argues that the objectification of myth was virtually revolutionary. He states that "Protagoras made a crucial analytical leap: from repetition of poetry to the critical analysis of poetry. His analysis was metapoetic in the sense that poetry became an *object* of study rather than simply the medium through which the world was understood" (*Protagoras,* 57). Protagoras's objectification was a sign of the newfound ability to move outside of myth rather than swim within it and a sign of the concomitant ability to talk critically about discourse: "Protagoras was one of the first thinkers to put into practice a *metalanguage*" and hence "to turn *logos* into something to be examined. . . . He introduced a new way of thinking and speaking about the world, the world of discourse in particular" (197). The fragments of Gorgias's work indicated that he actively speculated about language and its power, if not, as Protagoras did, its correctness.

So, contrary to the impression left by less sympathetic writers, some of the Sophists were indeed innovators, who presented in both form and content sometimes radical advances from the mythic-poetic tradition. However, considering the method of commonplaces as narrowly as Kennedy and Ong do does not capture the capacity of the Sophists to use methods to invent new constructs or to make argumentative connections through prose composition. One of the problems is that Kennedy, Ong, and even Cole fix on that feature of commonplaces that makes them appear to be simply *things*, relatively static elements—phrases, for instance, to be committed to memory and then moved around like blocks. The deficiency of such a conception and the need for a more dynamic view of commonplaces become more evident when we look at them with the compositional needs of the Sophists firmly in mind, especially as those needs involved inventing from oppositions and from the emerging needs of the moment.

There were three major needs or purposes that circumscribed the development of the Sophists' methods of composing. First was the idea, given currency especially by Gorgias, that persuasion to a single immutable truth was impossible and that the purpose of rhetoric was the creation of possibilities. Because there existed multiple truths, the purpose of argument was balance: persuasion to one side necessitated persuasion to its opposite. Persuasion did not aim at the resolution of contradictory appearances for the purpose of establishing a truth but aimed at awakening the public to the possibilities of multiple and contradictory truths (Jarratt, 22). The purpose of any *technê*, therefore, would be less to create coherent proofs than to generate unexpected possibilities and permit them to play out. For Gorgias, at least, the generation of possibilities in language should, in turn, effect changes in opinion, *doxa* being unstable and susceptible to the vivid appearances of truth painted by language: "The crucial function of *logos* in argument . . . is not to represent reality and not to defend truth, but simply to bring about a change of opinion" (Mourelatos, 157).

The second factor influencing sophistic methods would be the perception of the "physicality" and autonomy of *logos*. Possibilities were actualized through *logos* and existed only in articulation. Hence, *logos* was a strong master, as Gorgias said in his "Encomium to Helen," working essentially by impinging directly on the psyche in a virtually physical way, much as substances could have an impact on the body. *Logos* worked independently of things, but with an impact similar to the impact that physical things could produce. Alexander P. D. Mourelatos and Jacqueline de Romilly both see the audible, the visual, and the *logos* as described in "On the Nonexistent" to work analogically: each worked in a similar physical way on specific organs of the body. One outcome of this notion of *logos* as physical was to consider that *logoi* could, almost physically, move into and out of relationships with other *logoi*. Any *technê* helpful to sophistic composition would be consistent with this sense of *logos* as having physical properties.

A third purpose shaping sophistic composing was a *kairotic* sense of linguistic possibility and even truth. Because *logos* was not naturally reflective of a reality, its purpose was not to align itself with reality; in other words, the purpose of *logos* was not to reflect an existing truth. Methods that would try to make *logos* more nearly reflect a truth would not be appropriate for the Sophists. Instead, any truth was temporary and might emerge as a possibility only through concentration on the moment, which could permit "the right thing at the right moment." The Sophists required a method that would allow the concentration on the moment by which possibilities could force themselves. In addition, in order to fulfill the persuasive potential of language to excite and impress the senses, the Sophists required a method in which the force of possibility of the word would be complete and immediate.

The question becomes, how could commonplaces fill such needs? How could they be at once sayings, little conservators of traditional wisdom usable in a variety of situations, and still provide a means of innovating and impressing new realizations upon audiences?

In order to articulate the method of commonplaces in the more dynamic form required by the Sophists, we need to look with more sympathy to the oral improvisational methods of the poetic bards who preceded them. The similarity between the Sophists' teaching methods and those of the bards has already been noted; furthermore, poetic "formulas" seem to be the ancestors of what we call commonplaces. Moreover, the Sophists saw themselves as inheritors of the bardic tradition (Guthrie, *Sophists*, 42, 104) in their roles as teachers and keepers of culture. Like the poets, the Sophists (Gorgias especially) were revered for their ability to compose extemporaneously and with improvisational wit (Guthrie, *Sophists*, 42, 43).

With this line of descent firmly in view, the dynamic nature of the Sophists' *technai* becomes clearer as the similarities between the compositional needs of poets and Sophists are foregrounded. It may seem ironic, considering what I said earlier about the conservative nature of epic culture and the well-documented need of the poets to remember and make memorable the epic stories, to think that the key to understanding sophistic originality lies in an understanding of oral epic art. But if we focus on the composing singer instead of his composition, we will see that the demands of memory and improvisation led to a highly dynamic means of composition. Sophistic method, while representing a clear advance on oral poetic singing, has its genesis in the demands of the immediacy of oral performance.

From "Commonplaces" to "Commonplacing" in Oral Composition

If the genesis of the commonplace is in the formulas of oral poetic, then conceptions like Kennedy's and Ong's may be off-center and reflect a post-alphabetic way of thinking of oral composition. Their definitions fail to answer a compositional question that, though of very little concern to a composer versed in writing, is of primary concern to the preliterate composing singer: What do I say *next*? If we take this clue from poetic composition, then the better label for the method would be "commonplacing." This label emphasizes the nature of the action that the method aids the composing singer in making—the action of "placing" one sound group, word, phrase, or idea next to another in order to advance through time in a performance.

The need for commonplacing seems to have developed from circumstances specific to preliterate culture. This conclusion is drawn in part from work by Eric Havelock. Havelock's controversial thesis, originally developed in *Preface to Plato*, was that the preliterate culture and the psychology of its members were conditioned fundamentally by the lack of writing and the necessity of oral recitation. The thesis has been enormously influential, and Havelock has had numerous detractors and supporters among those interested in the history of literacy.[4] His conclusions have been challenged on various fronts, particularly with respect to whether the development of literacy was the revolution to culture that Havelock claimed it to be. Although some of the analysis in this chapter relies on Havelock's work, I am concerned more conventionally with the influence of the lack of literacy on the compositional methods of oral composers than with the influence of oral recitation on the development of culture.

From Havelock's work and Parry and Lord's pioneering studies in the 1930s with illiterate Yugoslav poets, we may infer some key requirements of the compositional art of the ancient bards.[5] Milman Parry and Albert B. Lord isolated specific compositional requirements as they studied contemporary representatives of an oral tradition that began in preliterate times. First and foremost among the conditions to be observed by the oral poet was the requirement that he perform his various tasks simultaneously. For the true bard, "the moment of composition is the performance" (Lord, 13). Lord emphasizes that the art of the bard must be regarded as the art of one who is singer, composer, poet, and performer all at once: "Singing, performing, composing are facets of the same art" (13) There was no composed song waiting to be remembered and repeated, word for word or line for line; the poet improvised the specific performance of the traditional epics. The problems with which the art was involved were the problems of spontaneous composition out loud, for an audience, in the traditional epic rhythm. The importance of rhythm may have been connected to the virtually religious functioning of the performance. Lord notes that the poet was required to "compose rapidly in the traditional rhythmic pattern" (25). He suggests further that "patterns were born for magic productivity, not for aesthetic satisfaction" (67).

The constraints of memory in an oral culture also meant demands for constant revivification of information for an audience. The songs encapsulated traditional heroic tales and myths. In the absence of writing, these needed to be impressed again and again on the memories of listeners. Havelock speculates that the success of a singing centered on its capacity to be experienced again and again as a lived event and thereby made memorable. Havelock says that, for instance, "you threw yourself into the situation of Achilles, you identified with his grief or his anger. You, yourself, became Achilles and so did the reciter to whom you listened" (*Preface to Plato,* 45).

Additionally, the poet was expected to satisfy the specific demands of an audience at a particular performance. Both Lord (25–26) and James A. Notopoulos (14) emphasize the point that the audience influenced the composition-performance of the singer. The audience influenced the length of the song and its sections, and the order of the parts of the narrative. The Yugoslav singers were sensitive to the moods of their audiences and had to shorten or lengthen songs accordingly (Lord, 16–17). In either case, the singer required a fluid form of composition and a method for composing that allowed him to conveniently either stop or extend his performance.

The virtuoso poet could use this fluid form to adapt in other ways. The poet was adept at including those passages that would enlist the sympathy of the particular audience, whether it was made up of the rich and distinguished or the poor and humble. Despite his willingness to include passages that would "arouse the sympathy of distinguished people" if the audience were well-to-do, the singer was quite willing to pitch the facts differently for a different audience (Radlov, qtd. in Notopoulos, 17).

Hence, the singer, in performing and composing at once, while at the same time satisfying the requirements of tradition and art, exercised a form of active, highly attentive judgment. Although the traditional song offered a superstructure (Peabody, 216–18), the singer had many decisions to make along the way and on the spot. These were decisions that required concentration on, and responsiveness to, the moment. Notopoulos said, "The physical, technical, and psychological factors at work in the creation of oral poetry make the poet live largely in the moment and only secondarily in the larger framework of his material" (15).

The method that developed to enhance concentration on the moment and permit active judgment was the method of themes and formulas. Thus, the first model of commonplacing is found in the way the poet used themes and formulas together in order to allow one moment of narrative to evoke another, or one sound group to evoke another.

Themes and Parataxis

Themes, according to Lord's definition, were "the groups of ideas regularly used in telling a tale" in traditional songs (68). Lord emphasizes that a theme had a verbal flexibility; that is, it "is not any fixed set of words, but a grouping of ideas" (69). Examples of themes might include various catalogues, like guest lists; letter-writing themes; council meeting themes; and themes in which the hero or his horse was ornamented for battle. The singer would learn a number of themes that, with little or no adjustment, he could use in different songs. With a repertoire of themes at his disposal, the singer was able to either linger over a certain theme or simply go to the plot line and advance the action quickly.

However, simply having a repertoire of themes at his disposal was only a small part of the singer's skill at actually using them; reproduction alone was not sufficient to produce art. Lord observes, in fact, that it is the modern critical mind that, seeing themes that recur in several songs and finding few apparent relationships among the themes within a song, concludes that a stock of culturally approved themes comprised the singer's method. The singer himself, however, would have found it as important to think in terms of a related ordering of themes as to know a stock of them. In other words, for the singer, the themes needed somehow to present themselves as leading into—*evoking*—other themes. In practice, the themes must have had a relationship. Disposition, or execution, of the themes together was part of the invention of the song. Lord suggests that often the means by which one theme evoked or led to another is by the action of the narrative: "Usually the singer is carried from one major theme to another by the demands of further action that are brought out in the developing of a theme" (95). The logic of the narrative would draw him forward, as would a second force noted by Lord, the "consequent force of habitual association" (96).

The movement from theme to theme that Lord describes is a movement from moment to moment essential to preliterate commonplacing. Basically, something that happened at the end of, or by the end of, one unit of composition evoked the beginning of the next; so the composer "inched" his way through the song by drawing beginnings and endings into a common place. By developing a facility for thematic thinking, the singer formed the skill of associating one theme with another, which means, essentially, finding or creating the *means* of putting endings together with beginnings.

The poet's rather primitive way of moving through time becomes plainer by contrast to the sophisticated compositional artistry with which we are familiar. The earlier art form was "paratactic and inorganic" (Notopoulos, 1) in contrast to the organic structure of later art. "Parataxis" indicates the presence of apparently discrete or loosely related parts occurring one after another, whereas "organic" refers to the use of an overarching thesis to determine selection and organization of parts. The organic we find not only in post-Aristotelian drama but also in modern essay writing. Oral, paratactic art does not recognize such subordination; as Havelock has said, the most sophisticated transition between parts in an epic poem is "and next" (*Preface to Plato,* 180). Digressions are not merely tolerated but are encouraged, possibly as means of storage and transmission of folkways: "The digressions . . . are actually the substance of the narrative, strung paratactically like beads on a string" (Notopoulos, 6). The ability to linger over digressions that appear to us to break up the narrative constituted a part of the poet's virtuosity. Laszlo Versenyi suggests there was a "tremendous concentration on the present moment dictated by the necessities of the singer's art. . . . Since long lines of argument are precluded and a careful preparation for what is to take place much later in the poem is unessential, all that matters is the present event. It must be presented vividly, firmly, directly, and laid open to sight so that it shines forth with a dazzling flash of light that leaves no shadows and allows nothing to remain hidden or undisclosed" (*Man's Measure,* 7).

This tendency toward parataxis did more than free the imagination of the poet and, later, the Sophist. For both, of course, it aided the spontaneous invention required in improvisation. The looseness of linkages and the discreteness of parts allowed the singer to linger over a digression and the Sophist over an argument. For the Sophist, the same ability to linger with one argument permitted him to play out its possibilities and to vivify and embellish.

The preliterate singer's method for making connections derived from *his* needs. This is significant. In oral art, the constraints on plausibility, while not nonexistent, would have been less severe or at least different than in a more analytical culture. Although needing to stay within the constraints imposed on the overall story by the mythology, the composer would have been making connections between specific themes with less immediate regard to what the audience might find plausible. Under pressure to invent quickly and in oral performance, he would be creating and enacting moments of feasibility (although not principles of feasibility) as he went along. The logic by which the oral epic singer worked, therefore, could be described as a logic guided by an alerted responsiveness to what had gone before and what could come after, a responsiveness heightened by the artistic pressures of performance.

Formulas and the Echo Principle

Commonplacing happened by virtue of the developed capacity of composers to hook together elements in a composition by finding or recognizing points that the elements hold in common. The chronological "hooking together" of themes in a narrative, however, does not begin to describe the sophisticated commonplacing habit that the Sophists seem to have inherited from the poets. That more sophisticated commonplacing began in the poets' use of formulas.

Parry defined a formula as "a group of words which is regularly employed under the same metrical conditions to express a given essential idea" (Lord, 30). This original definition of the formula as a group of words led later scholars to think of formulas (and their offspring, commonplaces) as "ossified clichés" that could be found repeating in various different epics (Lord, 108). However, with the formula reexamined, as Lord suggested, "not only from outside in terms of textual analysis, but also from within, that is, from the point of view of the singer of tales and of the tradition" (30), the notion of the formula as a cliché to be memorized evaporates. Reexamining the formula also helps us to overturn inadequate conceptions of the commonplace.

From the perspective of the singer, what was at work in the use of formulas is better called "formulaic expression," defined by Lord as "a line or half a line constructed *on the pattern* of the formulas" (4, emphasis mine). Lord emphasized that the singer needed, not simply a stock of formulas, but a method for calling to mind at the moment of necessity a phrase that would fit with story, mood, theme, meter, and previous phrases. He needed, it seems, not phrases, but a sense for "patterns" (37).

The developing singer, according to Lord, acquired the patterning skill necessary for formulaic expression in much the way any of us acquires language. We do not acquire a stock of words, phrases, and sentences; instead, we learn the grammar or patterns of a language so that we may produce spontaneously an infinite number of sentences. Similarly, the novice singer, through concentrated listening and imitation, learned to think habitually in the patterns that underlay the formulas, rather than to memorize the formulas per se.

The mature singer used formulas in much the same way that the mature language user produces language. He produced formulas, not mechanically, but more or less spontaneously under "the necessity of singing" (Lord, 33). The thoughts the singer produced usually took the formulaic structure he had learned. He produced formulas through an analogic or substitution system like that of language. In use, "language substitutes one subject for another in the nominative case, keeping the same verb; or keeping the same noun it substitutes one verb for another." In the same way, a singer with "an essential idea to produce under different metrical conditions" substituted a key word in order to adapt to the appropriate metrical conditions (35).

The constraints of oral performing required the singer to move through time by moving from one sound group to another. Idea was constrained by sound, and the fundamental method of movement in time was that movement by which one sound follows another. The easiest way one sound may follow another is repetition, which is basic to formulaic expression. Repetition grounds many aspects of what is now called poetic style. Meter is based on repeated sounds and silences of various lengths; assonance and alliteration are based on repeated vowel and consonant sounds; rhyme is based on repeated sound groups.

Havelock called the general use of repetition and its variants the "acoustic echo" (*Preface,* 187). The acoustic echo aided the formulaic expression of the singer by the evocation of "a variant word or phrase" (187), which was of great psychological help to the poet. This evocation could take many forms, some less sophisticated than others. For instance, "The easiest and laziest form of memorization is sheer repetition" (147): the phrase "Hector is dead" may be followed by the phrase "Hector is dead." As the oral mind grows "bolder," it might repeat the meaning of "the same essential image—a dead man who is Hector" while varying the "words and syntax":

> Hector is dead; fallen is Hector;
> Yea Achilles slew him
> Hector is defeated, Hector is dead.
>   (147)

With only textual evidence and little appreciation of the echo function, the literate mind can make little sense of such pleonasms, or redundancies.

Understood as a means of improvisation, however, pleonasms are responses to an echo that allow the singer to continue. The repetition allows him literally to "play for time" until memory and meter allow him to advance the song.

The poet may also have had "a parallel system of repetition of sound alone without reference to meaning" (Lord, 147–48) and a number of other forms of patterning that used repetition to achieve variation. So, for instance, Lord finds "formulaic" those lines that "follow the basic patterns of rhythm and syntax and have at least one word in the same position in the line with other lines" (47). In an example from a singing of the "Song of Bagdad" that survives translation well, notice the functioning of the phrase "to the city of Kajnida":

"Lead me to the city of Kajnida!
I know not the road to the city of Kajnida."
It was a beast and could not talk,
But the steed knew many things.
He looked over the mountains
And took the road to the city of Kajnida
(46)

These patterns, though based on repetition expressly, operated through an analogical movement of thought. The singer moved through a song in part by identifying potential similarities in order to generate one sound or meaning group from another. For instance, in the oral medium of preliterate singing, a knack for bringing to mind synonyms as well as a knack for pleonasm became important, allowing the singer to vary the verb form according to the length of the noun subject in a line of poetry so that the meter of the line could be maintained whatever the noun subject. Similarly, if the sense of a line would be made clear in half a line, sound, not sense, was nevertheless the determining factor of utterance: the metrical line still had to be completed. So in order to take an entire line to make the utterance, the singer needed ways to stretch out an idea; he must repeat the idea in the second half of the line: "He spoke, he uttered a word." On the other hand, if he needed to do so, the singer could often complete the sense of an action within the line; he might also complete the sense in less than a line and use a variant phrase to satisfy the metrical requirements of the line (Lord, 34).

In some respects, this kind of adjustive use of formulaic structures was probably even more necessary to early composers of prose, freed as they were from the constraints and/or options of meter. Of all types of echo adaptable to prose, the one most interesting to the study of the development of ideas is the one most plainly inherited by the Sophists: the balance in its various forms, eventually including parallelism, antithesis, and simile. All are generated by virtue of echoes. Although sophisticated balances like the antitheses favored by Gorgias have roots in Heraclitean opposites as well, their oral roots are in rhythm, particularly in the balanced rhythms of the back-and-forth movement between singer and audience. This back-and-forth pattern was standard in oral poetic (Finnegan, 29, 122) and might have taken the form of periodic oral responses made by the audience in rhythm with the speaker (call and response).

We make rhythmic balances like antitheses by playing out the beginnings of a rhythm we seek to complete; these rhythms are based on repetition. The balance achieved by the listener's response to what the singer has said is present in more compact form in the similes, antitheses, oppositions, and parallels of early prose composition. In a discussion of Scottish ballads, Buchan writes, "The habit of thinking in balances, antitheses, oppositions and parallelisms is intrinsic to the oral mind" (qtd. in Finnegan, 128).

That habit of mind enabled the poets to move forward in their composition by generating one thought or sound group as the antithesis of what had come before or by generating a sound group from what they had identified as similar in the one before. Thinking in balances permitted the poet to have "the right sound at the right moment." Having the right sound at the right moment, not first ownership of the utterance, is the oral poetic standard of originality. Significantly, creativity consisted in a facility for metrical pattern and for making "sayables" on the spot: "the formulas themselves are perhaps less important in understanding this oral technique than the various underlying patterns of formulas and the ability to make phrases according to those patterns" (Lord, 44).

The potential of this sort of originality was apparent, however, in three habits of thought, all inherited by the Sophists and developed into a fledgling *technê* of commonplacing. The first, of course, is a sense of rhythm or balance, inherited by the Sophists as a proclivity toward generating balanced forms and ideas. It was the need to move forward that made this poetic use of rhythm a hallmark of a particular kind of improvisation.

The second is what B. E. Perry called "the early Greek capacity for viewing things separately" (qtd. in Notopoulos, 14). Havelock attributes the entrenchment of this habit in oral culture to the fact that before writing there was no "timeless copula" by which eternal verities or statements of knowledge could be uttered, such as "'human beings are responsible for the consequences of their own acts'" (*Preface*, 181–82). He notes that the "kind of knowledge which is built up in the tribal memory by the oral epic poetic process . . . is a knowledge of 'happenings' (*gignomena*) which are sharply experienced in separate units and so are pluralised (*polla*) rather than being integrated into systems of cause and effect" (180).[6] The capacity to view things separately is also evident in the paratactic structuring of the poems, which was inherited as the "running logic" of early prose. With such structuring, various parts of a song could be kept in paratactic distinctness and available to be moved into contact with one another.

The potential of this distinctness of parts for innovation is important. Typical of the epic mentality is the potential to bring separate parts together

while maintaining the integrity of each, allowing attributes that are sometimes not only distinct but even disparate to exist side by side without question. The result is, first, an ability to put things into association—create
associations between things—without having to account for the principles
of that association. Versenyi speaks, for instance, of the attribution of both
power and wisdom to the gods by the poets: "That they did not even feel the
need to account for this association is typical of the epic mentality. The uni-
formity of belief characteristic of an age of living myth does not give rise to
critical reflection, and the paratactic view of the world requires, and can
provide, only conjunction (in this case of knowledge and power) and not
connection or underlying rationale" (*Man's Measure*, 25).[7]

A further outcome of the capacity to view things separately is a fluidity
in the associations made between elements. If elements could be put into
association, they could also be removed from familiar associations, and new
relationships could be asserted. The potential existed for making highly
imaginative intellectual moves. Thus, alertness to the possibilities of balance
and contrast could guide poets, and later Sophists, toward evolving and creatively asserting possibilities.

The third quality of mythic composing is an outgrowth of the first two:
the ability to move those separate things into and out of contact with one
another through a sense of rhythmic or balanced response. The value of this
habit of thought was not as a basis for reasoning to conclusions about the
world but rather as the basis of an artistic *technê*, a rational—although perhaps not reflective—method for developing and producing from an alertness to balance. It was this alertness to balance that the Sophists would have
found could guide them toward similarities and opposites in order to create
possibilities.

Plausibility, Opposition, and Sophistic Originality

The fact that the Sophists were indebted to oral poetic improvisation is apparent in their proclivity for performing before audiences, for inventing arguments impromptu, and from the similarity between the structure of early prose
and epic poetry, including parataxis, or the "running logic" of arguments.
Untersteiner points out that a part of one of Protagoras's fragments employs
"the linked composition peculiar to the archaic style" while subsequently
breaking a poetic pattern (54). Havelock comments that the "first philosophic
prose" of Heraclitus and that of Anaxagoras, Zeno, Mellisus, and Diogenes was
characterized by an advance on bardic poetry rather than a break from it (*Literary Revolution*, 246). In this prose "we can still see the self-contained statement, pregnant and often balanced, being strung with its fellows on a
continuous string to provide a running logic" (246).

Beye points out the same thing with respect to the prose historians. Of
Herodotus, he says that the style resembles "*lexis eiromenê* (speech strung

together)" a style that is "paratactic in its construction. It is similar to the appositional style in epic poetry: an idea or action is described, redefined, and expanded through the addition of words, phrases, and clauses in apposition" (207). These characteristics are an achievement over the aphorism, but still show qualities of the balanced forms and the "paratactic" style of the bards. The style of the early historians bears a stronger relationship to oral poetic (and may be a response to the constraints of orality) than to, for instance, Aristotelian argument.[8]

Jarratt sees parataxis as so prevalent in sophistic rhetoric that she labels it as one of the two chief "syntactic structures" employed by the Sophists (21). These loose associations, like "beads on a string" permitted the generation of arguments that were uncluttered by the demands of organic unity present in later art and composition. In "organic" composition, an undergirding thesis determines selection and organization of parts. Modern essay writing, for instance, requires "hypotactic" structuring, which means that the work must be built on that thesis: "Imagine . . . hypotaxis, as vertical and visual. . . . The end is prefigured from the beginning—the whole structure is built in a vertical form, 'hypo' suggesting an organization 'from under'" (27). Sophistic composing, however, allowed a freer ranging imagination; Gorgias's essays frequently link arguments simply with the phrase "and another argument."

But the Sophists were operating under different composing constraints than were the poets; composing impromptu was not a demand of the Sophists' art in the same way it was for preliterates. Whereas the singing poet needed to be enabled to bring to his own mind the next thing to say, the Sophist had to be able to bring to an audience's mind what must or may follow from something else. In other words, he had to be enabled to invent plausibilities. Furthermore, Sophists were firmly in the realm of *logos*, manipulating words rather than sound groups. The required connection making would have to have an impact of immediacy on the audience, as Gorgias said that *logos* had on Helen, neither requiring nor inviting analysis. The Sophists adapted to *logos* the idea that virtually any elements could be put side by side if some linguistic connection could be generated. They adopted from improvisation the *kairotic* notion that connections could be developed through performance rather than through explanation. This may be one reason that we see in extant works of the Sophists' performance set pieces with commonplaces rather than handbooks of explanations and systematizations.

Like oral poetic commonplacing, sophistic commonplacing rested on the generating of new ideas from a responsiveness to similarity or echo. We have textual evidence of sophistic commonplacing operations. An illustrative example lies in the plays on words so often mistrusted by Aristotle. Plays on words take many forms, but all perform similar operations within an argument. One example is Aristotle's own, cited from Gorgias: "Also Gorgias' address to the swallow, when flying above him it dropped its excrement, would have been excellent in a tragedy—'Shame on you, Philomela.' For to a bird it would not be shameful to do what she did, but to a girl it would be. So he berated her effectively by addressing her not as what she is but what she was" (1406 b14–20, Lawson-Tancred trans.). *Philomela,* Greek for nightingale, was also, in Greek mythology, the name of an Athenian king's daughter who was changed into a nightingale. Gorgias's pun rested on the similarity in the name of what was and the name of what is. Puns, of course, may rest on other kinds of similarity between names, but in all cases, the commonplacing operation is the same: the speaker seems to draw one thread from a complex fabric to stitch it together loosely with a different complex fabric. Just as the acoustic echo is based purely on sound, the play on words is purely linguistic, generated by what we might today call the productive ambiguity in words. Furthermore, just as the acoustic commonplacing of the poets had the potential for bringing together at one point in time elements that are different or even opposed, so the commonplacing of the Sophists had the potential for bringing together disparate elements into one place, as happens in the "Philomela" pun.

Other examples abound and, significantly, extend into argumentative situations. The play of balances between two forces reveals a form of argument reminiscent of poetic style. Sophists frequently make use of "twos": these are present in the use and overuse of antithesis by Gorgias, for instance, and in his recognition of "either/or" patterns in arguing. Most of the Sophists are supposed to have enabled their students to argue on both sides of a subject. Nowhere was this capacity considered more reflectively than it was by Protagoras, to whom is credited the statement that "to every subject there are two-*logoi.*" The supposition that everything could be challenged by generating an opposing argument may have led him to state that the gods' existence could not be proven, a statement considered by some at the time to be heretical.

Balances and oppositions were very much the intellectual water in which the Sophists swam; the "two-*logoi*" argument and similar ones are thought to derive from the Heraclitean metaphysical belief in the flux of opposites. However, the use of oppositions as a *technê* to create arguments may not have derived so directly from Heraclitus and provides evidence for an origin in the *technai* of composition. Schiappa argues that, unlike Heraclitus, Protagoras couched his assertions about opposition in the presumed ability to use language and make arguments, an ability that was couched, in turn, in his ability to think of "language itself as an object of inquiry" (*Protagoras,* 97). Not yet able to objectify language, Heraclitus could not step back and challenge the naive theory that each entity had a single name, despite the fact that that conclusion may have been implicit in his aphorisms

(97–98). Schiappa argues that Protagoras's "two-*logoi*" fragment may be "a nascent version of the logical form P and not-P" (98) and that surely he was responsible for "seeing opposites as essentially linguistic," which was "a necessary step to a more abstract conceptualization" (99).

The distancing of words from things permits the manipulation of language for the heuristic purpose of creating ideas about things. Schiappa favors translations of Protagoras's two-*logoi* fragment that indicate the distinct capacity for *words* or *arguments* rather than *things* to be in opposition, interpretations like Plato's quotation: "If you speak of something as big, it will also appear small" (*Protagoras,* 99). Plato's rendering indicates not only the capacity to speak of speaking-of, but also the logico-heuristic potential that speaking of one thing has for speaking of its opposite: speaking of something as big logically generates thoughts of it as small if we are thinking in terms of that form of balancing which is opposition. The translation reveals yet another nascent balanced form, the if-then argument.

Protagoras's paradox concerning his student Euathlus, discussed in the previous chapter, may be regarded as an instance of commonplacing that draws into a common place two apparently opposed entities: winning and not winning. The two entities are drawn together in a variation of punning: a paradox works by locating the thread of similarity in opposing formulations. A paradox cannot be explained as well as it can be performed, but Lyotard's very modern explanation comes close to serving: physics permits phrases to be moved into one category as both origin of a series and element, even if propositional logic does not. In invoking the world of physics and the movement of physical entities, Lyotard plainly describes commonplacing.

The "Defense on Behalf of Palamedes" of Gorgias shows how a fundamental antithetical move may be elaborated imaginatively.[9] Even conventional oppositions like that in Palamedes' claim to innocence show how antithesis may work. Palamedes claims, "You accused me through spoken words of two directly opposed things, wisdom and madness, which the same man cannot have. . . . If . . . I am wise, I have not erred; if I have erred, I am not wise" ("Palamedes," 25–26). Because the antithesis works by moving elements out of one place and into two (literally, wisdom and madness may not be found in one body, according to the antithesis) it creates a connection of opposition and hence impossibility where none had previously been presented.

The wisdom-madness opposition was, as Segal points out, a conventional one, "a topic which must be mentioned" in a defense in which human will plays a part (118). Nevertheless, the antithesis is not actualized until performed in and for the concrete situation. Gorgias's own emphasis of the importance of the *spoken* utterance bespeaks his awareness of both the evanescence of speech and its importance: wisdom and madness exist together, by virtue of the accusation, until, by virtue of another linguistic performance, they are made to oppose one another. Moreover, despite the conventional nature of the opposition, the fact is that the situation called out the opposition as response; the opposite does not exist without being made plausible in the particular circumstances. The opposition itself, along with the particulars of the accusation against Palamedes, generate a plausibility that exists in the oral world of the particular accusation and defense.

The "Palamedes" proceeds by elaborations of the same antithetical move, resulting in the progressive elimination of possibilities. Gorgias never attempts to prove Palamedes' innocence but merely shows the apparent impossibility of his guilt by generating and eliminating possibilities. Antithesis works to create the possibility of impossibility in the concrete situation.

Antithesis thus used is different from, but similar to, the plays on words that are also evidences of commonplacing. Unlike plays on words, antithesis does not rest on limitless potential semantic ambiguities in words. However, antithesis is like pun in that it exists only by virtue of language. Contrastable terms like *wisdom* and *madness* form the basis of antithesis. Experiences do not contrast neatly, but terms may. In sophistic, terms may have a life of their own, apart from things. Terms may be brought into contact through a relationship of opposition, whereas examples drawn from experience may disconfirm the opposition. As Aristotle disdainfully pointed out, Sophists and early orators stayed away from the facts of experience and developed arguments based on probability instead. In fact, Tisias and Gorgias both argued the superiority of the probable to the true (Kerferd, 82). Establishing the probable required more art and used the potentials of language appropriately; hence, probabilities were superior. Making the connection plausible, however, often meant extending conventional oppositions as Gorgias did in the "Palamedes."

We have seen how the generative possibilities of antithesis are brought to truly artful form in Gorgias's "On the Nonexistent," whose functioning rests on the generative possibilities of opposites. Gorgias is unwilling to accept a conventional wisdom that things may be as they have already been expressed; in this case, he will not concede that Being exists. One reason for his unwillingness is this: acceptance that what is simply *is* favors the perspective that the world is complete, that we may know it, and that language may reflect it. Gorgias refutes those points. Secondly, like Protagoras's assertion that the gods may not exist, the very existence of Gorgias's treatise insisting that nothing exists presents ironic testimony to the generative potential of language and the sophistic insistence on generating "sayables" by generating oppositions: if we can say that something is, we can say equally well that it is not. Proofs stand, not to demonstrate what is, but to make present what is not. Again, both in form and substance, Gorgias takes on this generative challenge in "On the Nonexistent."

Finally, and most important for present purposes, Gorgias uses commonplacing to exploit fully the resources of language. By doing so, Gorgias lays bare possibilities that would not have existed had he not articulated them. He relies on conventional categories and original connections among them to reveal the novel to be possible. For example, Gorgias employs the *topos* of the one and the many, an obligatory subject in pre-Socratic philosophical discussion, in order to make one of several arguments showing that nothing exists. As he does in the "Palamedes," Gorgias seeks to progressively generate and remove possibilities. In the "one and many" section (Sextus, 73–74), Gorgias seeks to show that existence is neither one nor many and hence does not exist. As in all the arguments in the treatise, Gorgias proceeds by finding where a point of contact between two elements could be made or removed through language, and he does so without actually offering proof. In this case he posits that existence is one and then seeks to disconnect "existence" and "one." He does so by indicating that the one is many: if existence is one, "it is an existent or a continuum or a magnitude or a body" (73). Any of these is many as well as one; for instance, "if it is a body it will be three-dimensional, for it will have length, and breadth and depth" (73). Language permits this fusion of types, which in turn allows both dimension and extension to be discussed as numbers. Gorgias does not dwell long on this argument and seems uninterested here in the larger implications of his collapse of the one and the many. Plainly, the argument is advanced as part of the "running logic" by which each argument is generated as a variation of the one before it in a way characteristic of improvisation—here for the purpose of rendering possible the nonexistence of the existent, not in order to explore more remote connections.

Commonplacing itself made possible in a subtle way the criticism and explanation that was to be the stuff of spectator logic. The Sophists, as transitional figures, helped to draw a habit of thought born of oral necessity into the world of writing. The poets, in an acoustically based performance in time, pulled units together into one moment in time. The moments were over as their utterance faded into the air. The Sophists, with their works often written down, pulled together different ideas (based in phrases) into one *place*, or removed them from one place into two. A sense that there were categories of meanings, of operations, and of elements burgeoned in all pre-Socratic thought. For the Sophists, this burgeoning interest meant potential shifts both in method and logic. Sophistic commonplacing operations could be discussed, categorized, and methodized; no longer would mere performance of connections be sufficient. Moreover, the places or categories in which new connections were generated were open to the naming and analysis that permitted some kinds of connection making and forbade others. Similarity and opposition themselves became categories under discussion for Aristotle. Aristotelian logic expressly forbade many of the kinds of connection making generated by loose philological relatings like those in the examples I have used here. The questioning that came with logic developed inevitably after a more visual sense of categorization was made possible by writing.

Realist linguistic theories like Aristotle's would not be friendly to commonplacing. Commonplacing worked by pulling out a point of similarity between two elements and drawing the two together on the suggestion of that similarity or removing them out of one place on a suggested point of dissimilarity. Like the points of similarity generated by a pun or a paradox, these points may have had little bearing in reality. Still, all similarities and oppositions were treated by the Sophists as the same types of things, because in any given "performance" all were able to provide a connection. In most cases, however, the operation itself obliterated relationships of part to whole. Whether we can speak of it this way or not, it simply is not true that (as was suggested in "On the Nonexistent") number applies in the same way to the many as it does to a single whole, or that the similarity that appears to hook together winning with not winning is a "complete" similarity.

However, when we remember that commonplacing was generated in circumstances of oral performance, the *kairotic* nature of sophistic *technê* and the forcefulness of *logos* are foregrounded. Commonplacing was developed and necessitated by the pressures of oral performance; in sophistic prose, it developed in circumstances in which the need to create possibilities was greater than the need to forbid them, as later logic and correspondence theories of meaning would do. Inventiveness was given high priority in sophistic rhetoric. We need to remember also the characteristics of oral performance that remained constant in commonplacing. Commonplacing rested ultimately not on a system but on a habit of being constantly responsive to potentialities of *logos*. This responsiveness, in prose discourse as well as oral poetic, arose from the pressures of the moment. In a circular sense, the habit seemed to rely on its actualization: a person was responsive only while doing, acting, and making.

The idea of a method based on responsiveness in practice transforms the roles of judgment and invention. Judgment becomes the ability to recognize potentialities, and invention becomes the ability to choose from among them so as to make something of them. In practice, the two are concurrent: a single rational activity, neither arbitrary nor random. In sophistic they rest on the development of potentialities based on identified similarities and differences. Commonplacing, as an operation of responsiveness rooted in the demands of oral performance, is a model of active artistic judgment.

Aristotle's Rhetorical Topics
Judgment and Practical Wisdom

There is a deep irony in the tradition that Aristotle helped to initiate. Aristotle is at once one of the noblest defenders of the autonomy and integrity of *praxis* and *phronêsis* and also the philosopher who sowed the seeds for the denigration of practical philosophy.

Richard J. Bernstein, *Beyond Objectivism and Relativism*

What if the machine is wrong and I feel peaceful about it. . . .? That's self contradictory. . . . If you really don't care you aren't going to know it's wrong. The thought'll never occur to you. The act of pronouncing it wrong's a form of caring.

Robert M. Pirsig, *Zen and the Art of Motorcycle Maintenance*

Despite its virtues, sophistic commonplacing cannot entirely fulfill its potential, nor can it fully develop a discourse to replace the vapid practical discourse left today in the wake of the epistemological project. The reasons for this lie, ironically, in many of the same elements of sophistic that give it value. Sophistic seems to deny the problematic nature of incommensurability rather than give rise to a discourse that engages incommensurate positions. The major reason for this limitation is the lack of a thorough consideration of practical discourse, which we find subsequently in Aristotle; incommensurability becomes problematic in practical moments.

In this chapter, I take up the shortcomings of sophistic invention and examine the ways the commonplacing introduced in sophistic is transformed in Aristotle's consideration of rhetoric as problem solving. After examining the transformation of commonplacing into topical thinking, I return to the topic, introduced earlier, of the subject-object dualism that is often seen to limit our view of *technai* of invention. As the first active "technologizer" of rhetoric, Aristotle offers an appropriate opening for reconsidering whether this dualism is inevitable and vicious.

Limitations to Sophistic Commonplacing

The first difficulty with sophistic is in its performative functioning. Oral rhetoric, as we have seen it so far, is a performative rhetoric. *Apatê* supposed a sense of fiction to all discourse, with all discourse possessing the same quality of distortion. The composer performed the distortion in a way not dissimilar to the way in which a priest performed an incantation.[1] When the Sophist spoke, he performed the act of making possible the impossible. What he did not do—and did not try to do—was argue the point in a way that might satisfy a logician. He accepted the incommensurability of the two worlds—that of the logician and that of the Sophist—thus eliminating the problem of incommensurability only on terms set by the Sophists.

We may see the problem this presents most clearly with reference to those contemporary discursive realms in which incommensurability is *not* regarded as a problem. For instance, incommensurability is not a problem in the universe of postmodern fiction, where disparate, incongruous worlds collide, brought into contact through innumerable devices. This universe, as Brian McHale points out, is "heterotopic" in a sense introduced by Foucault: "the coexistence in 'an impossible space' of a 'large number of fragmentary possible worlds' or, more simply, incommensurable spaces that are juxtaposed or superimposed on each other" (Harvey, 48).[2] Fiction may be a sort of master discursive universe for postmodernists.

Similar conclusions have been drawn in the field of speech communication. In a critical examination of the science fantasy film *E.T.,* Janice Hocker Rushing considers the necessity of bringing together in a productive way two contradictory impulses toward nature. She concludes that perhaps the guiding trope for our age must be the oxymoron, a contradiction in terms reminiscent of sophistic. She further suggests, however, that the oxymoron may be possible only within the genre of "space fiction": "It may be that space fiction or fantasy is the most important contemporary genre for presenting and responding to the rhetorical exigence of fragmentation" (200).

Any way of enacting possibilities that otherwise appear impossible is to be encouraged as an enrichment of our discourse. The creation of worlds in which the otherwise impossible does exist is perfectly consistent with sophistic goals and their genesis in poetic. What this contemporary instantiation of sophistic cannot do, by definition, is make the impossible worlds commensurate with actual worlds.

More to the point, sophistic "solves" the problem of incommensurability by suggesting that a variety of conceptual frames may exist and remain, as Rorty would put it, "forever incommensurate." This may represent an appropriate solution until practical matters force—or appear to force—decision making between incommensurate frames.

A second, related limitation to sophistic is a formal one. In practical circumstances, sophistic offers no way to bring together incommensurate views into debatable space. To put the point differently, sophistic suggests no way to negotiate conflicting views about what counts as good discourse. The troublesome nature of this weakness is nowhere more evident than in disputes in which the effectiveness of sophistic discourse is itself challenged in ancient or contemporary forms. For instance, Rorty sees the discourse of epistemology as having little value to philosophy today, because epistemology seeks agreement and, hence, end points to discussion. Rather, he much prefers discourse that seeks to be "edifying" and that thereby encourages more conversation. The Sophists, likewise, engaged inventiveness in the service of what might be considered an ongoing conversation. Gorgias, for instance, saw language as serving a transformative function, and invention as serving to correct the misconceptions of *doxa* by substituting vivid new conceptions of truth for accepted opinion. Hence, to adopt Rorty's terminology, language and invention were bent to the work of developing "edifying" assertions—those that could awaken a listener to new worlds of thought—and the conversation thus could be prompted to continue, one illusive opinion following another.

However, Rorty, like the Sophists, is not immune to criticism about the directionless nature of this construct; his views about discourse are themselves incommensurate with those of epistemologists. Matteo, for instance, suggests that to join the ongoing conversation Rorty desires, the philosopher must abandon any search for truth and put aside standards (like the law of noncontradiction) for evaluating statements purporting to be true. The conversation, Matteo claims, would be devitalized because it would lack "a direction and serious purpose" (257): there would be no way of sorting sense from nonsense (242), and the conversation would be guided only by the hope "that somehow progress will be made in an utterly *ad hoc* fashion" (243).

We may leave aside for our purposes the questions of who is right or wrong, whose needs for what kind of discourse should be met, or whether Rorty's response to critics like Matteo would promote good conversation. In fact, we are not concerned here with standards for conversation like those the spectator judge might seek. The question before us really is whether edifying conversations—much less progress toward any "truths"—may take place in the face of conflicting views about what counts as good discourse. Can an ongoing conversation have vitality for the thinker who is seeking end points and progress? For whom are we seeking edification?

In many circumstances, these two conceptions of conversation and edification might remain forever incommensurate, as Rorty hopes. In other cases, however, when decisions must be made, a difference in standards for and about discourse muddies the possibilities for productive discussion in a potentially damaging way. We saw one example of practical moral discourse that was confused in just such a way when we examined the exclusionary rhetorics of the secular humanists and the fundamentalist Christians. So mutually exclusive were their accepted forms of discourse that they were unable to find a way to talk to each other, much less reach the hoped-for agreement on legislation on such subjects as abortion.

A third limitation to sophistic invention is the gap it presents between action and incipient action. This gap is particularly apparent in the *kairos* and the reshaping of our expectations about choice and *logos*. *Kairos* presumed that truth was changing and provisional and that it developed out of the moment. Thus, commonplacing took place by virtue of a habit, learned through experience—and, perhaps, tuition through example—of being responsive to the potentials for invention *in the particulars* of a situation.

But how would the discourse that was to be invented relate to the crises that presented themselves in real situations? The *kairos*, in a speaking situation, prohibits the predetermining (or prescribing) of an end in action in advance of the situation itself. That is, if the justice of the decision grows from the moment, then there is no advance truth in improvisation. Soldiers in battle, pressed into the need to act, find truths that are beyond the rational *logos* that might serve them in ordinary circumstances. There is a loosely drawn analog between the action taken by the soldiers Gorgias honors in the "Funeral Address" and the action of the rhetor inventing ideas. In each case, a form of justice is served. Justice is served to the soldiers in the dramatic moment of decision. But justice is served by the rhetor in another way, at least by some interpretations: in acting "inventively," he is also doing justice to the moment. In responding improvisationally, he is discovering a truth that must ever be reinvented in response to the ever-changing moment. But the analog is not perfect: although invention of ideas is plainly a form of acting, it also represents *incipient* action in situations of practical crisis. What is said is *preparatory* to taking action.

This gap between action and incipient action is important because it brings to bear the idea of virtue and its distinction from cleverness, or *deinotês*. Sophistic invention seems to propose no final end in action. To respond cleverly, to invent plausibilities that invite radical reconsideration of accepted thought, such action seems to be its own end. The separation between the invention itself and the rightness of an act it may point to is unaccounted for. In the Sophists' own terms, it did not need to be accounted for; but Plato, and later Aristotle, found this separation disturbing. For Plato, recommendations for action needed to be determined out of knowledge of what was right or just, knowledge that had to precede rhetorical invention. Contrary to the *kairotic* improvised statements of the Sophists, the statements of knowledge credited by Plato could not be generated from the moment itself. Knowledge was to be prior in every sense of the word. The difference between the *kairos* of the Sophist and the notion of virtue promoted by Plato allowed Gorgias to claim he was teaching justice, while Socrates could claim otherwise in the *Gorgias*.[3]

If we take the gap between action and incipient action seriously, sophistic *kairos* is an incomplete response to those practical moments in which incommensurability discloses itself. The requirement for action shapes practical discourse, and the pressure of the need for action adds another dimension to invention. These are not reasons to oppose the *kairotic* as it exists in sophistic as Plato did, but rather reasons to refine or expand it. The same may be said of *apatê*. The sense of language as powerfully transformative should not be abandoned; rather, the distortive impulse the Sophists observed and obeyed should be redirected. "Edification" and "abnormal discourse" require more than the production of *any* iconoclasm; they may require a radical disruption that is directed toward action about something in particular.

These demands bring us to Aristotle and his theory of rhetorical topics. At first Aristotle may seem a peculiar choice for vitalizing and redirecting notions of *apatê* and *kairos*. Unlike the Sophists, he plainly held that language could and ought to serve a representative function. In a frequently quoted passage from *On Interpretation*, he stated that "spoken words are the symbols of mental experience, and written words are the symbols of spoken words" (16a. 2–4). Moreover, Aristotle inherited from Plato a belief that truths exist prior to speaking. His *Rhetoric* plainly seems to be directed to defenders of truths discovered through other means: "Things that are true and things that are just have a natural tendency to prevail over their opposites, so that if the decisions of judges are not what they ought to be, the defeat must be due to the speakers themselves" (1355a. 20–23).[4] Aristotle sought to ground rhetoric in the same logic that could direct a thinker to demonstrable truths and to guard audiences against what he saw to be the deceptive power of language and emotion—a power that Gorgias saw as the proper functioning of rhetoric.

Given these interpretations of Aristotle's rhetoric, his system of topics would seem to be inconsistent with commonplacing. Indeed, most interpretations of topics have seen them as ways of finding proofs, presumably for truths already discovered. Typical is Kennedy's definition, which states that the inventional objective of the speechmaker was to develop rhetorical arguments, or enthymemes. The topics, therefore, were to help the speaker in inventing enthymemes (*Persuasion*, 100–101). Ong also saw Aristotle's rhetoric as a form of argument and therefore regarded a topic as "some kind of 'place' . . . in which were stored arguments to prove one or another point" (*Presence*, 80). Missing from both these definitions is any remnant of the dynamism of commonplacing. Typical interpretations see Aristotle's rhetoric as an art of producing conviction and topics more or less as static categories of argument.

These interpretations are strongly warranted; Aristotle's *Rhetoric* may easily be seen as an effort to make the thinking involved in collective decision making more rigorous by allying rhetoric with logic. However, we need to remember that such a view sees Aristotle through a post-Cartesian veil. Aristotle's intellectual forebears included the epic poets as well as Plato, so an interpretation of Aristotle as inheritor of a tradition grounded in orality

is also warranted. The practical needs of speaking orally before an assembly
are also being met in the *Rhetoric*. Foregrounding the rhetor's needs places
logic in a supporting role, in the service of those needs. Aristotle's own definition suggests the viability of this function for rhetoric. He is at pains to
point out that rhetoric is not a science of producing conviction: "It is also
clear that its function is *not* persuasion. It is rather the *detection of the persuasive aspects of each matter* and this is in line with all other skills"
(1355b.9–11, Lawson-Tancred trans.). Rhetoric is an art of discovery,
directed toward specific situations: "the faculty of observing in any given
case the available means of persuasion" (1355b.27–28). As Kennedy points
out in a translation note on this passage, "The actuality produced by the
potentiality of rhetoric is not the written or oral text of a speech, or even
persuasion but the art of 'seeing' how persuasion may be effected" (Aristotle,
On Rhetoric, 36).

Looked at from the point of view of the rhetor in a particular situation,
rhetoric becomes inextricably bound to solving problems identified by the
orator in a practical situation calling for talk; hence, rhetoric becomes, not
an act of persuasion, but an art of problem solving: the rhetor has to find
something to say that will aid in solving a particular problem perceived by
the rhetor. In developing rhetoric as a problem-solving art, Aristotle did
more than create an ability to ground claims in strong argument. He developed a form of invention in rhetoric that wedded acting well with discovery,
and judgment with acting well. He attached to rhetoric virtues that helped
ensure that inventing well became one form of acting well. This was an
advance over the Sophists; Aristotle's rhetoric attempted to assure that
virtue lay in trying to find a response that could help solve the problem at
hand. Infused as it was with problem-solving virtues, Aristotle's rhetoric also
responded to certain of Plato's concerns. With rhetoric regarded as problem
solving, the concepts of both *kairos* and *apatê* can became identified with
virtuous behavior that permits the bringing together of contradictory arguments into public debate.

Kairos, Work, and Problem Solving

Rhetoric and Problem-Solving Work

Sophistic developed in part from the forcefulness of the moment on judgment,
the importance of *kairos*. Any moment, unique as it was, called out for its own
particular response. A similar notion of *kairos* is detectable in Aristotle. In his
more analytic world, however, different barriers to the forcefulness of the
moment presented themselves and had to be overcome. These were to be
overcome, not by force of a logic, but by force of ordinary language. We may
follow Aristotle better by referring to discussions of the later Italian humanists,
who faced in Descartes even greater challenges to the importance of moment.

The resemblance of later rhetorical invention to sophistic *kairos* is made clearest in Vico's opposition to Descartes. In a fully developed statement of rationalism, Descartes eliminated as unnecessary the study of those things of which one could not have knowledge. Because he presumed that we could have knowledge only of those things that could be grounded in constancy, Descartes rejected from consideration all those fields that were concerned with the "constantly variable individual case" (Grassi, 40). These rejected fields included history, politics, and rhetoric. Although there were various reasons for Vico's rejection of Cartesianism, two are relevant to understanding the relationship of *kairos* to work. One is the concept of *verisimilia*, or truth-likeness, and the other is the concept of *similitudo*, understandable as meaningfulness.

The notion of *verisimilia* reflected the humanists' understanding of Aristotle's conception of knowledge. If "Aristotle maintains that knowledge can exist only of something which occurs regularly and of necessity" (Grassi, 39), then "whatever manifests itself differently, i.e., whatever changes, cannot be an object of knowledge" (30). Of these things, human beings could have only likeness to truth, that is, probable truth or *verisimilia* (39). Vico saw Descartes' exclusion of the probable as wrong-headed, since the problems of varied individual cases are those that press themselves upon us during real work. Descartes' philosophy denied the importance of preparing for specific cases, that is, of knowledge of the probable.

Probability is different when thought of as "likeness to truth" than when thought of as "likely truth." The "likely truth" interpretation foregrounds a modern, statistical sense and introduces concerns of relativism to knowledge; that is, when we say we have only probable truth, we imply uncertainty and a sense of less than the best. No such relativism is present in the humanist *verisimilia*. What is foregrounded, instead, is a different kind of knowledge, gained in a different way; that is, knowledge gained immediately, through image and through the imagistic in language—the dazzling flash of light. Also foregrounded is the importance of appearance to knowledge. What we act on, given the attainment of truth-likeness, is the appearance of truth.

Similitudo gains importance for Vico because of the primacy of meaning to human work and problem solving. The problems presented to us in our work are very much like those with which we have been presented from the time that Hercules cleared the primeval forest in order to make space for the first human community. They are the problems presupposed by the fact that "nature possesses a meaning only in regard to human needs" (Grassi, 6, 7). Hence, for Vico, knowledge consisted of "a relationship, a *similitudo*, between what the senses reveal to us and our needs" (7). Rhetoric held a privileged place among those studies involved with the probable because its use of topics reflected original metaphorical thought by which such relationships were most fundamentally revealed. First—that is, original—speech brought first knowledge to human beings (Verene, 182).

Vico saw metaphor, and topics as well, operating in a way very similar in some ways to commonplacing. Knowledge of the probable was not reached systematically and methodically but through a sudden insight "for finding what is common between things" (Verene, 174). The "right thing at the right moment" was to be found through concentration in work and through study, not through a single critical-deductive method like that of Descartes. What we have called the *kairos* emerged through work and yielded knowledge of a world that is not independent of us but is made present by us through our needs. In other words, the constantly changing needs presented by our variable challenges and problems are what yield to us meaning or *similitudo*, which is understandable as insight into the *significance* of what we see.

Aristotle's Rhetoric as Problem-Solving Work

Aristotle's claims for rhetoric were much less sweeping than the humanists' claims, and the problem-solving work for which it was suited were more narrowly defined. Within the confines set by Aristotle, rhetoric becomes understandable as an art of public and political work. But in a sense suggested by the humanists, rhetoric is engaged in to reveal the meaning of elements in our work. It is directed toward removing blinders to seeing the significance of elements in specific situations.

Aristotle's rhetoric may be seen to be in the service of a particular type of problem solving, directed toward very specific tasks of governing the city. Aristotle was concerned with the ability of the *demos* to act well. Rhetoric became necessary when action had become impossible, not for every reason that it might be impossible, but only for certain reasons: the reasons that cause people to deliberate. People do not deliberate about what they already believe to be settled or about what they believe, as a body, to be impossible or, alternatively, inevitable. They deliberate about "matters . . . that ultimately depend on ourselves, and which we have it in our power to set going" (1359a.37–39). These matters are contingent on our decision making, in which, plainly, no one clear path of action recommends itself.

There are no doubt countless reasons that a clear path to action might evade citizens of a *polis*. Aristotle did not try to enumerate them, but his writings suggest several possibilities. One reason certainly was the fact that there was no scientific way of knowing the best course of action. Aristotle was careful to distinguish among the theoretical sciences, the practical sciences, and the arts. Only in the theoretical sciences (biology, theology, and physics) could assurance and, presumably, common assent, be obtained. The practical sciences of ethics and politics, however, which were concerned with human action, could achieve only likeness to truth, or probability. In matters in which action was in dispute, however, no one way shone more clearly than another as being likely. Aristotle did not adopt notions like *verisimilia* and *similitudo* as such,[5] but he did indicate that, although the scientific method of demonstration could not provide knowledge in practical situations—or perhaps *because* it could not—there was importance to the task of deliberating about matters that did not permit of the same certainty.

There was a related reason that a clear indication of action might elude the thinkers: a loss of practical wisdom. A confusion of the methods of theoretic with practical sciences and arts might make the discovery of the significance in the practical situation impossible. The ability to discover and act on the significance of the particular situation was a function of practical wisdom, *phronêsis*, not scientific knowledge or the contemplative wisdom that was directed to distinguishing truth from falsehood. For Aristotle, practical wisdom was that part of the intellectual faculty that allowed human beings to bring true reason into agreement with right desire in order to create good action (*Nicomachean Ethics*, 1139a.20–30). Practical wisdom was incipient action; it was the capacity (potential or power) to act with regard to things that were good or bad for human beings (1140b.5–30). Its objective was to preserve a good judgment about things that are to be done (1140b.10–15). Moreover, practical wisdom was to be directed toward particulars as well as universals, since a circumstance in which action must be taken requires more than recognition of "universals only—it must also recognize the particulars; for it is practical, and practice is concerned with particulars" (1141b.14–16). The practically wise person was excellent at deliberation (1140a.30–35), which, as a general rule, consisted of aiming to find the universal rule that best suits the particular situation (Milo, 60).

Most human beings should have the potential for practical wisdom, and that wisdom ought to make discussion about action unnecessary in most cases. However, despite the tendency of all things to act according to their natures, obstacles could arise: the acorn that would tend naturally to oak, for instance, might be transferred to infertile ground. Aristotle comments, for instance, that our view of causes might become distorted: "The man who has been ruined by pleasure or pain forthwith fails . . . to see that for the sake of this or because of this he ought to choose and do whatever he chooses and does" (*Nicomachean Ethics*, 1140b.17–19). The practically wise could fall into error with respect to knowledge of a universal or a particular (1142a.20–23).[6]

On this view, rhetoric was to remove impediments to practical wisdom and, more remotely, to good action and happiness for the *polis*. The rhetor to whom Aristotle's *Rhetoric* is addressed was to use the tools of rhetoric in order to act wisely and remove such impediments to wise action by the group.

We may now see more clearly how rhetoric could be brought to bear in circumstances in which a course of action was not clear. The practically wise person recognizes a breach in the collective public harmony that makes public decision making and communal action possible. The need for common deliberation signals this loss. Sensing a loss of insight into what should be done, the rhetor, as practically wise person, seeks to remove impediments. Those impediments are blinders he perceives as having kept the participants from seeing clearly those aspects of the problem that are of common significance. Rhetoric, as a practical and productive art yielding not truth but probabilities, was invoked to yield insight into the significance of what was before the group. In more familiar terms, rhetoric did less to produce discovery than to remove blinders and to allow the *kairos*, the right thing at the right moment, to force itself.

An example might be helpful. Imagine an academic department engaged in the process of designing a new departmental curriculum. No single curriculum stands out as a strong possibility. The intellectual worldviews of the members diverge dramatically in some cases, but that inhibits the work of the group little until they must make a common decision relative to those views. The group becomes so driven by dissent, distracted by individual needs, and plagued by the lack of a common vision that they are rapidly losing their capacity to act wisely or, as Aristotle would more likely put the point, to discern the truth. At this point, rhetoric is needed. The moment may disintegrate without a response, in the way that Lloyd F. Bitzer, in his analysis of the rhetorical situation, points out; but the moment itself is what calls rhetoric into existence. Not just any response will recall the group to its capacity as a deliberative body, however; the response must fit the needs of the moment.

The idea of "fittingness" of response, employed by Bitzer and others to describe rhetoric, has led to some confusion of the Greek notions of *kairos* and *to prepon*. Modern interpretations have suggested that the force of timeliness recognized so acutely by the Sophists was subsumed in Aristotelian rhetoric as *to prepon*, which, in Roman times, would become the more familiar *decorum*.[7] The subsequent foregrounding in rhetorical theory of *to prepon* would imply that rhetorical invention should be directed toward ascertaining the appropriate way in which a proposal should be couched or the best time and place for it. *To prepon* restricts rhetorical activity, suggesting, for example, that it is inappropriate to speak on or near Martin Luther King's birthday without referring in some way to the civil rights struggle or to African-American history. Furthermore, *to prepon* commands that we teach our children that there are moments when some things should *not* be spoken.

This emphasis would make invention an art of, at best, finding a way to adjust our ideas to the demands of the moment and the situation. The demand of appropriateness in successful rhetoric implies that little that is original can come from rhetorical invention. According to this interpretation, the audience, the public, or the conventional wisdom is the determiner of what ought to be said, and when and how it ought to be said; topics have, in fact, sometimes been described more or less as categories of conventional wisdom.[8] *Kairos* suggests, however, that "the right thing," if it happens at all, is forced by the uniqueness of the moment, not by human design. In a problem situation, the right response is right when it reveals a clear sense of the significance of the moment, a *similitudo*. In rhetoric, invention assists the rhetor in finding a response that may transform the cacophony of elements threatening decision making in such a way that the group might act wisely as a deliberative group.

Aristotle plainly saw the influence of the moment of urgency as a force for rhetoric. He speaks of the conditions that make an art of rhetoric necessary by distinguishing between the work of the legislature in making laws and the work of the citizenry in reaching decisions in particular circumstances: "Well-drawn laws should themselves define all the points they possibly can and leave as few as may be to the decision of the judges; and this for several reasons. First, to find one man, or a few men, who are sensible persons and capable of legislating and administering justice is easier than to find a large number. Next, laws are made after long consideration, whereas decisions in the courts are given at short notice, which makes it hard for those who try the case to satisfy the claims of justice and expediency" (1354a.32–1354b.4).[9] At this point, Aristotle specified the ways in which the nature of the decision making may lead to a collective loss of wisdom: "The weightiest reason of all is that the decision of the lawgiver is not particular but prospective and general, whereas members of the assembly and the jury find it *their* duty to decide on definite cases brought before them. They will often have allowed themselves to be so much influenced by feelings of friendship or hatred or self-interest that they lose any clear vision of the truth and have their judgement obscured by considerations of personal pleasure or pain. In general, then, the judge should, we say, be allowed to decide as few things as possible" (1354b.4–13).

Plainly, Aristotle, unlike the Sophists, saw the pressures of the moment as limitations to decision making and suggested good laws and good rhetoric as the necessary remedies. He acknowledged that the need for an art of rhetoric arises because not all decisions can be left to the legislators. In admitting the influence of the immediacy of decision making and the resultant barriers to wisdom, Aristotle also implicitly invoked the oral, face-to-face situation as the model emphasizing urgency in decision making: only real and immediate situations call forth the need for rhetoric. As William L. Nothstine has summarized, "Choice becomes meaningful (and rhetoric called for) only when resources are limited, or time is constrained, or foresight is incomplete, or interpretations are in conflict" (158).

In foregrounding the urgency in a political problem-solving situation and assuming oral, face-to-face decision making, Aristotle also identified the key element that created the pressure in the situation: the presence of the other whose disagreement is to be taken seriously. In this respect, rhetoric bears similarity to dialectic, but differences are also apparent. Aristotelian dialectic was structured around an adversarial relationship between the participants. Although both were engaged cooperatively in an intellectual examination, that examination necessitated that each be committed to holding up his side of the debate against the other. Rhetoric, however, was occasioned or generated out of disagreement among those who had to act together if action were to take place. Their inability to act in concert and to act well would create a problem. Consequently, the perspective of the other *must* be taken seriously by the rhetor. The problem situation he sought to influence was constituted of disparate voices.

This describes, recognizably, a hermeneutic functioning to Aristotelian rhetoric. However, Aristotle did not foreground understanding and interpretation as aims of his rhetorical art; he emphasized invention and the urgency of finding a response in a situation in which there is no obvious response. This distinction is important, because it is the pressure of finding a response that shapes the moment for the rhetor. Rhetoric was an aptitude based necessarily in understanding of the other. It involved the capacity or aptitude to invent links between self and other in the moment when those links are needed. The ability to see the need, grasp the moment, and invent appropriately were all bound into the rhetorical art. In order to see the place for topics themselves, we must examine the relationship between *phronêsis* and understanding.

Action and Understanding

Acting wisely is a matter of action as much as understanding. In his examination of Aristotle's theory of political judgment, Beiner emphasizes the point that *phronêsis*, while grounded in a conception of good judgment, is not *fully* describable as good judgment. The good judgment we accord the wise person is an important element, but *practical* wisdom is validated only as action: "*Phronêsis*, then, is judgment that is embodied in action; it is judgment consummated in the efficacy of good *praxis*. If I *see* what a situation requires, but am unable to bring myself to act in a manner befitting my understanding, I possess judgment but not *phronêsis*" (*Political Judgment,* 74). Likewise, the loss of an ability to act signals a loss of practical wisdom in the *polis*.

Moreover, excellence in practical decision making goes far beyond the capacity for making sound personal decisions. Practical wisdom is in the service of community action. How can we have wisdom about what would constitute good action for the community? The answer is that the practically wise have, and act on, a sort of fellow-feeling with members of the community. Furthermore, because wisdom and judgment are not to be separated from action, this fellow feeling has been gained from the experience of *acting* with the community. Aristotle distinguishes between the *pathos* and "suffering with" that the young might endure with others, and the *praxis* that constitutes acting together with the community in creating decisions, and thereby creating and recreating the community itself (Beiner, *Political Judgment,* 77). If I am a practically wise person, my sense of judgment is activated in situations in which I am practicing citizenship. That is, I should be able to "act with you" in situations in which you and I together recognize that our ultimate interests are in what is good for the community (what Aristotle designated as the interests that are assumed to invoke rhetoric) even though other points may separate us. In these situations I can and will be actively engaged in putting myself in your place.

This ability to act with another calls into play a set of intellectual and moral virtues. The virtues involved in understanding another and in knowing how to act on that understanding are of equal bearing. Hence, practical wisdom is not just judgment but is an active "judging with." Beiner points out the importance of "the *hexis* (habit or settled ability) that is *phronêsis* [which] . . . equips the virtuous and prudent man with a capacity to project himself into the genuine situation of another" (*Political Judgment,* 78). The Aristotelian rhetor acting with *phronêsis* feels a sense of oneness with the public he addresses. Rhetoric comes into play for reasons that are therefore personal to the rhetor. His sense of the community's loss of practical wisdom and alienation from self is felt as discordance in his own mind. In fact, his sense of oneness with the public—with a community of thought—allows him to be aware of the loss of wisdom. This loss is the imperfection, the problem, to which he responds. He seeks to restore both order and his own peace of mind by removing the public's blinders to the significance of certain factors in the situation. This interdependence of speaker and public makes them partners. A situation in which the real meanings, in the sense of *similitudo*, become clear comes about only as the result of successful interaction between rhetor and public.

The inventional art appropriate to Aristotle's rhetoric would, in this view, need to unite wisdom with eloquence, "judging with" with speaking well. Beiner points out that "rhetoric is the counterpart in the realm of speech to what *phronêsis* is in the realm of *praxis*" (*Political Judgment,* 88). The rhetorical topics would need to be ways of speaking eloquently just as much as they are ways of coming to understand the public.

Rhetorical Inventiveness and Transformative Language

This account is highly abstracted, however, and does not tell us, as Aristotle wishes to do, how to be good at rhetoric—a subject matter that takes on particular importance when it is tied so inextricably to citizenship and problem solving. How are we to respond to the unique pressure of the presence of the other, whose ends we recognize as our own, and act inventively as the moment commands? We must find the ability not only to gain an understanding of the other but also to act in speech. How may the moment be seized inventively and with wisdom?

Invention functions rhetorically to transform. For Aristotle, the cacophonous voices of the group during decision making signal an unclear situation. The rhetor hopes to guide the interaction within the community so that he may transform a situation in which there is disorder or lack of clarity into one in which there is clarity. Gerard A. Hauser, in a distinction between what he calls determinate and indeterminate forms, suggests a notion of the clear situation that accords with this interpretation of Aristotle. A clear situation is "determinate" in at least two senses of the word: first, it has absolute boundaries and outlines, a recognizable and specifiable name and shape; and second, one course of action appears logically deducible from it. In other words, the determinate situation is one that, in Aristotelian terms, has the power of first principle in that it seems to command us to a particular course of action.

These two senses of determinance coalesce for the practically wise person who, acting as problem solver, needs to transform a chaotic situation into a clear one in which action may be restored. The transformation of an indeterminate into a determinate situation takes place in speech through a transformation of names and meanings; but similar transformations may take place in any problem-solving work. Novelist Robert Pirsig provides a contemporary example. He maintains that the need for practical wisdom is forced upon the individual in problem-solving work. The work of Pirsig's motorcycle enthusiast illustrates the importance of a moment's shining forth so that old, unproductive habits of thought may be broken and the force of the unique moment be permitted. One of Pirsig's most vivid descriptions, of a motorcycle mechanic trying to remove a stuck screw, reveals precisely how such "original seeing" (Nothstine) might take place and how situations may be seen as semantically constituted.

Pirsig tells us that a motorcycle is nothing more than a system of concepts worked out in steel (94). The mechanic struggling with the stuck screw must reinvent the screw and the universe of concepts that contains it—that is, the motorcycle itself. Because a screw is usually considered "cheap and small and simple," the worker at most times finds it unimportant, routine; he takes it for granted (280). Only when the screw is a problem does it (and the moment in which the problem is encased) stand out. When the screw influences the entire motorcycle, it takes on great importance: "Right now this screw is worth exactly the selling price of the whole motorcycle, because the motorcycle is actually valueless until you get the screw out" (280). In a sense, the system of concepts that was the motorcycle no longer accommodates this more important screw. The screw and the mechanic's previous conception of its significance are a problem to him. He is himself stuck, not knowing what to do, as long as he thinks of the screw as he has thought of it in the past and as a rule. He suffers from a sort of learned incapacity: "In the past when you separated subject and object from one another in a permanent way, your thinking about them got very rigid. You formed a class called 'screw' that seemed to be inviolable and more real than the reality you are looking at. And you couldn't think of how to get unstuck because you couldn't think of anything new because you couldn't *see* anything new" (280).

This result of overreliance on abstracted, a priori principles and habitual, lawlike patterns of thinking was the essence of Vico's complaint against Descartes: the loss of the capacity to prepare for individual cases. In a similar way, the loss by the *polis* of practical wisdom—because of an overreliance on theoretical thinking or on habitual, timeworn approaches—blinds them to the particulars of the situation and their significance.

In the case of the motorcycle, the worker must remove himself from this state of stuckness before he can remove the screw. Fortunately, he is aided by the forcefulness of the problematic moment itself: his very involvement with the problem allows—or may allow—the worker to overcome that learned incapacity: "If you concentrate on it, think about it, stay stuck on it for a long enough time, I would guess that in time you will come to see that the screw is less and less an object typical of its class and more an object unique in itself. Then with more concentration you will begin to see the screw as not even an object at all but as a collection of functions. Your stuckness is gradually eliminating patterns of traditional reason" (280).

Pirsig implies that patterns of traditional reason are changed only by the force of particular real problems that overwhelm old habits of thought. This sense of the moment's force implies a pragmatic variation on the Gorgianic *kairos*, situating it phenomenologically in work, problem solving, and the uniqueness of experience. Moreover, *kairos* here also relates to the way the caring mechanic has become able to gain a new vision into the problem: he has become enabled to look, not at what a thing is, but rather at what it does. Another way of making the same point is to say that the mechanic has looked not at what the screw *is*, but at what the screw *means* to the situation. "Meaning" in this case, implies "significance," the significance of a thing to a situation. Startled into recognition, the worker is also forced by the moment to acknowledge a sense in which names and meanings are *apatêloi:* they are impermanent and distortive. Naming may cause blindness as well as restore sight. A useful method would seem to have to enable the worker to focus on the moment at hand and gain awareness of the significance of a thing to his needs. Eventually, rhetoric presented itself to Pirsig also as the key art in isolating such a method.[10]

The implications of the relationship of meaning to the clear situation are apparent. Situations may be seen as slipping into and out of clear, meaningful configurations. A half-empty gas can, for instance, may sometimes attract little notice and have little meaning. However, when a person notices that the half-empty can is in a basement near a hot water pipe and a pile of oily rags, the configuration of elements in the situation changes. The gas can becomes alive with significance; no longer simply a gas can, it is an agent of destruction. The newly configured situation transforms the thing. The situation itself is also transformed into a "dangerous situation."

Because terms slip into and out of various relationships with one another, a situation can be unclear from the outset, its significance not apparent. For the same reason, a situation may be transformed into a clear, determinate one. From the perspective of the actor or worker, what the situation is lies in its *appearance*. A situation is indeterminate because it *appears* to be so, and it is determinate because it *appears* to be so. Such appearances are the realm of rhetoric. Furthermore, the appearance of determinateness, the power of first principle, has the force of truth and reality. Aristotle, in a remark fraught with significance, observed in the *Rhetoric* that likeness to truth and truth are recognizable by the same faculty to listeners (1355a.15–16).[11] In the same way, the humanists equated truthlikeness (*verisimilia*) with probability: the probable situation is not just one that might be true, but it is one that has the appearance and forcefulness of truth.

In seeking to clarify the significance in the situation, the rhetor seeks to make concrete for listeners the relationship between their present needs and the data revealed to them by their senses. Because the meaningfulness of anything varies from situation to situation, a priori rules, so necessary to the sciences in describing a stable reality, are of no use to the uncovering and producing function of rhetoric. Pirsig's motorcycle mechanic was prevented from seeing the function of a screw in a situation because he knew only what the screw was and not what it meant. In the same way, the incapacity of a community to depart from the rationalistic methods of contemplative wisdom can present a barrier to practical wisdom. Rhetoric is the agent for restoring practical wisdom, real meaning, and hence, knowledge of how to act in a situation.

The impetus to invention for Aristotle's rhetor, then, was the need to transform a situation that was indeterminate because it appeared so, into one that was determinate because it appeared so. He thereby transformed a reality through providing a forcefully clear definition of the situation. He could make such a transformation by taking advantage of what might be called a vulnerability in semantic categories that allows relationships among terms, and thus the configuration of a whole situation, to be changed.

Topical Thinking

The inventional methods implied by typical definitions of topics do not serve the needs of the speaker who requires insight into a situation and a way to transform it. If rhetoric is to be directed toward discovering an original, forceful way of seeing a situation, a random generation of thoughts or arguments from categories would be spiritually defeating and unproductive to the speaker. Having a catalogue of ideas at his disposal would not guarantee that he would find within that catalogue the insight he needed at that particular rhetorical moment. Not all the ideas that might be generated could suit the need for finding and revealing what is significant in a particular situation. The rhetor needs a method of invention that will help him discover a way of looking at a situation with an eye toward transforming it; that is, he needs a form of *judgment* to accompany inventional method.

Dialectic

Aristotle harnessed the transformative potential of language in his method of topics, which he most likely introduced in his work *Topics*, a treatise on dialectic or disputation. Conventionally, the topics of dialectic are regarded as a loosely related group of logical principles to be used to examine an intellectual proposition. As such, they have been criticized for their logical weaknesses. However, when the oral, improvisational nature of dialectic is emphasized, as it is in Eleonore Stump's analysis, the *Topics* becomes "less a peculiar treatise on logic than a handbook on how to succeed at playing Socrates" (173).[12] A dialectical topic, in this context, is "primarily . . . a strategy for arguing" rather than a logical principle (168). As strategies in dialectic, the topics take on a commonplacing function by which similarities and differences are created within a particular dispute. In rhetoric (with which Stump does not deal), topics as strategies create new situations in the perceptions of rhetor and *polis*, again by creating similarities and differences.

In an oral disputation of the kind envisioned by Aristotle as his dialectic, the improvisational nature of the debate created pressure on the disputants. The debate was to begin with a question that was open to serious disputing, and it was to be worded in such a way that one interlocutor would uphold the position as it was stated and the other would dispute it. The disputant upholding the proposition would ask the other participant questions that could be answered yes or no. The objective was to lead the assenting answerer along, question by question, so as to force him to accept the proposition as the end of a train of reasoning.

The requirements of the oral contest forced a melding of memory and analytical skills in a challenge that resembled the one faced by the poets as well as by Gorgias when he spoke extemporaneously. The oral poet, for instance, under pressure to compose, had to be able to recognize and generate phrases on the basis of similarities and differences. More to the point, he had to be able to have one phrase remind him or prompt him to think of another. One phrase, sound group, or idea evoked another for the singer or

Sophist. The habit of thinking that facilitated this evocation seemed to encourage the identification of similarities and differences not readily apparent to the mind *not* sensitized to looking for them. The operation of commonplacing itself allowed singer or Sophist to put together phrases or ideas that might not otherwise have suggested themselves as being related.

The problem and the solution for Aristotle's disputant were more complex but not dissimilar. He too needed to have presented before him, based on his opponent's statements, the materials relevant to making a response. Like the poet, the interlocutor engaged in dialectic needed a ready response. Whereas for the poet the response was to what he himself had just said, the response of the interlocutor was to his opponent. The disputant needed to exercise judgment as to the implications of his response: it had to lend itself either to the completion or the destruction of a chain of reasoning. He needed to hold the relevant materials before him in order to determine a response from them; and in order to do so, he had to have a commonplacing operation that would bring into one place the particular subject matter of the debate, his final objective, the ideas advanced by his opponent, and the implications to his opponent of those ideas.[13] Once enabled to see those factors together, the disputant might be able to generate an advantageous response. He could not do so without conjoining those elements for consideration. The topics were to help him accomplish this conjoining in a timely enough fashion to produce responses.

Stump, whose analysis is one of the few to emphasize the oral and *kairotic* nature of the debate, offers an example:

> Take, for example, one of the Topics mentioned earlier: '[You must see] if the genus and the species are not in the same [category,] but one is a substance and the other a quality, or one a relative and the other a quality. To speak generally, the genus must be under the same category as the species.' This Topic can be used to refute a number of arguments, namely, all those in which the opponent maintains that one thing is the genus of something else and the two things in question fall into different categories. Aristotle gives an example in the same passage. Suppose the arguer's opponent maintains that knowledge is a species of what is good; the arguer chooses the strategy of seeing whether the putative genus and species fall into the same category, and he sees that they do not. Then he makes his argument as follows. He gets the opponent to admit first that goodness is a quality and then that knowledge is a relative; he then brings the argument to a conclusion by implicitly or explicitly using the principle that a species and its genus must be in the same category. (173–74)

Thus, an individual topic functioned on the basis of the vulnerability of semantic categories. That is, elements of a proposition did not belong in one or another category absolutely and eternally; the boundaries of categories were not that secure. Elements like "goodness" or "knowledge" could be removed from one category and placed into another for purposes of examination. The topics suggested ways in which these "placings" could be accomplished. Composed of Aristotle's four predicables, each of which indicated a type of proposition, and his ten categories, each of which described a type of predicate, the dialectical topics could alert the trained thinker to potential new placings. The proposition "knowledge is a species of what is good" is a genus-species proposition that the speaker may create by considering the *quality* that might be predicated of knowledge; "quality" is one of Aristotle's ten categories. The unschooled arguer faced with the contention that knowledge is good might have gone down to defeat, since knowledge seems so obviously to be a good. A disputant familiar with thinking topically, though, would instead recognize that there are always other ways of seeing what may at first appear to be the obvious, only way. The different potential topics, hence, provided a means for discovering and generating a different perspective than that which might already have been present in the debate. The interlocutor needing to respond to the contention that knowledge is a species of what is good had to look at knowledge *as if* he were going to apply a relevant topic. He might have asked himself, for instance, "If the good may be regarded as a quality, can knowledge be regarded as something else?" Because a proposition was generated out of the particular pressures of a particular debate, the proposition was given viability by the debate itself—forced by the *kairos*. A consideration of knowledge as something that is relative might be something as new to the interlocutor introducing the idea as to his opponent.

A different, more visual image emphasizes the point that topics are actions or strategies rather than the descriptions of conceptual relationships we might expect from a logic. The subject matters with which dialectic is concerned may be regarded as multidimensional, multifaceted gems masquerading in the dispute as having only two sides. Thinking with the aid of topics may be considered a means of turning a subject so as to see its various facets. In the example we have been using, the topic offers a means for turning the subjects of the proposition, knowledge and good, so as to view sides of each that might suggest that the proposition "knowledge is a species of what is good" is false. "Turned" so that one of its aspects is brought into focus, knowledge may be regarded as something that may *not* be a species of the good. With some "turnings," the two propositional terms, knowledge and good, might be seen as compatible; with others, they might not. With some topical moves, the terms could be disjoined and a distinction created that had not been present before the debate. With other moves, terms could be conjoined and a similarity created.

The importance to dialectic of similarities and differences was made clear by Aristotle in the beginning of his treatise on topics. The identifying of similarities and differences was as central and necessary to the art of dialectic as was the selecting of propositions for debate. The ability to identify similarities and differences, in fact, is divided into three parts that serve as three of the four "means whereby we are to become well supplied with reasonings' (*Topics,* 105a.20–25). Following the breakdown of the ways by which reasonings can be found are pieces of advice for looking for similarities and differences among terms in a proposition.

The emphasis on strategic thinking should not distract us from the advantages of looking at the topics as part of an oral exercise motivated by a need to think *kairotically* about intellectual questions. "Strategies" might more broadly be considered actions, and the importance Aristotle gave to dialectic is testimony to the importance he gave, not to acting *against* an opponent, but rather to acting *on* the intellectual world with words, under the pressure of a specific dispute.

Therefore, a type of *kairos* is an important formative element of topical invention in Aristotelian dialectic. Insofar as dialectic was predominantly an oral mode, it was dominated by the requirements of improvisation. The actual moment in the dispute had to evoke the response, and topics aided the disputant in making a response that was relevant and forceful. A "just" response contributed to the sound examination of the proposition at hand.

Rhetoric

In rhetoric, however, *kairos* was quite different, as was topical thinking. Aristotle wished to see clarity of vision restored in situations in which rhetoric was called for, and good judgment and right thinking made possible. Rather than engaging in talk that might further obscure or prejudice the judgment of the public, the rhetor needed to create circumstances in which the truths in the situation might emerge clearly. Therefore, Aristotle saw the intellectual and moral virtues of the good rhetor as merged: the rhetor was obligated to see his proposal in terms intellectually plausible to the other, and he was further bound to create his own proposal in terms they would all see as constructive of the common good. The rhetor discovered and shaped a true response to the situation by viewing his proposal in terms by which the others would judge it.

In a moment calling for rhetoric, "truth," "significance," and "probability" would be related and perhaps even merged terms. The rhetor had to view his situation as a lack of clarity among the decision makers. Either there were competing voices, or no dominant perspectives had captured the minds of the *polis.*[14] To this mix, the rhetor acting with practical wisdom must try to provide an eloquent response. To do so would be to fulfill the obligation to act wisely with words. The wise rhetor recognizes that there is not *a* truth when novel and contingent moments are being decided, but a variety of truths, some hidden and some already disclosed. While many truths may be disclosed, the true significance of some elements in the situation remains hidden until deliberation is completed. "Truth," in the case of a specific decision-making incident, is highly pragmatic; it is what is recognizable to the group as significant to solving their problem. Other truths may not meet the needs of the moment in either of two closely related ways: either the truths are unresponsive to the moment, or they are unrecognizable to the group. Those limitations to truth are related because the problem is inseparable from the talk about the problem. To act rhetorically, the practically wise citizen must discover the significance in his perspective to the needs of the *polis*, and he must reshape the perceptions of the decision makers so that the significance shines forth clearly and brilliantly. Probability, or the forceful appearance of truth, is created out of, not prior to, the situation in which the rhetor finds himself.

The topics as they were developed by Aristotle offered ways of seeing the indeterminateness of a situation in terms by which the *polis* itself might see it; topics made use of relational categories the group itself was likely to use in decision making. The topics also suggested to the rhetor ways of producing clarity in the situation. Like the dialectical topics, the rhetorical topics suggested ways that elements could be moved into and out of different relational categories so that the situation could be transformed. The rhetor used the general and material topics to remove elements from one set of relationships and place them in another so that the situation itself was reconfigured.

How might the topics have worked? The rhetor might have begun by asking himself what it is that is not clear in the discussion or that is causing conflict and continued deliberation. He could have done this by learning the point at which deliberation becomes unnecessary, because, as Aristotle says, "we turn a thing over in our mind until we have reached the point of seeing whether we can do it or not" (1359a.39–40). The rhetor might ask what subjects people do not need to discuss. People do not deliberate over those things they take to be already determined: things that exist or will exist (past fact or future fact), and things that cannot possibly exist (possibility or impossibility) (1359a.30–39). Whether the speaker was to be talking about ways and means, war and peace, national defense, imports and exports, or legislation (1359b.15–25), he could turn the problem in question over in his mind and determine whether disagreement and confusion are over a past fact, a future fact, a possibility, or an impossibility. Having hit upon one or the other of these as sources of conflict or unclarity, the rhetor also would know that he must bring precisely that point into clarity.

The procedure was not that simple, of course. Aristotle pointed out that the subjects over which we deliberate until we see them as determined are *means* directed to achieving two ends. The two ends, which are consonant with the relationship of rhetoric with ethics and politics, are happiness and the good (*Rhetoric,* bk. I, chs. 5–6). When human beings feel that the general happiness is secured or the good is being served, their decision is made and there is no need for deliberation. Past fact, future fact, and questions of possibility all serve to analyze and determine happiness and good *in the particulars of the present situation.* Happiness may be secured, according to Aristotle, by good birth, wealth, and other factors. Turned a certain way, an element in a situation could be shown to be associated with the fact or the possibility of wealth, for example.

Possibility, past fact, and future fact are three of the four general topics (bk. II, chs. 18–19). The fourth, degree, is itself generated out of the particulars of the situation. People may be thrown into indecisiveness or disagreement even if there seems to be clarity about the facts or possibilities in question; there may be questions about the relative good or happiness involved. Aristotle said about utility, an important good to be considered by the deliberative speaker, that "it often happens that people agree that two things are both useful but do not agree about which is the more so" (1363b.5–10). In looking at a situation, the speaker could determine if the source of conflict is the relative size or amount considered. For this purpose, Aristotle included special topics to which the speaker's attention was directed. For instance, the rhetor could bring about clarity if he could show that, turned a certain way, an element in the situation revealed that his proposal showed the greater number of goods. Alternatively, he could contribute to clarity by removing a proposal from a category by similar means; for example, he could remove a proposal from the category of "wealth" by showing that the proposal would deplete the coffers of the city.

Having isolated the key elements that needed to be transformed and the basic connection that needed to be made in order to give significance to those elements, the rhetor could then consider more specifically the strategies he would adopt for making the transformation. These strategies are listed clearly under each of the four general topics, and they are straightforward discussions of verbal appearances.[15] The strategies under the Possible, for instance, include such suggestions as "That if of two similar things one is possible, so is the other. That if the harder of two things is possible, so is the easier" (1392a.12–14). These are "topics" readable in the same general way as the strategies listed in the *Topics.*

The formal topics also show how the rhetor might act so as to create perceptions of clarity, or the forcefulness of first principle. The twenty-eight formal topics are related to the enthymeme, which Aristotle described as a "rhetorical syllogism" or demonstration (1355a.5–15). It is difficult to overrate the importance of the enthymeme to Aristotle, who called it "the substance of rhetorical persuasion" (1354a.15). As a syllogism, the enthymeme is a logical construct, reflecting a fundamental pattern of reasoning used in demonstration and dialectic as well as rhetoric. Aristotle recommended that the reasoning developed in the premises of the enthymeme not be carried too far back "or the length of our argument will cause obscurity." He also suggested that because of this need for clarity, the uneducated might be better than the educated at speaking enthymematically (1395b.25–31). If we emphasize the logical properties of the syllogism in interpreting Aristotle, his description might imply that the enthymeme is inferior to the other syllogisms, in which the premises must be specified and held up for examination. As Robert Price puts it, the enthymeme so regarded "stands to the syllogism proper as (defective) practical argumentation to (perfected) theoretical argumentation" (147).[16]

However, if we emphasize the urgent nature of the situation, the enthymeme may be regarded as an agency of clarification. The deductive movement of mind, from premises to conclusion, seems naturally to lead to the impression of necessity in the minds of listeners. Aristotle, in his description of the enthymeme, may simply have been suggesting that the rhetor must present his reasonings in such a way as to make the appearance of necessity crystal clear so that the rhetorical effectiveness of the syllogistic form is not undermined.

The place and the function of the formal topics suit this description of the enthymeme. Donovan J. Ochs argues that the formal topics represent structural elements upon which enthymemes may be constructed (424). These elements consist of the crystallized descriptions of ways in which the mind might move so as to see a conclusion to be clearly determined. For instance, topics consist of ways of picturing relationships; "opposites" and "correlative ideas" are two such relationships (1397a.5–30). The logical grounds of these elements are not discussed in the *Rhetoric*, nor do they seem to be important. What seems important is that the formal topics represent ways in which appearances of conclusiveness may be recognized by an audience and may be constructed. Rhetorical *logos* consisted, in part, of the use of language to construct conclusions that had probability: the appearance and forcefulness of necessary truth.

Rhetorical *topoi*, like dialectical *topoi*, provide a habit of thinking by which hidden aspects of a situation may be brought to light. More importantly, put to use rhetorically they offer a means of making connections between elements of a situation where those connections did not exist before, thereby transforming a situation by reconfiguring it.

Rhetorical Topics and Active Artistic Judgment: The Subject-Object Dualism Revisited

If we are not careful, we might envision topics as an inventional method to be applied mechanically. In other words, the rhetor or the arguer engaged in a dialectical contest would sort through the topics provided by Aristotle, decide which one to apply, and use it. This conception of the topics, however, would present the thinker—and the art of rhetoric—with almost insurmountable problems. First and most obviously, the topics would be an unwieldy system, almost impossible for the thinker in either case to use. Secondly, the topics would represent no means of active artistic judgment; rather, they would be a closed universe of possibilities, given in advance and not responsive to the unforeseeable circumstances for which they would be needed.

The response to the first problem, however, suggests a response to the second. In the dialectical topics, the apparent unwieldiness would make the system useless for the purpose for which it was derived. There are hundreds of strategies listed in the *Topics*. If the arguer were to have sifted through the entire list, he would have found himself suffering from an embarrassment of riches. After having gone though the time-consuming process of looking at all the strategies, perhaps the arguer would have found several that might seem useful. He would then have had to discard the other strategies and examine those that appeared promising in order to determine the best. Only then could he employ the strategy with his specified subject matter. Generally, then, he would have been presented with considerable material that would have been irrelevant to his particular situation and would have gotten in the way of his generating a response.

Stump points out, however, that the dialectical topics are organized in such a way that they would not invite such a random form of exploration. The topics are "generally ordered according to the predicables," which include genus-species, property, accident, and definition (174). As Aristotle saw it, any proposition necessarily concerned itself with one or another of those relationships or attributions (*Topics*, 101b.17–25). The topics are further ordered, Stump argues, so as to allow a student trained in them to develop a familiarity with the predicables and a way of thinking about them: "One can use the *Topics* to become thoroughly familiar with the nature of the predicables and the way they work. . . . Because one understands the nature of the predicables, strategies and principles having to do with them will suggest themselves naturally" (178).

The *technê* that Stump describes constituted, therefore, a way of developing a special habit of thinking about certain matters in order to take part in disputation. Much more is at stake here, however, than ease of use for the thinker. Considering topics to offer a habit of thinking—*topical thinking*—de-emphasizes the influence of the specific topics and emphasizes instead the qualities of the habit. Topical thinking, if not application of specific topics, suggests a form of active artistic judgment. In dialectic, the interlocutors became habituated in responding to the particular momentary circumstances of a real debate with something to say that was directed to a specific end. They were enabled to respond because of an attitude toward language. The fact that ideas are inevitably (for Aristotle) couched in ordinary language is not a limitation to our discovery of truth but rather an invitation to bring to mind any of an infinity of potential truths. Within a particular debate, the multifaceted terms permitted the disclosing of some truths as others were enclosed. Dialectic prepared the thinker to be responsive to the other party and to specific circumstances, and it prepared him to regard the fluidity of semantic categorizing as an opportunity rather than a limitation.

The opportunity for active artistic judgment is brought to maturity, however, in rhetorical invention, not in dialectic. The skills of the good dialectician are technical, in that they claim some universal applicability; they should apply to all subjects. On the face of it, the skills of the rhetor are just as technical. Pirsig's motorcycle enthusiast with the stuck screw, for instance, seems at first to require a sense for topical thinking similar to that required by the rhetor. The motorcycle enthusiast was looking for the meaning of the screw to his situation in order to take action. At the outset, he was not hoping to develop just any idea about the situation but to find some clear indication of what he ought honestly to consider the screw to mean in and to the circumstances. A priori rules or if-then strategies—old, nonsituational ways of thought—would inhibit his thinking as much as the pure generation of random ideas would. A topical method, however, involving responsiveness to the circumstances, an assumption that the meaning of the screw could be shaped by the circumstances, and a way to put the different meanings of the screw into the same place *with* the circumstances so as to see what appeared as most compelling—such a method might help him. At the point of his "stuckness," the mechanic does not ask that the new way in which he envisions the screw be "right" or "true"; he asks only that he have some way, whereas previously he had none, in which to form an honest opinion.

However, a rhetor, as the practically wise person envisioned by Aristotle, is not a mechanic of any sort. He belongs to the political forum and political situations, and he brings to them more than technical knowledge and self-interest. His voice is, in part, the internalized voice of the *polis*, developed from the experience of acting with the community. Topical thinking brings to him the know-how to make good in action his understanding of that voice; it provides him with a way to act wisely, by seeing and showing the significance, heretofore undisclosed, of elements of the situation. Like the interlocutor described by Stump, the rhetor accustomed to thinking topically is accustomed to seeing subject matters as transformable; terms may be moved in and out of categories so that similarities and differences may be created. However, these truths are not created willy-nilly or as an exercise. He seeks specifically to have a voice *useful* to the particular deliberation in which he finds himself.

The question of the topics as mechanical method and of Aristotelian *techné* as inherently instrumental cannot be laid to rest as easily as this, however. Whether the method is applied mechanically or virtuously, Aristotle's rhetoric seems to be a highly manipulative art; the rhetor is taught to manipulate audience perceptions and situational elements. This, I think, is just what Aristotle had in mind. As I stated earlier, he directed his advice about rhetoric to those who have truth on their side. He invited, in part through the topics, the manipulation of the elements of the situation so that the rhetor might make clear to others a truth he had already seen. Interpreted in this way, Aristotle did indeed pioneer that dualism between rhetoric and philosophy by which truth was discovered by philosophy, and rhetorical invention was charged with transmitting it. Rhetoric, while important, was left with no truths to discover and little that was novel to create.

However, there is a necessary and, I hope, productive ambiguity in my account of Aristotle that helps confront this issue. If rhetoric is to be directed, in its final cause, toward transformation of a situation from an unclear to a clear one, to whom is the situation unclear at the outset? It may be easy to read Aristotle's *Rhetoric* as a treatise on manipulating the perceptions of listeners, but it is equally easy to read it as directed toward remedying a lack of clarity in the rhetor: the topics of invention exist, of course, to meet the rhetor's need for discovery.

The idea that the rhetor seeks clarity for himself helps us to envision a less manipulative rhetoric and gives light to a particular type of discovery distinct to rhetoric. However, even with this rhetoric firmly in mind, the picture of Aristotelian *technê* as inherently instrumental is not completely laid to rest. The problem of a subject-object dualism, to which I alluded earlier, remains: if a rhetorical *technê* provides a means of refiguring the situation at hand, isn't *technê* still reduced to instrumental means to an end? And is not the human being figured as the agent of discovery and creativity—an originative, unmoved mover?

These questions are confronted in a related way by Heidegger, whose consideration of human being pressed upon him the need to grapple with the problem of the originative place of *Dasein* with respect to art.[17] Heidegger points out problems inherent in the technological thinking with which we, as inheritors of Western (and especially American) culture are burdened. Among these is the Cartesian subject-object split that precedes technology and enslaves us to technological thought. Once we conceive ourselves as subject, or actor, and the rest of the world as acted upon, we begin to see everything as material or resource, or what Heidegger calls "standing reserve" ("Question Concerning Technology," 17, 18ff.). Ironically, human beings themselves become reduced to objects, to resources to be manipulated and controlled; and language becomes, largely, a tool toward that end.

A full application of Heidegger's thought to Aristotle's rhetorical *topoi* is beyond the scope of this chapter, but a brief review of two essays that provide a Heideggerian analysis of invention and *topoi* will help restate the question and point to a response.

Language and its relationship to Being have become distorted, according to Heidegger's thinking. Once we become dominated culturally by a scientific, subject-object dualism, the function of thought becomes representation. Language, used scientifically to represent, manipulates the world by portraying it as object, and, we might suggest, by indicating that the world is *only* object.

One result of representational thinking is the loss of the early Greek sense of *technê*, which, Heidegger suggests, meant a "bringing-forth" ("Question Concerning Technology," 13) or an "unconcealment" ("Origin of the Work of Art," 168ff.). Our modern use of the word foregrounds making, crafting, or manufacturing.[18] When we come to think of the subject-object split in terms of manufacturing or constructing, as if human beings manufacture or construct their own worlds, then human beings begin to regard themselves as ground of truth. This is a tragic eventuality for human beings. In according humans absolute power to determine what is real (whether by applying measuring sticks of their own design or by "creating" reality), Cartesianism withholds peace and contentment, Heidegger says. Human technologies are bound first to appear to offer absolute knowledge, and then ultimately to fail: "Such efforts are finally unsuccessful because human being always comes upon a limit, a refusal: There always remains something hidden, something beyond the purchase of theory and system" (Worsham, 207).

Lynn Worsham, in an examination of teaching writing "skills," finds good reason to reject the sort of technologizing Heidegger condemns. She then turns her attention to what might be substituted once we have rejected mechanical systems of invention. Among the mechanical systems she rejects are "problem-solving" approaches (210–12) much like the problem-solving form of invention I have attributed to Aristotle. Although Worsham does not speak explicitly of Aristotle, rejection of Aristotle on this basis should not be surprising. Aristotle is the first master-systematizer in Western history. As I have pointed out, he appears in most of his works to have a sense of language that supports the effort to systematize: he generally regards language as representational and instrumental. More to the point, problem solving implies something entirely instrumental, the adaptation of technological means to an end—even if the end is a personal discovery by the rhetor rather than manipulation of an audience.

What becomes problematic, however, is the fact that in Aristotle's problem-solving art of rhetoric can be found a type of invention that sounds much like the Heideggerian sort for which Worsham searches. Aristotle's topical thinking, I have said, works for us when we think of language as presentational, as revealing what has been concealed, thereby transforming our vision. An even more pointed similarity may be found in the sort of "reflective" writing that Worsham turns to as offering hope for a nontechnical form of invention. Worsham cites a work by Cyril Welch to describe reflective writing: "The kind of writing that Welch introduces is one whose topos and ethos are potentiality and possibility. The task of writing is not to add to the store of knowledge, but to subtract the familiarity and the 'alreadiness' of what has been said. The reflective writer must let go of the traditional ground on which she stands. She must let go of what is taken for granted and instead move toward 'an appearance in which the alreadiness momentarily gives way to what one can never know and claim but only acknowledge and uphold'" (232).[19] "Subtracting the familiarity" is a well-made distinction and describes effectively what I see Aristotelian *topoi* as doing. But how can these opposing ideas—a problem-solving art and noninstrumental invention—yield such similar descriptions?

Perhaps the important difference is in the discrepant ways in which Worsham and I consider the impetus or occasion for invention. Worsham is concerned in her essay with the teaching of writing. The impetus for writing, she suggests, is poetic, both in our conventional use of the term (236) and also, implicitly, in the more ancient sense (*poiêsis*, or 'bringing forth') that Heidegger reminds us was part of the ancient lost sense of *technê* (Worsham, 208).

But Heidegger pushes the idea of *technê* further than does Worsham, to locate the position of the human being with respect to the origin of the work of art. In recapturing the relationships among *poiêsis* and *technê*, he searches out the place of the human being in "occasioning" or "being responsible" for "starting something on its way into arrival" ("Question Concerning Technology," 9). Having rejected the manufacturing model of the human contribution and the portrayal of the human being as originator, Heidegger seeks, in "The Origin of the Work of Art" to reconsider the activity of creating, which may be regarded as allowing emergence: "To create is to let something emerge as a thing that has been brought forth" ("Origin," 180). This bringing to truth is not in the hands of human beings as causal agents; *Dasein*, the human thinker, the being whose essence is in seeking self-truth is, however, necessary for the disclosure; he "is but the instrument, the scene, as it were, of the happening of truth" (Versenyi, *Heidegger*, 100).

What *Dasein* requires in order to be the scene of disclosure is the freedom to seek self-truth; for Heidegger, freedom is part of the essence of human being. Freedom, however, is not possessed by human beings as a quality or characteristic; instead, freedom possesses *Dasein*. Freedom grants itself to human beings and, in so doing, permits the possibility of the emergence of truth. Freedom, not human power, permits creation. By similar token, *technê* has no power of its own to produce truth. The most that *technê* can do, this implies, is enhance that human freedom that permits disclosure.

Therefore, if *Dasein* might be considered scene of disclosure, *technê* might be considered occasion, or even opportunity. Whereas Worsham acknowledges the need for human being as scene of disclosure (208), she does little, when she turns to a discussion of writing, to consider the occasion or occasioning of the disclosure of truth. It is not clear what spurs creativity or the allowing of disclosure. What pushes the writer along in the rather monumental task of letting go the traditional ground on which she stands? It is clear from Worsham's own concerns about the problems of teaching literacy that human beings are not, at all times and in all places, ready, fertile ground for discovery. What provides the necessary occasioning for inventive speech?

I see the occasioning as coming from a problem-solving urge. An illustration, drawn from Nothstine's Heideggerian discussion of *topoi*, will be helpful. Nothstine regards *topoi* (not necessarily Aristotelian *topoi*) as directed toward providing clarity (in terms of sight or insight) to the rhetor rather than to an audience whose perception is to be manipulated. He states this in several ways as he draws out the associations of the "place" metaphor from within a hermeneutic ontology: "'Place,' 'topos' can suggest not simply location of objects separate and independent from the self, but rather the situation of the self within a world of things and possibilities. The 'place' metaphor may refer to a position affording a particular point of view, a perspective, from which one regards one's world" (155). Truth, in the Heideggerian sense as "unconcealment," may mean "selecting a vantage-point which allows what is hidden to be seen" (156). Nothstine implies, as Worsham does not, that we do more than leave a "familiar ground"; we also move to locate a specific standpoint. But how and why do we give up familiar ground?

Nothstine indicates a response to that question. He goes on to point out that we are afforded only a limited stance from which there is a limited point of view. We may be afforded a new viewpoint and a new stance on the occasion of challenges to the old: "Rhetoric always involves the attempts of finite humans to come to terms with their condition and their finitude through language-use, to orient themselves to the world of tensions and discontinuities in which they always already find themselves" (158). Furthermore, the attempt to orient ourselves in the world "is performed through choices of action and utterance in the public realm" (159). The problem faced by the human being and prompted by the public world is the need for a literal coming to terms with her self, occasioned again and again as she tries to orient herself with other selves. It is this problem that enables and occasions original (in the sense of originating from the *situated* self) seeing. Unconcealment occurs when the human being finds and speaks from a position she finds revealing in the situation. Although Nothstine does not deal with inventional *technê* per se (he turns his attention to rhetorical criticism), topical thinking participates in the occasioning of original seeing by leading the thinker to a subject position where unconcealment may take place. Arising out of the tension of "the inevitable discontinuities of life" (158) the self is literally given worldly existence only as she is positioned.

One of Nothstine's examples, the writing of the columnist Ellen Goodman, reveals the writer as constantly responding to the challenge of positioning. Goodman often responds in her writing from the standpoint of the comparer; she reveals a "preference for comparison as a vantage point or topos" (161).[20] Goodman does not write in a vacuum, however; she writes rhetorically, out of a sensed need to respond, in her own authentic voice, to what is going on around her. We might think of topical thinking, in this case, as the habit of finding a vantage point that permits fresh insight. Such a vantage point melds personal voice with public moment so as to occasion an authentic response: "Goodman's unique claim upon us is her ability to show us how easily categories upon which we rely may be juxtaposed, and thereby to teach us the humanizing limits of such categories. This is the contribution of her rhetoric, what her 'standpoint' enables her to 'see' and offer to us; it is an expression of her individuality that transcends any assertions we (or she) might make about it. It is an insight that cannot be arrived at through the standard treatment of topics or argumentation" (161). It derives from a problem-solving urge in the sense I see implicit in Aristotle: a sense that the world that surrounds me needs a truth to be told.

Despite her protestations to the contrary, Worsham seems to see the importance of this kind of problem solving. In seeking a substitution for mechanical-technical invention, she points out that "the literacy crisis points to a sense of homelessness, a sense of alienation, and lack of belongingness to the earth and to the world. . . . The literacy crisis, in short, is a crisis of involvement. . . . Involvement begins with the radical and creative questioning of social practices and their effects on our lives" (236). This is an important insight; in addition, it confirms the idea that rhetoric is in some way a political art. There is a danger, however, in disconnecting involvement in the world from the urge to act with language (and I do not believe that Worsham ever intends to do this). Doing so once again robs rhetoric itself of invention by implying that the truths to be written about come prior to the urge to write. There is danger, also, in this consignment of all truth to prior discovery: I may be involved with my world and the people in it and be led simply to repeat what they say, their "party line." Rhetoric is then consigned, once again, to the task of only dressing up what I say. So to think that invention may be yielded from involvement alone is to risk introducing another duality: it is to separate rhetoric from discovery and writing from thinking. And these are separations I am certain Worsham does not intend. Whatever the flaws of Aristotle's rhetorical topics, the fact that he drew them from what he saw as the standpoints for problem solving commonly used in a community suggests that they exist to promote *phronêsis*.

To recognize the potential of topical thinking for us today means first finding Aristotle and then giving him up. Aristotle's rhetorical topical thinking brings a conception of *kairos* to the conception of *phronêsis*. Insights come when the particulars of a new situation are connected with old or understood or agreed-upon forms of decision making; this occurs under the goad of the conflicting voices that are taken seriously because of the demand for action as a community. Whether I am acting as citizen, philosopher, or scientist, original thought becomes possible for me at the point at which I am pushed to regard other voices as impinging on the categories I take to be common sense. The seriousness with which I take those other voices is an obvious necessity in practical situations in which the challenge to reconfigure the elements in the situation is the challenge to find my own voice.

Fully realizing voice, however, means giving Aristotle up, in the sense of giving up thinking of topics as instrumental. The idea of *techné* needs to yield, in contemporary thought, to the twin notions of *hexis* and *phronêsis: techné* must be rethought as a habit of allowing wise responding through the occasioning of invention. Thus, *techné* helps provide the rhetor with a focused concentration on the problem at hand. To recognize topics as an ability to turn a thing over in our mind or to find our standpoint with respect to the specifics of a situation is to eradicate subject-object divisions, specifically separations among rhetor, audience, and situation. Topical thinking allows invention to spring from the momentary bringing together of speaker, public, and situation; it frees us to judge actively.

Stasis

Argument as Active Artistic Judgment

Considering topical thinking to constitute a type of active artistic judgment invites a host of other questions. For instance, the topics that Aristotle conceived grew from a particular community of thought. The ability to use topics to act well was conferred and seasoned by experience with that community. The problems with which the rhetor was engaged occurred within a community with shared conceptions of the good. If rhetoric is, in part, an art of creating ideas by moving between two points of view, can it be effective when different communities of thought are involved?

This is precisely the question that arises when we consider the problem of incommensurability, which is often experienced as a clash between whole systems or communities of belief and knowledge. What makes some disputes "two worlds" disputes (as Sonja K. Foss calls them) is partly the fact that on each side rival conceptual worlds—conceptual systems—are involved. On each side key conceptual terms are linked to other more transcendent terms in an interlocking structure of relationships. In a "two worlds" dispute, each side would like to assume that it may argue persuasively with the other by moving a particular conceptualization (an act of abortion, for instance) from one category to another (in abortion, from the category of elimination of tissue to that of murder of a live human being) in the kind of action topical thinking might enable. However, such arguments have historically not been compelling. And although the other side may respond with arguments against such transformations, these too tend to be "straw" arguments. The reason that the desired epiphanies rarely take place is the same reason that arguments in defense of one's own side in the dispute may be generated with comparative ease: we tend to generate arguments *in terms* of our own framework or system of thought rather than any other way.

Topical thinking would seem to assume a single unified and relatively stable conceptual system within which to develop arguments. Aristotle was able to identify a conception of "the good" as it existed within the political consciousness of fifth-century Athens and to advise rhetors in ways of drawing entities into a relationship with the good. When conceptions of ultimate terms (like "the good") or conceptions of their importance differ—as they do in incommensurate systems—a topical method would seem to offer few resources for a fruitful meeting between systems.

The difficulty, however, is less in inventional methods like the topics than in a limited understanding of argument, an understanding that makes inadequate use of all the resources argument has to offer and fails to permit the full potential of active artistic judgment to emerge. Argument has come to be seen as functioning to link particular terms with more general and transcendent terms in a single conceptual system. Argumentative moves are persuasive, therefore, when they are themselves sanctioned within that system. In the service of any conceptual system, argument and the judgment that allows it function visually and by sanction to clarify and refine the hierarchical tree of relationships among terms. The adequacy of this "normal" form of argument is challenged in circumstances of incommensurability at those very moments at which the validity of particular systems of thought are challenged by other systems. Those moments invite reconsideration of what argument can and cannot do.

Visual and rule-governed argument cannot eliminate the challenges of incommensurability, nor can it enable moments of incommensurability to act as goads to the creation of new and unanticipated relationships. However, argument that itself is generated from the discomforting and disconcerting moments of clash between adherents to incommensurate systems can, in fact, guide arguers toward the development of conceptual relationships neither might have imagined. This sort of argument arises from the oral and improvisational demands of active artistic judgment.

The Ciceronian method of antithetical argument suggests a way in which active artistic judgment may be engaged in moments of incommensurability. The method of antithesis allows arguers, by virtue of their disputatious exchange itself, to realize their own and the other's systems of thought in concrete, specific, flesh-and-blood terms rather than as abstractions. The result may be the breaking down of each system and the development of new conceptual relationships that would not have come about within one system or the other.

Locked as we may be into the expectations of the systems thinking and visual argumentation that we have come to accept as normal, we may see incommensurability as threatening chaos, and the only response a return to stability. The possibilities of oral argument, however, allow us to accept incommensurability as a goad to creativity. Therefore, in order to really understand oral argument and its potential fully, we need to contrast it with the visual nature of the systems thinking we are accustomed to. In what follows, I demonstrate the pervasiveness of static thinking characteristic of visual systems,[1] the way in which argument has been drawn into that visual universe, and the limitation to creative judgment that has resulted. I then develop an alternative, with Cicero's method of antithetical arguing suggested as a model for oral improvisational argument.

The "Visual-ization" of Argument

"System," defined loosely, refers to a cluster of elements that are somehow related. Littlejohn's rather general definition in *Theories of Human Communication* will serve: "A *system* is a set of objects that interrelate with one another to form a whole" (41). The idea of systems may have its genesis in Western observations of natural sciences; for instance, we may identify a solar system through its relatively consistent relationships among planets and to a unifying sun. The example highlights what, for my purposes here, are some of the key characteristics of systems: the idea of a structured set of relationships, in some way hierarchical (as with the planets tied together by the pull of a sun), and with describable rules for the ways the elements behave in relationship to one another. In general, systems thinking assumes that these structured relationships are available to our thinking through conceptualization. We capture knowledge of systems and achieve order to our thoughts when our conceptualization of the world provides a visual or at least visualizable array of elements in relationship.

Systems are often said to act persuasively, prescribing acceptance of certain truths and actions by the strength of an internal logic. Importantly, however, the internal logic of a system gains its persuasive power because it is visually conceivable. Richard B. Gregg, who has made a thoroughgoing treatment of the sensory nature of ordering, has indicated that symbolic classification and categorization operates from a visual base and that the "symbolic inducement" underlying much persuasion derives from a human need to order that derives, in turn, from a need to order *visual* percepts. The importance of "symbolic inducement," a term derived from the thinking of Kenneth Burke, highlights a similar point about conceptual systems; Burke suggests that we may be induced to see things and believe in things in ways constrained by the conceptual systems we have adopted, tacitly and otherwise. Although examples of symbolic inducement are numerous, the examples I will draw on here from Kuhnian science are themselves persuasive.

Kuhn's language during his early attempts to describe the scientific paradigm is provocative. He envisioned a paradigm in much the way we have been talking about a conceptual system. He said, for instance, that a scientific paradigm has elements of "an accepted model or pattern," although he admits that this analogically derived sense of "paradigm" is not neat (*Structure*, 23). Lawrence J. Prelli summarizes by suggesting that "a paradigm constrains the vision of those who accept it; it suggests what is to be anticipated in respect to situated phenomena" (87). He goes on to explain the constraining effects of a paradigm by relating Kuhn's concept to Burke's notion of "terministic screens," itself an idea that clearly pays homage to the relationship among vision, symbolic inducement, and conceptual systems. By "terministic screen," Burke meant to describe the way any conceptual system filters out some percepts at the same time it allows others in. Prelli states that "once we are induced to accept particular terministic screens, we gain entry to the orientation invoked by those terms. We will treat those terministic screens as unquestioned presuppositions, if only provisionally. We cannot enter the orientation otherwise. . . . An orientation patterns or structures our experiences and prescribes how otherwise disconnected items should be related in sensible, orderly, and compelling ways" (89–90). Walter B. Weimer has said straightforwardly in writing about the rhetoric of science that "truth is relative to conceptual framework" (11).

It is not difficult to see why incommensurability seems to be an inevitable outcome of systems thinking. The hierarchical and visual nature of a conceptual system, with tightly logical relationships among its elements, seems by its form to reflect isomorphically what is real or natural. Consequently, for adherents to a particular conceptual system, the acceptance of its basic rules and relationships may be tacit, unquestioned, and reflective of a natural order. In addition, for adherents to a particular conceptual system, any alternative system automatically represents a challenge to a conception of reality. Both systems cannot be isomorphic with what is real, any more than two dominant paradigms can exist unproblematically in science.

Moreover, the hierarchical organization of systems is itself persuasive of a standard of correctness, as the etymology of the word implies: in Greek, the *hierarchês* is the figure in charge—the steward, priest, or keeper of sacred things. Hence, the overarching principle in a hierarchical system is regarded as a universal first principle determinative from the outset of the relationships within the system. Conceptual systems are therefore relatively static, at least in their structure beneath an overarching first principle, permitting no interplay with competing conceptual systems. Knowledge growth is limited (it would seem) to improving the presumed accuracy of the logical array of elements within a system. Kant's comment about human nature describes what is recognizable as a systems bias with respect to belief and knowledge: this bias "regards all our knowledge as belonging to a possible system, and therefore allows only such principles as do not at any rate make it impossible for any knowledge that we may attain to combine into a system with other knowledge" (*Critique of Pure Reason* I, pt. II, div. II., ch. 2. sec. 3., B502). With no provisions within the logic of any such system for interaction with some other system, each occupies its own plane, untouched by the logic of the other.

While it may be clear that systems may be visual and hierarchical, it is not so clear why argument and rhetorical judgment need to be similarly modeled, but in contemporary times they are. Argument, as a rational activity, is generally associated with a composition developed as a logical defense or with the logical development of an overarching principle. The most prominent definitions of *argument* focus on this feature; typical is this one from the 1989 *Oxford English Dictionary:* "A reason urged in support of a proposition."[2] The model of such argument is perhaps the paragraph or the composed position paper. If we try to picture this version of argument, we can picture a "vertical and visual" form, as Jarratt calls it (27). The inclusion of particular pieces of evidence or particular assertions in a position paper is determined by the dominance of a theme or thesis: the "proposition" to be defended. This structuring is what Jarratt calls "hypotaxis," wherein "the end is prefigured from the beginning—the whole structure is built in a vertical form, 'hypo' suggesting an organization 'from under'" (27). Whether the "proposition" in a composition is considered to be the "foundation" of the structure or the "overarching," universal idea being given "support" by the particulars, the key point of the metaphor is that argument is a vertical, hierarchical form.

Argument thus envisioned does not require the presence of another thinker; in fact, when we consider "having an argument" with someone else, the whole notion tends to take on the flavor of something irrational and unmethodical. For just this reason, the visual notion of argument limits the possibility of active artistic judgment and offers no resources for communication between incommensurate systems. In fact, hypotactic argument, like any other systems thinking, is concerned with arraying things—in the case of argument, arraying assertions and evidence—according to their appropriate visualizable relationships in a hierarchy (the use of outlines to plan composed arguments is testimony to the assumptions of hierarchy). To show an excessive interest in such arraying is to show an excessive concern for "proper place" and to reflect the underlying assumption that, as in nature, everything has its proper place, has no other place, and has only one relationship with every other thing in *its* proper place.

The supplanting of the term "judgment" by the term "arrangement" in Ramist rhetoric provides an illustration of that excess of visual interest and its consequences to rhetorical judgment. Ong (1958) describes the ancient shift in terminology:

> Ramist rhetoric is a rhetoric which has not only no invention but also no judgment or arrangement of its own. The field of activity covered by the terms judgment or arrangement (*dispositio*) has likewise been dissociated from voice by being isolated from rhetoric and committed to Ramist dialectic or logic. In the process, judgment—which necessarily bespeaks utterance, an assent or a dissent, a *saying* of yes or no—simply disappears, and with it all rational interest in the psychological activities which such a term covers. Arrangement or 'positioning' (*dispositio*) secures exclusive rights as the only other phenomenon besides invention which occurs in intellectual activity, and as the sole principle governing the organization of speech. Unlike judgment, which cannot be conceived of independently of some reference to saying, to utterance, and thus to the oral and aural world of personalities,

'arrangement' can be conceived of simply by analogy with visually perceived spatial patterns. ("Ramist Rhetoric," 252)

Ong makes it clear that specific ontological assumptions underlay the Ramists' visual rhetoric. The Ramists conceived of the arts "by analogy with extended, and hence quantified surfaces, and . . . two extended objects cannot occupy the same space" ("Ramist Rhetoric," 240). Hence, the arts had to be distinct, and within each art all the parts had to be distinct. Ramus called the rule of thought "Solon's Law" after the building ordinance in Athens that required a clear space on every side of a structure to separate it from the others ("Ramist Rhetoric," 240–41). *All* things were to be in their separate or distinct compartments, or places.

Given Solon's Law, judgments as to how ideas could and should be fitted together—their logic—were derived from principles like those Ramus adopted from Solon, principles arrived at externally and prior to the ideas themselves. In a completed philosophical system, for instance, the elements would typically be included by reference to an overarching a priori principle. The visually biased form of judgment that generated such a priori systems makes use of a form of argumentation reflecting the same bias. Argument itself becomes an inactive method of pronouncing judgments already made (relatively) obvious by the rules operative in the system. As Ong says of Ramist rhetoric, such forms of judgment and argumentation usurp the active work of the human judge by locating the task in rules and principles outside him. The external standards characterizing a priori systems and the static character of judgment in argument are both instances of visual, nonrhetorical bias. Justification is made "in terms of" the logic of the system. Insofar as words and things are thought to be related, things (like core beliefs or first principles) justify other things (subsequent propositions, assertions, and evidence) in a way that can be visually rendered as a hierarchical tree that appears static and permanent.

These "trees of justification" are inadequate for overcoming problems of incommensurability. Hauser notes that the effectiveness of argument as a means of settling disputes of various kinds has been impaired under twentieth-century conditions because of a withdrawal of human judgment in favor of judgment conferred by the logic of a system of thought. He notes that "conditions of diversity, interdependence, and awareness . . . have undercut the historically prevalent notion that a proposition may be justified by appeal to self-evident assumptions" (261). He suggests that, as a consequence, when people encounter differences that are based in separate sets of self-evident assumptions, they are unable to discuss their differences fruitfully: "Consequently, when one party insists on the truth of his or her starting premises and the irrational character of an opponent's, communication becomes an ineffectual means for settling differences" (262). The problem he cites can be considered to be one of human agents' yielding their powers of judgment to a principle or rule. Hauser points out, for instance, that "core beliefs, after all, justify subsequent propositions only to those who subscribe to them" (262).

The abortion rights controversy active in the second half of twentieth century in the United States provides a ready example of Hauser's concerns. Celeste Condit identifies the controversy as being a "competition between two powerful, incommensurable discourses" (202). In familiar (and simplified) terms, we might say that a particular strong position on abortion rights may involve an entire belief system, including a powerful superordinate belief. I may be against the right to abortion if I believe that *by nature* life begins at conception and that consistency with this belief dictates that the right of the fetus to life must be protected. I may be for abortion rights if I believe that a woman's right to control her body *as a natural right* overrides other considerations and that consistency with this belief dictates that the right to her decision making must be protected. Of course the commitment to one side or another is more complicated than this, involving religious beliefs, cultural and socioeconomic differences, and differences in experience. But by 1985 the discourses could be accurately labeled "pro-Life" or "pro-Choice" and could be understood in contradistinction to one another and as incommensurate. By the early or mid-1970s, in fact, a "set of competing terms" or "competing vocabularies" on each side already jockeyed for public dominance (Condit, 96).

As a competition between two competing and incommensurate moral vocabularies, the abortion rights dispute offered no way for an "interaction of beliefs and values" of the agents (Condit, 163)—or, more to the point, the dispute, framed as incommensurate, offered the two sides a logically sound way to refuse any genuine negotiation. As we might expect, persuasion became impossible at that point at which the different sides gave different significance and weight to different value terms. Efforts at understanding the other side help little when these efforts occur in terms of one's own vocabulary. For example, "pro-Choice" supporters were fond of pointing out to some conservative groups taking a "pro-Life" stance their inconsistency in also supporting the death penalty. The objection formed neither an effective challenge nor an effective attempt to understand and adapt to the vocabulary of the other side. Condit explains that the "pro-Life" stance of conservative groups had consistently implied a "pro-natalism" rooted in a longstanding valuing of the natural preeminence of motherhood and "maximal human reproduction" (61–62). In the 1960s, Condit states, "Sanctity of human *life*, rooted in a conservative concern for pro-natalism, was translated into the liberal individual discourse of a basic human right—the Right to Life" (62). Liberals, in adopting a translation of pro-Life terms according to the vocabulary of liberal individualism, failed at their efforts to uncover a fatal flaw in conservative belief systems. Liberals did more to sustain the consistency within their own vocabularies and tighten the logics of their own belief systems, which they then recognized as "consistent" and "logical" in contradistinction to the "inconsistent" and "illogical" beliefs of the other side.

The judgments produced during argument do not necessarily have to follow the visual form of systems thinking that we see exemplified in abortion rights rhetoric. Judgment can, instead, be humanly pronounceable rather than generated by the internal logic of a system. If arguers had some genuine stake in the pronouncements of those opposing them, they would be forced to assume the burden of communicating their ideas in such a way that those ideas could be judged reasonably by the opposition. If "self-evident assumptions," "a priori principles," and "core beliefs" were no longer accepted as self-evident (literally as *speaking for themselves*), the visual bias of apodictic argument would have to be abandoned. In other words, anyone arguing points for a human judge whose position opposed that of the arguer would have to develop relationships among terms and attributes that would be apparent and have validity, not necessarily in her own frame of reference, but in that of the other.

If justification in terms of core beliefs or a priori principles means finding the proper places for things, allowing or substituting human judgment means finding common places between one system of ideas and another. The granting of priority to human judgment necessitates the placing of one's own ideas in common with those of others.

This distinction between proper and common places is more than a play on words. It suggests a key difference in what we may mean by a system and in what we may believe can be done with things. It is fairly easy to recognize a visual and hierarchical formulation of "system," just as it is easy to understand argument as apodictic and therefore visual. Thought of visually, argument and system are identified: both are forms of demonstration. Proper places are found for things by applying a logic that is fundamentally deductive in order to reason from an a priori principle and demonstrate what falls under it. However, when we think of argument as oral, the obligation of finding places in common between differing vocabularies implies something entirely different for the arguer. She is not obligated to discover the logically proper place a thing ought to occupy; instead, she is to create new sets of relationships by finding points of commonality between elements in her system and those of the person with whom she is arguing.

Suppose for the moment that ideas within a system are understandable in terms of their similarities to, and distinctions from, other ideas within the system. If this is the case, the process of creating new sets of relationships has the potential to be ongoing once human judgment is introduced. Each time an idea or a system of ideas must be submitted to the judgment of another, new sets of similarities and differences must be created. Argument thus allows movement through time and space by virtue of the fact that a person must find ways of taking challenges to her ideas seriously and must invent ways of providing responses that will be taken seriously by the other. Therefore, thought of orally, arguing necessitates crafting relationships among terms from each disputed side. This crafting of relationships is a dynamic, ongoing activity, in contrast to the static and apparently *completed* presence of a visual system.

A model for such argumentation lies in the ancient methods of *stasis*, especially as they reached their mature statement in the antithetical method of Cicero. In attempting to develop a role for rhetoric that would usurp the dominance of philosophy, Cicero articulated the way that constant responsiveness to argument offered a kind of system unmaking and remaking. Dynamic argument would displace static systems of relationship. Before we move on to a consideration of Cicero, however, the distinction between visual argument and oral argument must be sharpened.

By Contrast: Oral Argument

If visual argument is perceivable as hypotactic and concerned with array, argument that involves clash between members of two distinct hierarchies of thought may be regarded as paratactic and unconcerned with arraying ideas. Instead, argument as oral is a version of commonplacing. Much as the poet responded actively and artistically to what he had already sung, rhetors can respond actively and artistically by picking up novel strains of thought from one another and developing new, but not random, differentiations and identifications. As outgrowths of discussion, these novel differentiations and identifications make no pretense to permanence or to the scientific isomorphism with nature to which visual systems aspire. Instead, they present themselves as temporary moments in time that function as starting off points for later creative discussion. Differentiations and identifications work temporarily and in the context of discussion.

A clearer and fuller articulation of what I have in mind may be found in a careful reading of Harold Zyskind's description of "rhetorical first principles" (376) and "arenas of action" (378). Zyskind conceives of rhetorical first principles that act as counterparts to philosophical first principles. Whereas philosophical first principles are the "givens" or assumptions that undergird apodictic argument, rhetorical first principles are simply suggestive references, "novel and generative firsts, or rather, firsts because novel and generative" (376). In their concrete manifestations, rhetorical first principles may be vast insights or nothing more than minor references to a term. Rhetorical first principles do not gain their force by initiating a web of causal necessity, but they have a similar forcefulness: once laid down by a human agent, they are recognized as indicative of further action. Rather than being unquestioned assumptions about reality, these first principles are inextricably linked to the vision and action of a particular human agent who finds them persuasive at a particular place and time in the context of a discussion that has preceded him.

Hence, the importance of the particular discursive framework in which the agent becomes actor is important. Whether the agent seeks involvement in a philosophical discussion, a discussion of political action, or a discussion of moral consequences, the broad framework in which that talk has happened and is happening is a place of discursive action. Zyskind sees the discursive framework as an existential place, an *"arena of action"* (378) in which the agent acts in order to "establish a place" (380) for herself. In a very real sense, the person may be seen as trying to constitute herself as an actor in this arena. As she exists by virtue of her talk, she *becomes* a point of view or perspective within the arena. Hence, the person becomes actor by finding in the arena some persuasive beginning in what has already been said and by assuming that following up the implications will win her a place.

Although Zyskind is interested in following the "battle" implications of the arena metaphor (stating, for instance, that "successful self-defense" is "the model actional principle" of rhetoric [380]), the analogy to the commonplacing activity of the poets is more instructive here. Especially important is the image of the actor moving through time in an arena of discussion that precedes her (Zyskind calls it "making one's way" [387]) and that she hopes will be changed by her presence and action. She moves within that arena by the creative operation of picking up on points that mark concluding moments from the conversation that preceded her, discovering what it is about them that would or should provoke more discussion, and following up their implications. So engaged, she is finding beginnings from end points, much as the poet composed by finding the suggestion for another line of song in what had come before. The arena that Zyskind describes has room for both the dominance of the discursive framework and the individual creativity of the agent who may find in it any number of suggestive firsts and may act on the discussion in any of a number of ways.

The discursive framework has multiple dimensions. A spatial dimension is constituted by the many clashing perspectives within the arena. Multiple perspectives brought together to be responded to provide the "stuff" of rhetorical action; consequently, interaction among any number of perspectives is expected to emerge. But for action to occur, there must be a recognition of the mutual dependency of the perspectives. Clash and movement can happen only because "each part or agent, each group, *being* a perspective, *must proceed by taking the others into account*" (Zyskind, 392). This is an existential truism, because in the arena, each agent knows herself, just as any perspective may be known, "by the *impress they can make on other minds*" (391). The truism also points toward an inventional principle, suggesting the usefulness of topical thinking: the rhetor can find points to make

in the particular discursive arena *in part* by finding and actualizing relationships of similarity and difference with existing perspectives.

There is also an important temporal dimension to this arena. In actualizing relationships of similarity to, and difference from, existing perspectives, the actor creates new positions, issues, or subject matters to be
responded to within the arena. But these patterns of relationship are themselves vulnerable and temporary. Rhetorically, any point in time in a discursive arena serves as a jumping off point for the creativity of others. The
arena is thus "an ongoing stream of successive times" (Zyskind, 392).

This characteristic has the potential of an inventional principle too, and
it implies a purpose of oral argument distinct from the purpose of visual,
vertical argument. The rhetor, moving through time, may think of herself
moving horizontally and paratactically through the space created in the
arena; she does not think of herself engaged in constructing a piece of a
hierarchical system, as she might if she were engaged in visually realized
argument. She is not charged with arguing so as to establish a logical coherence with a preexisting framework of thought. She is charged, instead, with
being responsive to what has preceded her and with recognizing that, if
provocative, she will be responded to herself. Therefore, rather than resisting contradictions or inconsistencies, she seeks them out as generative
forces; she also will allow and respond to challenges by others to her discovered pattern of relationships. The eagerness to embrace inconsistency or
contradiction is a major element distinguishing rhetoric from visual logic.
Whereas a visual and vertical perspective on knowledge as a completed system idealizes consistency, coherence, and permanence of structure, the oral
sense of argument, which is concerned rather with the ongoing generation
of ideas, idealizes inconsistency, clash, and temporariness. In fact, the only
consistency in such orally realized argument is the continuity of the arena
itself: argument continues through time while, and even because, there is
discontinuity, interruption, and redirection of streams of thought.

If we may borrow for a moment from vertical and hierarchical systems
an advantage of visual imagery, we might imagine the arena of interacting
participants and ideas as a matrix—a visual metaphor Zyskind also adopts.
This matrix has the spatial and temporal dimensions Zyskind suggests. As
such, it contains moments of interacting perspectives: nodes on the matrix
where differing perspectives have forced themselves into relationship.
These points of relationship are nothing more nor less than moments of
intersection at which interactants have met and invented subject matters as
issues for specific disputes. Subject matters, not systems, are in dispute.
Subject matters, unlike systems, are limited in scope and make no pretense
to permanence; instead, they develop from the need for concrete debate
and have validity only as they meet the need for disputation. However, as
discoveries emerging from the need for debate, subject matters do intro-

duce rhetorical first principles, or jumping-off points for other debaters from which other subject matters may be invented. Hence, the matrix exists prior to particular interactions and at the same time emerges out of inter-actions. Various interactants progress through time by bringing their per-spectives into intersection, picking up, as generative, threads from debates that have taken place, and thus inventing new subject matters for further debate. The direction of further debate and the creation of new subject matters—the horizontal dimension—is open-ended and does not aspire to completeness as a vertical system might do.

Implicit in the description of this oral model of argument is a way to think of incommensurate systems being positioned to be negotiable and arguable. Although there may seem no way for entire vertically organized systems to be brought into clash, specific subject matters for debate bring pieces of systems into a place of clash from which even more new subject matters may emerge. In these interactions, systems of thought may not be destroyed so much as deconstructed—dismantled—with some elements recombined with elements of other, clashing systems, their orders of prior-ity disrupted for purposes of the debates.

To understand the potential of these disruptions and recombinations fully, we must see this matrix as providing a means of invention. If we can-not see the inventive potential of this horizontal and paratactic activity, the matrix appears to be a way to trace rhetorical histories rather than actually create subject matters *for* history. Without an accompanying sense of inven-tional method, the matrix is a tool to aid the spectator who is interested in looking back critically at arguments that have taken place instead of an enabling perspective on argument for the actor/artist engaged in doing rheto-ric. There is a danger of hopelessness in becoming locked into the position of the spectator observing the history of clashes between incommensurate sys-tems in a culture where the concept of vertical and hierarchical argument dominates: unproductive debate may appear inevitable. This danger can be mitigated only when a method of invention for the arguer is recaptured and the notion of oral and paratactic argument redeveloped.

We may detect the potential for this method in Cicero's method of *con-troversia*, or antithesis. In fact, Cicero's method of *controversia* operated from a set of assumptions similar to the ones we have been using to distin-guish oral from visual argument: Cicero viewed rhetoric as being insepara-ble from its agents, having its own generative form of judgment, and being productive of subject matters. Most importantly, Cicero saw in rhetoric the means by which a forum of opinion was progressively shaped and reshaped through contact among contradictory positions: as the Sophists found con-tradictions generative of assertions, Cicero found the conflicts between incommensurate philosophies capable of forcefully pulling apart and repo-sitioning ideas into new patterns, definitive of new knowledge. In Cicero's method we will see the usefulness of topical thinking and the seeking out of contradictions as generative forces.

Cicero's Rhetorical-Philosophical Method: Seeking Out Contradictions

Cicero's method of *controversia*, like other so-called *stasis* methods that developed after the Greek Enlightenment, would seem to be ideally suited to tackling the apparently intransigent problems of incommensurability. Such methods are put to use where a standoff between positions occurs; these moments are points of *stasis*.

The term *stasis* has been given various definitions. Dieter, in his exhaustive effort to translate the term, indicates that the rhetorical term had its genesis in Aristotle's physics as "that which disrupts, or severs motion and robs it of its continuity" (349). Hence, a point of *stasis* might be recognized as a point where the articulation of an opinion stops because of the introduction of a counteropinion. It might also signify a disruption of common opinion, the point at which progress as usual halts because of the introduction of an equally strong counteropinion. Dieter, in fact, recognizes *stasis*, graphically represented, as the point at which two counterforces, represented as horizontal lines, meet to produce a standoff. Carter, in a conventional rhetorical description, defines *stasis* as "the method by which rhetors in the classical tradition identified the area of disagreement, the point that was to be argued, the issue on which the case hinged" (98). Although Dieter describes situations in which the equal weight of the reasons supporting the opinion and the counteropinion could prevent any rhetorical solutions (354), the method as practiced by rhetoricians like Hermagoras, Cicero, and Quintillian reflected optimism about the capacity for rhetoric to move the state of opinion beyond the enforced rest of the *stasis* point.

Cicero's method for analyzing and inventing arguments in instances of *stasis* is his method of *controversia*. The method constituted a dialogical testing of propositions that elevates ordinary conversation to serious debate. Although the method is rooted in courtroom debate, for Cicero its great value lay in pitting philosophical schools against one another in order to test their claims.

Cicero believed that the knowledge achievable by human beings was not absolute but probable knowledge. In accordance with his belief in the probable nature of human conclusion making, Cicero rejected the scientific methods of dogmatist schools like that of the Stoics and employed instead a method of philosophical examination adapted from the antithetical method of the courtroom. When used for philosophical problems, the antithetical method required placing two contradictory positions against one another. The adherents of each school would typically develop expositions of their schools' positions, each of which would be responded to with a searching refutation. This response was usually made by a Skeptic (sometimes Cicero), who refused "to state anything positive" himself and satisfied himself with identifying logical difficulties with whatever position had been set forth by someone else. Hence, as Michael J. Buckley points out, both invention and judgment were brought together in one method—a method of dialogue by which arguments in support of a position were invented by one person and examined or judged by another. From this procedure of invention and critique, the weaknesses and strengths of the various competing schools could be identified, and the surviving conclusions would emerge as the most probable.

Significantly, bringing together invention and judgment into one method reunited wisdom and eloquence, philosophy and rhetoric. Cicero complained that, with few exceptions, these had been progressively but erroneously separated since the point at which Socrates rejected the Sophists. Cicero argued that although the matters treated by rhetoric and philosophy might differ, one without the other would be useless to the wise man or to the life of the public: "Wisdom without eloquence does too little for the good of states, but . . . eloquence without wisdom is generally highly disadvantageous and is never helpful" (*De Inventione*, I.1.1). Likewise, the methods of rhetoric and philosophical inquiry were to be one; rhetoric and philosophy could be distinguished by the subjects they treated, but not by their methods (Buckley).

The need to reunify wisdom with eloquence—and invention with judgment—was far more than academic to Cicero. He saw philosophy as a practical matter, and his derivation of a philosophical method from the practical method of rhetorical invention reflects that view. In order to appreciate the importance of that point, we may reexamine the relationship between Cicero's antidogmatism and what he saw as the development of probable knowledge, a tenuous relationship that has as its corollary his ambivalent attitude toward Socrates.

Socrates' own antidogmatic, antithetical method reflected the belief that a philosophy having as its sole aim the rejection of all dogmatically held opinions should make use of a purely refutative, dialogic method. Socrates, opining in a well-known statement that all he knew was that he could not know, adopted a philosophic method that rejected development of systematic doctrine in favor of cross-questioning those who claimed they had knowledge. The method was oral and dialogic so as to fulfill the Socratic goal of getting interlocutors to reject dogma, examine premature claims of certainty, and reject those claims that could not withstand cross-questioning. Cicero endorsed these goals and hoped in this regard to recapture Socrates' career (Buckley, 144).

Socrates' rejection of the Sophists, however, signaled his backing away from the practical needs that gave birth to philosophy and his rejection of the importance of invention, at least according to Cicero. Because of this rejection Cicero, in his own turn, turned his back on some schools that claimed to be Socratic. Cicero's issue with them had to do with their apparently losing sight of the practical side of philosophy. Philosophy needed to be concerned, not simply with destroying all claims to knowledge, but also with establishing knowledge in some form that allowed human action. Cicero did not accept the claim of some schools that knowledge could not be attained at all. Instead, he followed Carneides and the members of the later New Academy, who believed that *probable* knowledge was attainable (*Tusculan Disputations,* I.9.17; Introduction xxii). Cicero's method was intended to lead to the finding and production (invention) of probable knowledge.

The practical need to produce probable knowledge was, of course, acute in a courtroom setting, where Cicero's roots as a prelate were. What would have begun as a situation of forensic *stasis*, with claims like "He did it" lined up against their precise counterclaims, had to move to some decision based on argument. Probable arguments in favor of each side needed to be discovered. The need for producing arguments also led Cicero to appreciate the generative function of rhetorical topics and to complain of the anti-inventive and cold logic of the Stoics. In Stoic philosophy, invention was neglected in favor of judgment; Cicero complained that "he [the Stoic] does not teach me how to discover what to say; and he actually hinders me, by finding many difficulties which he pronounces quite insoluble" (*De Oratore,* 2.38.159). Cicero's philosophical method was to recapture the need for practical discovery and action.

Cicero's Method of *Controversia*

Cicero's generative method, the method of *controversia,* was to be applied to a variety of issues, ranging from philosophical to forensic. In all cases, the value to practical disputation lay in the potential for the method to generate subject matters for debate and hence to provide an oral, dialogic corollary to visual forms of judgment.

Discovering a Rhetorical Subject Matter—The Work of the Method

The practical needs that generated the method of *controversia* are most apparent in Cicero's uses of the method in forensic speech. For Cicero, any controversy would be centered around one of four issues, or *constitutiones* (*De Inventione,* 1.7.10).[3] Each issue was articulated as a question, either a conjectural question, involving a fact; a definitional question, involving a word or expression; a qualitative question, involving the nature of the act under discussion and "concerning the value of the act and its class or quality" (*De Inventione,* 1.8.10); or a translative question, involving the proper place for the issue to be decided. These are fairly standard *stasis* questions among those Roman rhetoricians who used them, although some, notably Quintillian, did not include the final question (Buckley, 152).

The questions provided an analysis of a controversy by locating with precision the point upon which a dispute turned. In a courtroom dispute, which will provide my example here, the advocate would find this point by asking the questions in their logical order until he found one that applied and that had the potential to provide him with an advantage. The question of fact, for instance, would be the first question to be asked in a controversy and would involve whether a person had done, was doing, or would be doing something. If the question of fact was admitted by all parties, then the dispute could not turn on that issue and might turn on a question of definition: "The controversy about a definition arises when there is agreement as to the fact and the question is by what word that which has been done is to be described. In this case, there must be a dispute about the definition, because there is no agreement about the essential point, not because the fact is not certain, but because the deed appears differently to different people, and for that reason different people describe it in different terms" (*De Inventione*, 1.7.11).

If, for example, a person took a silver vase from his neighbor's house, and there was no dispute as to the fact, there could be a dispute as to what the act should be called. The person who took the article might insist that the act should be called "borrowing," while the neighbor might insist that the act be called "theft." Definitional questions gain importance in philosophical disputes, in which things and deeds may appear differently to different people.

If there is agreement on the first two questions, then the dispute may turn on a question of quality, that is, "about how important it is or of what kind, or in general about its quality, e.g., was it just or unjust, profitable or unprofitable?" (*De Inventione*, 1.9.12). The man who took his neighbor's vase might admit that the act could be called theft but explain that he took the piece with his neighbor's good in mind, out of concern that someone seeing the valuable piece might burglarize the neighbor during the night and threaten his life.

The final question is the translative or procedural one. As a question about the jurisdiction of the case or whether it is being tried under the appropriate law, the question is a technical one. As such, it could be evoked at any point during the debate at which the violation of a rule seemed possible or at which another ruling could be more applicable. In other settings, the so-called translative issue becomes an issue of *action*, when one inquires how and whether a decision can be translated into action. In philosophical debate, inclusion of the issue of action was a significant acknowledgment of the practical demands upon philosophy.

Locating the appropriate question for the debate was the first step in creating the subject matter of the dispute. Significantly, the subject matter itself took the form of a question to be answered, and it arose out of, not prior to, the debate itself. Quintillian is enlightening on this point in his own discussion of legal *stasis*. The proper subject matter of a legal dispute was not actually the case, or *causa*, with which a prosecutor began; the genuine subject matter was the problem or question (*quaestio*) generated during the dispute: "Some say that the state of the matter is the first conflict of legal matters . . . ; they have, I believe, sensed the right thing, but expressed themselves inadequately. It is not the first conflict—as, for instance, you have done it, I have not done it . . . but what comes out of the first conflict, namely the kind of question" (quoted in Grassi, 1980, 49).

Starting from a "conflict of pleas" (*De Inventione,* 1.13.18) like "You killed him" — "I did not kill him," the subject of debate or *quaestio* would be whether the accused committed the act, if this fact were the point the arguers agreed was in dispute. If it were, then knowing this point of dispute would permit the advocates to analyze the case as a question of fact and apply topics appropriate to such a question. The "reason or excuse" is the point that makes the conflict of pleas possible and without which there would not be a dispute. The excuse might consist of "You killed him, *because I saw you there*" — "I could not have been there, *because I was in another part of town at the time.*" From this excuse arose "the point of the judge's decision (*indicatio*)" (*De Inventione,* 1.13.18), here, "Was he at the scene of the crime or was he not?" In the conjectural issue in this example, the remainder of the analysis would consist of showing the proofs of the claimed facts. But in the other three types of issue, the advocates would proceed by being aware of the defendant's *foundation*, or strongest possible argument, which was the argument considered most relevant to the judge's decision (1.13.18). Therefore, after the development of the initial *quaestio*, subject matters would continue to be generated and negotiated through the progressive analysis and synthesis taking place during the argument.

Not all controversies, philosophical or judicial, would mimic this procedure exactly. In fact, if the procedure could be applied this mechanically, there would be little of the spontaneity and improvisation that would come from the particulars of a specific controversy itself. But besides demonstrating how Cicero's method works in a judicial setting, the example serves to show how this two-voiced method aids in the generation of new subject matters.

During the course of the two-person clash, the advocate for either side is forced out of his tendency and desire to support his position in his own terms. Forced to find the point that separates him from his opponent, he must build his case, not in the terms he might prefer, but in terms that are established in part by his adversary and in part by his circumstances. Dieter is at pains to emphasize that "statiatic" situations offer the potential for special instances of analyzing and synthesizing. Arguers proceed by attempting to block one another's progress: the plaintiff "intends his statement to be a final one," but his "'rest' is immediately disturbed, for the defendant . . . insists on using the plaintiff's resting place as the starting place of his own contrary motion" (359). With his rest stopped when his adversary introduces a counterassertion, an advocate must analyze his case in the terms generated by the action of the assertion and the counterassertion coming together.

The important moment is this synthesis, the momentary coming together of the two sides as *together* they generate the subject matter of the debate, the *quaestio*. Jeffrey J. Levy observes, "The development of the specific question at issue establishes a new subject-matter which is the product of two contrary arguments each trying to explain the same set of circumstances. What has happened is the generation of a rhetorical subject" (65). The *quaestio* sets the terms of the debate and thus takes it in a direction that neither participant might have dictated on his own.

Controversia as Oral Invention—A Contrast to Visual Proofs

The importance of rhetorical subject matter as probable knowledge generated from debate highlights a key contrast between oral argument and visual argument. In an oral, dialogic method like Cicero's, the continued generation of questions moving toward an answer aims to open debate and requires materially at least two voices. Visual systems, however, aim for closure and completeness of representation, and require only a solitary thinker.

Buckley makes a similar point by contrasting Aristotle's scientific method for grounding knowledge with Cicero's method for generating probable knowledge. For Aristotle, scientifically grounded knowledge consisted of knowledge of cause. In order for a person to say he had scientific knowledge, he had to have not only knowledge of the fact but also of "the cause on which the fact depends" (*Posterior Analytics*, 1.71b.10). Significantly, "cause" had a verbal component: it was the proof of the truth or the reason one could say that something was true. Aristotle constructed four questions that, used together, demonstrated the cause of a thing's being, and he considered them to comprehend all the possible questions that needed to be asked in order to seek cause, or proof (*Posterior Analytics*, 2.89b.20–25).

Levy argues persuasively that these questions can be reduced to two, both of which have to do with ascertaining the cause or the authority for saying our knowledge is scientific and not accidental: "Is there a middle?" and "What is the middle?" (Levy, 72). A "middle" is the connecting term of a philosophic demonstration or syllogism: "the 'middle' here is precisely the cause, and it is the cause that we seek in all our inquiries" (2.90a.5). For instance, we cannot assert *scientifically* that walking improves our health, even if our assertion may incidentally be true, without knowing the *cause* linking walking and good health.

For Aristotle, finding the middle term—the cause—impelled the thinker to a syllogistic demonstration that the alleged fact could really be considered a fact. A crude syllogism, for instance, might be, "A strong heart indicates good health; walking strengthens the heart; therefore, walking leads to health."

Cicero's rhetorical method was similarly precise, and in similar manner, Cicero regarded the four analytical issues or *constitutiones* of his rhetorical method to be logically comprehensive of every controversy (*De Inventione*, 1.8.10). The four issues and four types of controversy were to constitute a universal way of generating probable knowledge. However, it was only by applying the questions *in debate* that the nature of the controversy could be discovered, the subject matter determined, and the most probable claims on both sides ascertained. Cicero, like Aristotle, was concerned with finding a "middle." But instead of asking, "Is there a cause and what is it?" Cicero asked, "Is there a *stasis* (point of dispute) and what is it?" (Levy, 73–74).

Thus, if there were a dispute about walking and health, the disputants on the two sides would have had to come together and debate it. Ciceronian analysis would have helped them isolate the point of their dispute (which might or might not have something to do with strengthening the heart) and the question that needed to be argued on both sides in order to reach a conclusion.

There is more to distinguish the two methods than the different beliefs about knowledge they support. Arguably, Aristotle's scientific method, with its emphasis on proof, does not generate new ideas. It searches out a way of grounding ideas that have already been asserted. More to the point, what knowledge will consist of—what it can be called—is determined a priori, in terms set by the method itself; scientific method itself takes over the role of judging master. Therefore, determining cause has as its purpose eliminating the need for debate.

The analysis called for by the antithetical method, however, is directed first to discovering and generating the subject matter that will open debate. Subject matters can continue to be generated as analysis may progressively narrow down the topics for dispute. The subject matters generated during the debate come out of analysis undertaken together by the two arguers, with assistance from the *constitutiones*. Probable knowledge is generated from human judgment rather than from a justificatory method, since probable knowledge comes only as the outcome of debate.

The subject matter constituted from the coming together in debate of the two contrary assertions is a pattern or relationship between the two, a way for them to exist together but *linked only by what they form*. The Latin use of the word *constitutio* for *stasis* signifies a unique synthesis that emerges only during the contact of contraries or opposites; for example, "the bringing, or coming together and the resultant 'standing together' of contrary informations of a homogeneous nature, or an instrumental organ of the body, as for example a femur and a tibia are articulated to form a leg" (Dieter, 359–60).

In this type of synthesis, the contraries are brought into contact, but although they touch, they do not merge; the subject matter created at the joint of their contact does more to create further material for talk than to bring the positions together into the sort of hierarchical relationship we usually expect of a system. There is no attempt to bring the two sides together in some way that would make the positions compatible or to discover some transcendent principle or hierarchical term to subsume them both. As Buckley points out, speaking of the application of the method to Ciceronian philosophy, "The Ciceronian debate does not move Platonically from communities and oppositions to an assimilation of lesser truths in the greater. It is controversy" (148).

We can see the significance of this point with further contrasts. In the example we have been using, the subject matter generated out of the original clash, "He did it"—"He did not do it," is the new question, "Was he in the vicinity or was he not?" The material of the original clash is left behind for the moment because its purpose in the debate has been served. The adversaries will each use the other's ending points to generate new assertions and counterassertions and their proofs.

The analysis offered by the *constitutiones* is thus an inventive counterpart to Zyskind's matrix and a further contrast to visual systems. The subject matters determined for debate suggest the beginning points and the terms for further debate. From the early points of analysis, an advocate develops a case that is again parsed into its debatable points, which are then disputed by the adversary. Each of these points of agreement on what to dispute constitutes a form of knowledge—not scientific knowledge in Aristotle's sense, but limited in scope and conditioned by the debate itself. With respect to the topic of the debate, each participant is led to know his standing in relation to the other and the other's in relation to himself. This knowledge develops in a way that would have been impossible without the analysis and the debate. In a legal dispute, this is significant knowledge that leads to equally significant decision making by the advocates. They are led to examine and discover the various ways in which, say, a party can be said to be guilty or to be innocent. Dieter's description of *constitutio* reminds us that the invented subject matters represent the constitution of key moments of new relationship. The etymology is striking: "A *systasis*, *systema*, or *constitutio*, then, is a constitution . . . i.e., in rhetoric, the physical incorporation, natural organization, organic make-up or vital system of a controversy" (360). The dynamic nature of *systema*, as distinct from visual "system," suggests that the subject matter discovered relates the two sides in such a way as to generate more and better material for debate.

Incommensurability and Cicero's Antithetical Method
Moving to "Practical Philosophy"

How can the antithetical method make debate possible between proponents of different, even incommensurate systems, and what advantage comes from that debate? In order to answer these questions, we need to turn away from forensic settings and see how the antithetical method might function in discussions of philosophical systems. In a judicial setting, the method aided in breaking down the original accusation and defense into the point at issue. In philosophical discussion, however, the antithetical method had a different function: it forced interlocutors to parse up their own systems of thought and to recognize (if not accept) new patterns of relationship with the opposing philosophy.

Cicero's antidogmatism played a major role in his adaptation of the rhetorical methods of the courtroom to philosophical discussion. In his discussion of philosophical systems, Cicero revealed reasons for his antidogmatism. The language he uses to describe philosophical systems is strikingly similar to language I used earlier to describe visual systems and incommensurability. For instance, he characterized philosophical systems by noting that "it is a striking characteristic of philosophy that its topics all hang together and form a consecutive system; one is seen to be linked to another, and all to be mutually connected and attached" (*De Natura Deorum*, 1.iv.9). Moreover, philosophical schools, as Cicero discussed them, are analogous to visual systems. Each school included as part of its structure the authoritative, hierarchical positioning of a master. This hierarchical structure of authority acted tyrannically on the adherents to a philosophical school, robbing them of their judgment. Cicero denounced those who, like the Pythagoreans, substituted the word of authority for what Cicero thought of as reason: "When questioned as to the grounds of any assertion that they advanced in debate, [they] are said to have been accustomed to reply 'He himself said so'"; consequently, "they cease to employ their own judgement" (*De Natura Deorum*, 1.5.10). Plainly, Cicero believed that falling back on points of authority undercut and devalued the forming of opinions on specific matters (*Academica*, 2.36.114) and (as he stated hyperbolically) made it "a crime to abandon a dogma" (*Academica*, 2.43.133) by disagreeing with some things an authority says, while seeing value in others.

Cicero defined the reasons for clashes between two schools in visual, spatial, even geopolitical metaphors that are suggestive of the reasons I cited earlier as responsible for the apparent inevitability of incommensurability. He pointed out that each philosophical system saw itself as containing in its intellectual structure a clear and accurate representation of the relationships among all forms of knowledge. Consequently, each school vied for hegemony. For instance, members of a philosophical school undertook, among other things, "to set out a system of philosophy, to unfold a complete natural science, to mould our ethics and establish a theory of the chief good and evil and map out our duties" (*Academica,* 2.36.114) according to the doctrines of that school. All philosophical systems were this way, but of course since all of them claimed to be the true structures of knowledge, they could not all be right. In a competition between schools for the right to be right, only one school may prevail: "To take both is impossible, for the dispute between them is not about boundaries but about the whole ownership of the ground" (*Academica,* 2.43. 132). Once developed, a system of philosophy could not see itself as right only some of the time, or about only some things.

For the same reasons, competitions between two incommensurate schools of thought would seem at first to be futile: because neither can defeat the other in terms acceptable to both (there are no such terms), no one can take the whole ground. Cicero, speaking of the reasons for his own skepticism, indicated that, when juxtaposed against one another, each school was less than completely compelling and was plagued with inconsistencies and ambiguities; furthermore, the arguments by which each defended itself were of little help in deciding between two schools: "What of the fact that the arguments advanced seem to me both acute on either side and equally valid?" (*Academica,* 2.43.133).

And yet there remained practical needs to make decisions and personal reasons to abandon blind following of doctrine: "I am dragged in different directions—now the latter view seems to me the more probable, now the former. And yet I firmly believe that unless one or the other is true, virtue is overthrown; but they are at variance on these points" (*Academica,* 2.43.134). Sometimes the frustration at the point of standoff was more personal still. What if, Cicero asked, he allied himself with one school? Would the dogma of that school require that he then reject the views of a beloved teacher who was an authority in a competing school? (*Academica,* 2.36.115).

Hence, the struggles among the schools for hegemony robbed the thinker of active judgment. What seems to be a particular source of concern to Cicero is the claim to completeness by each of the schools. The claims to "whole ground" made it impossible to remedy the immobility of indecision by allowing the acceptance of elements from each. Cicero's philosophical method, therefore, needed to induce the antidogmatism of Socratic method so as to break up the power of hegemonic philosophical schools, but it had to do more. It had to permit the examination of the schools so as to discover the ways in which a school could be said to be both right and wrong. The capacity to judge actively meant being enabled to determine which elements of dogma could hold up to examination and which could not. The capacity to break philosophical systems into elements may have been more open to a skeptical listener like Cicero, who himself was sometimes cast as audience and judge in the dialogues of disputation: "You, Lucullus, if you have accepted the views of your associate Antiochus, are bound to defend these doctrines as you would defend the walls of Rome, but I need only do so in moderation, just as much as I think fit" (*Academica,* 2.44.137).[4]

Moreover, philosophical method was tied to dialogic testing for Cicero. Problems of knowledge presented themselves from the beginning for Cicero as competitions between and among schools of thought; knowledge issues were discernible as controversies, and probable knowledge would be an outgrowth of the judgment applied in a controversy between schools. Schools of thought could not be tested by a method like Aristotle's, for example, which employed a singular logic in order to test assertions to truth, because incommensurate systems could each produce "proof" that was compelling within but useless from outside the system. In addition, a purely reductive method for knowing like Aristotle's would not be sufficient. Cicero's needs required that the end point of method be a generation of statements of probable knowledge that might not have been apparent from the beginning, since (in contrast to Lucullus, for example) the active judge must be able to find ways for certain elements of various schools to exist together as among the probably true. A method that would satisfy Cicero's needs would have to bring together the competing schools in order some-how to compare the individual conceptual logics relating the elements within them so as to permit open judgment. Knowledge could be gained only as claims to truth were examined in terms of the counterclaims of rival schools.

Both the *constitutiones* and the debate were necessary, therefore, in the effort to break out specific elements from the systems in which they were significant and examine those elements through comparison. The debate was necessary for constituting the elements of each system as arguable assertions. Cicero's method is entirely and determinedly verbal. What I have been calling "elements" of a system—positions on specifics like ethics, logic, and epistemology—could be examined only as assertions to truth or untruth. Cicero's method assists in parsing the schools into arguable com-ponents—assertions rendered arguable, in fact, through comparison and contrast with another school. Buckley, in his own discussion of Cicero's philosophical method, summarizes thus: "Ciceronian method becomes an attempt to discover what is the case by taking such statements and locating through debate the senses in which they can be asserted and denied" (148–49).

The *constitutiones* offered a way of delimiting for debate the complex philosophies of each school and providing the examination of one claim to truth at a time. In judicial situations, the immediate cause of the dispute is an accusation about a specific act; the *constitutiones* were necessary to determine what it is about the act that is at issue. The points involved in a philosophical dispute are, presumably, less clear because of the complexity of the schools and the lack of clarity in their relationships to each other. Locating the *quaestio* yielded the precise nature of the controversy by pulling out of each school those specific assertions to truth that could be found to separate the two schools with respect to the topic at hand.

For example, in Cicero's dialogue *De Natura Deorum*, representatives of the major post-Aristotelian schools were brought together to debate their differing theologies. What began as a question concerning the positions of the schools on the existence of the gods quickly evolved into a question of quality or *kind*, as Buckley indicates (153): there was general agreement on the existence of the gods, but disagreement about what kind of existence they had. Specifically, the debate centered on whether the gods were actively present in daily human life. On this point, differences among the schools presented themselves as specific assertions and could be debated as particular subject matters, synthesized from the analysis suggested by the *constitutiones*.

Moving from Cure to Inventiveness

The basic moves by which *De Natura Deorum* proceeds do not fully capture the value of the antithetical system to incommensurate issues. Because of his practical concern that debate should lead to something consequential for the situation, Cicero's method suggests the ways in which lively debate makes something come of the collision between incommensurate frames. An important practical suggestion for us today has to do with what can be done about points of misunderstanding between interlocutors.

Buckley argues that the value of the debate format is in sorting out true points of separation between systems from points that rest on misunderstandings. His is an important rather than a trivial observation, because misunderstandings neither occur for trivial reasons nor produce trivial effects. Differences of interpretation occur because specific assertions of belief gain meaning and significance within each of the different "coordinate systems" or "frames of reference" of the schools in which they are situated (Buckley, 148). The debate format allows different frames of reference to be brought into contact and probed by their rival coordinate systems. This is important, "for the ambiguous terms common to all will only achieve determined significance and translations by reference to their own systems" (148). Because the agents who speak from one frame of reference identify the meanings of terms on the basis of that perspective, they may be unable to recognize either differences or similarities in the meanings being attributed by another perspective.

Because our perspectival definitions are limited, we must examine the meanings of others' assertions of truth from the perspective to which those assertions properly belong. No one can do that on one's own, and casual discussion will not suffice because the meanings of one frame of reference can be probed only during a challenge by a rival perspective. If we differ, for instance, on the issue of God's existence, I will not know until we debate it that my sense of "existence" bears certain similarities to, and differences from, yours. We make such a discovery only as we search for the issue that really distinguishes us. Only when we prepare to test our assertions by pitting them against each others' do we discover the full significance—the full meaning—of the term "existence."

However, an important issue of representation arises here if we follow Buckley in casting the value of Ciceronian method as eliminating misunderstandings. If we are not careful, we may begin looking at discrepant frames of reference as merely semantic barriers in need of elimination. Buckley's own language adds to that impression: "In some cases, the words alone may be really different and by understanding the divergent languages a community of agreement" upon a common truth can be discovered" (148). Cicero's method would seem reducible to functioning as a way of stripping off the obscuring veils of inadequate language in order to unmask the real agreement hiding beneath. Moreover, incommensurability would seem to be a curable problem, corrected out of existence with improved understanding and with the accurate representation of real essences that have thus far been inadequately represented. By extension, the importance of developing accurate systems of visual representation would be affirmed, and the distinction between visual systems and oral judgment would again be obscured.

However, the value of the antithetical method need not be read as resting on any such notions: that discrepant frames of reference should be eliminated as barriers, that overcoming the problems of incommensurability rests on achieving understanding, or that words obscure real essences. On the contrary, Ciceronian method, based as it is in ordinary language, sees discrepant frames of reference less as barriers to understanding and more as goads to invention and discovery. Specifically, Ciceronian discoveries need to be those that are consequential to the situation circumscribed by the discussion. These rhetorical discoveries enrich conversation and introduce new possibilities that would not have emerged without the methodical opposing in dialogue of the competing frames.

Possibilities emerge in dialogue because of, rather than in spite of, differences in language. Beliefs are realized and asserted in words, and words are multifaceted. Terms can be turned in different ways, by virtue of differences in context, to reveal different meanings. Through debate, new contexts establish new differences and similarities. Ciceronian method thus institutionalizes the insight of topical thinking.

The debate between Cicero and Lucullus in *Academica* offers one example. On its face, the debate is merely a good example of the basic movements suggested by the *constitutiones*. Lucullus, representing the Stoics, argued that the New Academics fell back on the authority of more ancient philosophers in order to make their case for skepticism. In so doing (he claimed), the New Academics falsely suggested that the old philosophers really knew nothing. Lucullus built his case through analogy to rebellious populist citizens who, when "raising a sedition . . . quote some famous personages of antiquity . . . so as to make them appear to resemble them" (*Academica*, 2.5.13). Cicero, speaking in defense of the New Academy, responded by attacking both the analogy and the accusation by disposing of them as not constitutive of a real difference between the New Academy and the Stoics: all Lucullus's concerns about whether the old philosophers support the New Academics really masked a different concern—a concern about whether it could be the verdict of wise men that nothing should be assented to. The issue of assent, in turn, could be disposed of by turning to an issue of fact, which was, Cicero claimed, "the one argument that has held the field down to the present day. For the point that the wise man will not assent to anything had no essential bearing on this dispute [between Zeno and Arcesilas]; for he might perceive nothing and yet form an opinion. . . . If the acts of opining and perceiving are abolished, it undoubtedly follows that all acts of assent must be withheld, so that if I succeed in proving that nothing can be perceived, you must admit that the wise man will never assent" (2.24.78). The issue Cicero moved on to is an issue of fact (whether anything can be perceived), but the argument for getting there is, in a sense, translative: an argument about the use of authority was the wrong place for this dispute.

The key point here, however, is that Cicero arrived at the specific articulation of the *quaestio* of perception *as a response* to Lucullus's argument. This is evident from the way Cicero got to the point of suggesting the *quaestio*. He did not simply dismiss Lucullus's argument about authority, nor did he claim that Lucullus simply did not understand the import of New Academic doctrine (although the problem of misunderstanding plays a role in Cicero's response). Instead, Cicero used the misunderstanding to discover the real point of dispute. Lucullus and the Stoics did not, as gauged from their argument, see the point of the New Academics' use of authority properly: whereas the sedition mongers wanted merely to associate themselves with respected statesmen, the New Academics were concerned with discovering truth. And the dispute about the truth of assent should be kept open, because there was enough ambiguity in interpreting the careers of the old philosophers to believe that truth had not yet been discovered.

But the apparent misunderstanding itself led Cicero to his statement of what was consequential and should keep the dispute open. In the important historic dispute between the wise men Zeno and Arcesilas, the open point turned on the question of whether true and false perceptions can be distinguished (2.23–24). Hence, Cicero's systematic elimination of what may have appeared to be points of dispute prompted him toward the point on which the debate should turn. In this case, the issue had to do with assertions about perception. Lucullus himself had identified the belief that perception was impossible as a cornerstone of New Academic doctrine. But the generation of the *quaestio* of perception came from the collision of positions, guided by Cicero's judgment and the *constitutiones* of the rival schools.[5]

Cicero did not establish a truth here by eliminating a misunderstanding. In fact, the search for truth does not rest on whether the misunderstanding Cicero picked up on is apparent or real. It does not rest precisely on whether his interpretation of the Stoics' use of the old philosophers was self-serving. In uncovering a point for debate, Cicero elevated the importance of the debate itself and of continuing it in directions consequential to understanding the material differences between the two schools. Cicero's realization of differences with respect to what would be considered proof from authority led him to a subject matter productive of debate.

Buckley's own insight into Cicero's *On the Nature of the Gods* offers another good example. This debate exemplifies for Buckley an instance wherein some of the differences important to the debate are "more verbal than real" (153). In fact, though, what occurs in the debate is not simply an ironing out of false differences, what occurs is Cotta the Academic's invention of an *identification* discovered while attending to those initial differences.

Cotta identified together the Stoics, the Aristotelians (or Peripatetics), and the Platonists with respect to their theologies and set them as a group against the Epicureans. The identification and differentiation turned on an even more specific point than broad theological positions, however. What began as a broad question concerning the existence of the gods quickly evolved into a question of *kind*, as I noted earlier: whether the gods were actively present in daily human life. On this point, convergences and divergences among the schools emerged. The disagreement of the Stoics, Aristotelians, and Platonists with the Epicureans on this point foregrounded the similarity among the first three schools: only the Epicureans denied "providence, divination, and fate" as attributes of the gods (153). The similarity emerged for Cotta when the issue was contextualized *in terms* of a specific theological point and allowed the debate to head into an exploration of a particular subject matter by virtue of arguments that would not otherwise have been introduced. Whether the identification of the three schools around this point is right or wrong is immaterial to the course of the particular debate; the foregrounding of the distinction of the three schools from the Epicureans permitted the examination of the key points of that distinction.

Importantly, the identification does not actually collapse the three schools nor merge their philosophies, but identifies them as similar only in terms of a specific point of theology. Hence, the schools may move in and out of relationships of identification and separation depending upon the specific subject matter of a debate and the judgments of those involved. The schools do not merge; rather, the relationship between them is prompted by a particular subject matter—here, the subject matter related to kind. This point of terministic contact produces what we might call a system only in the sense of that articulation of tibia and fibula.

The contribution to the ongoing intellectual conversation of such identifications is even more evident from a third example, the philosopher Varro's identification of the Platonists with the Aristotelians in the *Academica*. Varro identified the two schools in terms of their methods. The schools, he said, may be thought of as one, but only when a common difference from Socrates' philosophy is foregrounded: "both schools drew plentiful supplies from Plato's abundance, and both framed a definitely formulated rule of doctrine . . . whereas they abandoned the famous Socratic custom of discussing everything in a doubting manner" (1.4.17). But the schools could be pulled apart again on other bases, notably on the question of the Forms: "Aristotle was the first to undermine the Forms . . . which had been so marvellously embodied in the system of Plato" (1.9.33). Thus, when questions of lineage and method were at issue, the two schools could be identified, and a participant in the conversation would be invited to expound on a single philosophical system. When the Forms were at issue, the differences between the schools were foregrounded, and these differences might offer material for further development in the discussion. Moreover, as Buckley points out, the identification of the two schools in the one dialogue allows them to be identified in other debates, like the debate on the gods. The existence of a variety of schools in the conversational grid allows for more possible relationships of difference and similarity. Hence, we may first identify things for the purposes of particular debate on a particular matter, but subsequently the similarities may serve as "suggestive firsts" that might be pursued heuristically in other debates

Cicero's rhetorical/philosophical method might be thought to begin with his contention that competing schools of thought each want "the whole ground." Here Ciceronian method may be contrasted with twentieth-century "normal" rhetorics. These rhetorics, in adopting many of the assumptions of normal science, suggest that persuasion to an incommensurate view may occur only as a conversion experience or "gestalt shift." In terms we have been using here, adherents to any position must adopt "the whole ground." Normal rhetorics, geared toward building a case for those already sharing first principles and immersed in the same conceptual system, have no resources for performing conversions, which seem to fall outside the realm of rational decision making.[6] The alternative offered by a normal rhetoric would be uncovering and remedying essential misunderstandings that are falsely separating two schools of thought. The schools would then presumably accept as fact that they should actually be collapsed into one. This alternative is, of course, no help in the face of genuine differences.

Cicero's method, on the other hand, suggests that important conceptual changes may occur when schools are tested on specific points being contested by other schools. Despite a claim that all he does is "lay before my readers the doctrines of the various schools" (*De Natura Deorum*, 1.6.13), Cicero's antithetical method, as dialogue, allowed disputants to discover or invent points of conjunction and disjunction that would have been impossible within the conceptual system of only one of the doctrines in question. For Cicero, examining a point of contention carefully meant having to be open (as the Academic was open) to the possibility of discovering a vantage point from which discrepant philosophies may be more similar than different, or from which previously accepted similarities must be questioned. These discoveries would not eliminate all differences between philosophical schools or necessitate the defeat of one side or the other. As moments in a dialogue, discoveries are tools of invention for taking the conversation in new directions.

Moreover, thought of as a way of taking the conversation in new directions, Ciceronian debate rejects the notion that significant differences may be "cured" by achieving understanding; in fact, Ciceronian method rejects medicinal models that suggest incommensurability should be "cured" at all. Discovering a particular vantage point from which new similarities and differences emerge places value on discovering new things to say. Varro's discovery that the Aristotelians and Platonists differed little with respect to method indicates a place from which to expound further on this similarity. Cotta insisted that the Stoics, Aristotelians, and Platonists were more different from the Epicureans than from each other from the vantage point of the *kind* of existence attributable to gods, despite the denials of the three schools. This insistence alone would not persuade them to collapse the schools together, nor should it; but it would allow him to expound further on features of difference from the Epicureans. Here invention and the contribution to the continuing conversation take priority over persuasion.

Such discoveries are motivated from a practical desire not to be defeated by points of *stasis*, at which there appear to be no ways to make decisions and no new things to say. The discovery of specific similarities and differences during debate may permit better talk and the possibility of decisions based on new considerations.

Resisting the Dominant Discourse About Incommensurability: Contemporary Efforts

Cicero's antithetical method resists the dogmatic adherence to particular schools of thought, and in so doing it also challenges today's dominant discourse concerning incommensurability. The antithetical method offers a way to break up the conceptual power of systems and a way for there to be intercourse and testing between two conceptual schemes, each of which would desire the "whole ground." In suggesting a paratactic movement by which disputants representing incommensurate schools may invent new subject matters together, the method provides hope that conflicts between apparently incommensurate frames may be productive.

Our contemporary habit, however, is to regard controversies that invoke incommensurate justificatory vocabularies as intractable. In such controversies the so-called common ground that is often sought as a solution may never be found, nor may a conversion experience be achieved, nor will the public dialogue be fully appropriated by either side. Because both sides have evolved into schools of tightly woven logics, each of which excludes the logic of the other, the fight is for the "whole ground" and for the right to control public opinion and policy. The potential for creative debate between these incommensurate systems, however, can be found.

The contemporary abortion rights controversy offers an illustration of the way in which disputation about incommensurate positions is handled. The name-calling and demonic attributions from either side about the other are often cited as examples of the degeneration of public discourse. One radio commentator records activists on the picket line, for instance, saying things like "These babies . . . were born sucking their thumbs" and the response, "Who are you to decide what's going on in my body?" ("Conversation Therapy for Abortion Foes"). These may be particularly angry exchanges, but angry or not, they illustrate how each side talks past the other when even a civil dialogue on abortion is attempted. Differing conceptual frameworks dictate that, going into the conversation, each side sees different points to be at issue.

Accounts of the development of what have come to be called the pro-Life and the pro-Choice movements reveal why this may be so. The rhetoric is what we might expect of a collision of incommensurate positions: different interpretive structures providing different meanings and weights to key terms; the potential for conflicting conclusions from similar data; the incorporation in each vocabulary of the "other" as a demonizing force; the tightening of each vocabulary so as to make one's own position the only "natural" position to hold. However, the accounts also demonstrate that the incommensurate vocabularies do not exist fully formed before debate, as though each is isomorphic with some natural state. They evolve in response to fundamental challenges: each side develops, in part, by casting itself in opposition to the other. Faye D. Ginsburg, in her analysis of the life narratives offered by grassroots activists on each side of the debate in Fargo, North Dakota, notes that within these narratives, "the 'other' becomes a critical counterpoint on which one's own stance depends" (196).

Ginsburg's accounts show how the incommensurability of the pro-Life and pro-Choice systems seems to assure the impossibility of any meaningful exchanges between them. Key terms are incommensurate. For instance, the idea of "nurturance" holds an important place in the conceptual systems of each side; it is not only a repeated theme in the narratives of both sides, but it is a keystone on which the structure of rationale is built for each (196). Pro-Choice women see a nurturing role to be broadly defined to promote the feminine perspective in "a world that is viewed as materialistic, male defined, and lacking in compassion" (170). Thus, the nurturing role should be fulfilled through seeking broad social change that should feminize institutions and allow women more influence. For the pro-Life advocates, nurturance is more narrowly tied to having and raising children. Ginsburg points out the importance to all these women of nurturance in its association with their identities as women, with womanhood definable through opposition to masculinity and masculine experience. Self-identification as nurturers helps each side to view themselves as acting "naturally" as women "ought" to act, and the other side as not acting that way. Ginsburg summarizes this tendency to naturalize positions in the abortion issue as something that shapes the social arena for debate, "a social arena marked as a contested domain. . . . Therefore, to succeed, each side must see and present its understanding of the cultural and personal meaning of reproduction as 'natural' and correct. To legitimate their own position proponents must make a persuasive case so that the formulations of the opposition appear unnatural, immoral, or false. On an individual and organizational level, then each side constitutes itself in dialogue with the 'enemy,' real and imagined" (196).

In the Fargo narratives, as might be expected, the participants on both sides invoked similar life experiences to validate their own positions. Consequently, the self-validating interpretation of experience renders the data of experience inadequate to force conversion of one side to the other. The different interpretations each side brings to their experiences are dictated by their incommensurate conceptual frames. Implicitly, the narratives of each side valorize different behaviors, portrayed as responses to significant life experiences; hence heroism is implicitly defined differently by each side, as are feminism and reproduction. Pro-Life advocates saw as heroic the overcoming of a natural ambivalence about staying home with children instead of being out in the larger world; resisting the temptations of career in order to do the right thing was valorized. Similarly, some women reported how the choice of an abortion might have made their lives simpler at critical moments. Thereby, the pro-Life women absorbed a version of feminism as self-indulgence into their own stories as something to be gotten over, a form of adolescent rebellion that helped them separate from their mothers. The births of first children allowed these women their "conversion" from feminism to a more responsible adulthood in which family and children came first (194–95). Feminism, therefore, has its place in the pro-Life ideology; but pregnancy and birth, as sites of conversion (and passages to adulthood and womanly self-sacrifice) are preeminent experiences shaping their womanhood.

There is a certain inversion of this plot line apparent in the pro-Choice stories. The conversion experience was often a significant "encounter with the social movements of the late 1960s" (170). These themes prepared women for a feminism that was envisioned as a broader form of social justice. The place of abortion rights in that program was sometimes found after a traumatic pregnancy or birth experience. As was the case with one of the women, Sherry, pro-Choice activists may be "angered by this personal encounter with the inequities women faced in reproduction" (162). After losing her daughter immediately after she was born, Sherry concluded, "I don't feel anyone has the right to force me to go through that again" (163). Her form of heroism involved working for abortion rights. Whether the pregnancy and birth experiences were actually any more traumatic for pro-Choice women than they were for pro-Life women, these experiences were validated as the impetus for activism in seeking or keeping abortion rights reform.

The Fargo narratives typify the structural development of incommensurate ideologies. Importantly, these accounts and others also show that the positions do not develop, as their adherents believe that they do, to represent what is "natural" and "correct." Instead, at some points the conceptual structures develop "dialectically" in opposition, or at least in response to, the other side. At least one pro-Choice woman articulated pro-family values as a response against the stereotype that pro-Choice activists were "anti-family": "How bringing an unwanted child into a family strengthens it is something I have never been able to understand" (154). Ginsburg comments that such inclusions show "how each side reformulates its stance in relation to the opposition" (154).

Condit shows how a similar tendency appears in the rhetoric of the movement at large. Important concepts gained definition and redefinition in response to public perceptions that had been formed by the rhetoric of the other side. The complex transformation of the central term "life" in pro-Life discourse is an example. Despite their equation of the value of "life" with a "pro-natalism," pro-Life advocates found in the 1060s that "non-pro-creative sexuality was no longer as strongly negative for women." Bowing to public sentiment, they broadened the concept of "life" and eventually came to advocate "sanctity of human *life*" (Condit, 62). The reformulated concept of life was in turn adapted to the dominant, more liberal human rights rhetoric as a right, the "right to life." Once incorporated into the public dialogue, this shifted meaning changed the shape of the debate to an advocacy of "rights": "The public argument became focused on the contest of rights between women and fetuses" (63). This agenda was pursued more by pro-Life advocates than by the pro-Choice side. The pro-Life side attempted to support the individual right to life of the fetus through appeals to science defining the beginning of life; however, pro-Choice advocates chose not to respond to such evidence, deeming it irrelevant and seeing the matter strictly as "a matter of individual choice" (214). We can recognize this as the point at which the issues focused on by each side diverged in such a way that discussion became unproductive and debate impossible.

Condit notes the complexity of the "relationship between the argument, the rhetors, and the persuasive moves they adopted." (63) Public policy eventually reflected uneasy compromises between sides. Legal priority eventually was given to the rights of women after Roe v. Wade, a decision that has been challenged frequently since it was made. Condit comments that "extremist ideologues" (202) have kept the controversy alive. Without recourse to genuine debate, protests that sometimes result in name-calling became a dominant form of communication. There were also a number of highly publicized bombings of abortion clinics and murders of doctors who performed abortions. The legal remedy that emerged from the charge of finding for one side or the other has not helped to provide an alternative to extremist expressions on this issue.

These accounts of the abortion controversy in the United States can lead a listener to believe fruitful dialogue between the sides is impossible. Appeals to experience would seem to be useless, since both sides interpret similar experiences according to incommensurate interpretive frames. Each side sees itself not only as correct but also as reflecting the natural order. Furthermore, even attempts at bringing the sides into clash have resulted in a reactive tightening of the conceptual rhetoric of each. Finally, as the controversy developed, each side became less responsive to the demands of the other, insisting that the controversy should turn on different issues.

Accounts like Condit's and Ginsburg's are enormously helpful in understanding the incommensurate vocabularies that characterize this conflict. One of their greatest benefits is in helping us to understand that practical and moral forms of incommensurability, while powerful, are not based exclusively in differences in the account of nature reflected by each side but are also shaped by rhetorical and social forces.

We lose what we have gained, however, if we begin to see the course that the abortion rights dispute took as inevitable and inexorable, as it may appear to be from rhetorical histories. It may seem inevitable that each side would develop different interpretive frames and that each side would eventually naturalize its own position and demonize the other's. To infer this inevitability is to take the accounts as reflecting a kind of "natural history" of controversy. Just as likely, the course of the debates reflects a Western rhetorical climate that takes epistemology as its model: rhetoric is to be based on what can be justified. Clearly, with separate logics of self-justification built into the conceptual systems of each side, the rhetoric of each likewise becomes self-justifying rather than inventive.

However, we also make an error if we point to places where the history could have been changed so as to lead to some better outcome. To favor this sort of advice giving is not only to oversimplify but also to yield to the worst arrogance of the spectator: the temptation to privilege the place of the neutral observer as more detached and therefore more objective than the participants in rhetorical exchanges. To do either of these things—to view incommensurability as a natural and inevitable outcome or to see where it might have been avoided—is to underrate the artfulness and creative potential of a nonepistemic rhetoric in helping participants create new positions from some point at which they presently find themselves.

Still, the accounts can help illustrate a few possible points at which a method of *controversia* could help participants move through the complex web of issues to break the impasse and create debatable space. Doing so requires accepting the possibility that there are issues between participants that are tractable, and that those issues can be located.

At first blush, *agreeing* on a point of *stasis* would seem to be impossible for the disputants. Establishing the nature of the controversy might seem to require one side to give in to the other. If, for example, pro-Choice advocates were to agree to debate the issue as one of fact, that is, whether the fetus can be proven to be an individual with rights at conception, they would seem to have given in to the opposition. And left alone to be debated as an issue of fact, the argument over abortion would be intractable. However, the issue need not be left alone if subject matters of debate are being genuinely sought. If the difference of fact seems to be beyond debating, interlocutors might explore issues of definition that may be behind the question of fact; here, perhaps, the difference in approaches to "rights" might be discovered in the context of the pro-natalism of (at least some) pro-Life advocates.

We can look for these tractable issues where the vulnerability of concepts—their susceptibility to recontextualization—meets human judgment. These could be the points on the conversational grid that are (or can be discovered to be) least naturalized in the frameworks of the disputants, that is, those points that have emerged mainly in contradistinction from the other side. Condit describes one such point in the abortion controversy, the belief in pro-natalism that was transformed to a belief in the right to life. Rather than attempting to tackle a subject matter of fact, disputants discussing the action issue of producing children or not producing children might find material for debate. If the dispute could be articulated as the obligation to give birth as opposed to the right not to, there are further issues of action that might present themselves: Where, when, and how do obligation and choice with respect to reproduction conflict? Where, when and how do they coincide?

These speculations may already have gone too far, but I hope they illustrate the direction that debates might take if they are motivated by an interest in creating arguable subject matters rather than capturing public advantage. This direction might be better exemplified by reference to contemporary efforts. There are a few initiatives for dialogical exchange about value-laden issues like abortion that have the goal of taking advantage of points of *stasis* in order to discover debatable issues in apparently intractable disputes.

One such initiative is the Public Conversations Project developed in 1989 by a group of family therapists to test the usefulness of therapeutic, dialogic methods for dealing with public disputes.[7] Developers of the project have attempted to restructure conversation on the issue of abortion. From most perspectives, the methods of the Public Conversations Project could not be more different from Ciceronian antithetical method. With its roots in family therapy, the Public Conversations Project is dedicated in large part to providing a comfortable and safe zone for disputants on both sides of an issue to discuss an inherently risky topic. Cicero, while certainly not expecting a disembodied presentation of different sides in a dispute, did not see the quality of the dispute to be affected by interpersonal concerns. Representatives of different philosophical schools might conceivably be limited by their own debating skill but not by differences in power or trust, differences that family therapists are at pains to level. The differences between Ciceronian method and the methods of the Public Conversations Project are the differences between classic philosophical argumentation and modern interpersonal discussion.

There is perhaps an even more important deviation from Ciceronian method: the rhetoric surrounding the Public Conversations Project (much of it provided by its developers) implies a belief that allowing individuals to talk honestly together in a risk-free setting will lead to new discoveries by everyone engaged in the discussion. The idea that speaking together honestly provides a solution to conflict implies that beneath the discrepant vocabularies of the two groups lies a common representation that can be found through guided, risk-free discussion. Ciceronian method, I have argued, supposes no such thing. Moreover, one lesson of studies like the Fargo narratives is that the adherence of participants to rival conceptual paradigms is likely to make their honest sharing result only in a reaffirmation of the reasons for their differences. Nevertheless, the structural methods of the Public Conversations Project may be read as though their objective is solution through honest talk. The founders argue that polarized public issues lead adherents to align themselves more firmly with the groups to which they are loyal for social as well as ideological reasons. Aligning with a group "gives one a socially validated place to stand while speaking and it offers the unswerving support of like-minded people" (Becker et al., 145). However, these loyalties also mean sacrifices, like suppressing "inner value conflicts and differences between oneself and one's allies" (145). Hence, the developers of the Public Conversations Project account for the *stases* in public discussions in terms of group psychology rather than of incommensurate vocabularies. The methods of the project are designed in part to break the dependence of the individual on the group.

Despite key differences, both the antithetical method and the Public Conversations Project challenge the dominant epistemological model that has produced the idea that intractability inevitably accompanies incommensurability. Both express confidence in oral exchanges and the active judgment of real participants. The founders of the Public Conversations Project note that their ultimate goal is "to enrich public conversations, that is, to improve the way that the public discusses and deliberates divisive controversy," and to do this through guiding and enhancing private conversations (Chasin et al., 327). Both fight the crippling hold that polarized terms and parallel hierarchies of belief can exert on argument. The Public Conversations Project attempts to do this by contrasting "destructive debate" with "dialogue" (Chasin et al., 325) and then constructing opportunities for dialogue.

Consequently, when the differences between doctrinaire talk and anti-dogmatic methods are highlighted, Ciceronian method and the Public Conversations Project become more similar than different. Some of the same features that might seem to distinguish the Public Conversations Project from Ciceronian method may instead suggest similarities. The direction of the Project and its preliminary successes with the abortion discussion suggest concretely the potential of dialogic methods like Cicero's for improving transactions between incommensurate vocabularies. An awareness of Ciceronian debate can itself enrich such antidogmatic initiatives as the Public Conversations Project by indicating the kind of responsive judgment that may occur if the willingness to test assertions of truth transcends the urge for defensiveness.

Promoting a willingness to test assertions is where the Public Conversations Project begins. The keystone of their methods is the opposition between "dialogue," and "destructive debate." The aims of dialogue bear resemblance to some of the aims of Ciceronian method. Dialogue allows participants to locate ways of resisting what I have been calling doctrinaire or dogmatic thinking. Although the founders of the project do not discuss doctrinaire thinking as such, the notion of "destructive debate" reflects the recognition that disputants may be locked into their own conceptual frameworks. For instance, one feature of destructive debate (which, they say, is like the debate commonly seen on television) concerns to whom disputants habitually direct their remarks. In destructive debate, "participants speak to their own constituents and, perhaps, to the undecided middle." By contrast, in dialogue, disputants (called "participants" in the Public Conversations

Project) "speak to one another." Moreover, in destructive debate, "statements are predictable and offer little new information," whereas in dialogue, "new information surfaces" (Chasin et al., 326).

With similarities to Ciceronian method foregrounded, it is easier to contextualize the importance of some of the interpersonal features of dialogue for proceeding beyond the *stasis* of incommensurability. Emphasis on the need for individuals to speak honestly and safely "for themselves" instead of from their roles as representatives of a group (Chasin et al., 326, 334) may help disrupt stereotyping on each side (as the Project leaders hope). Just as importantly, from the perspective of Ciceronian method, the strategy also leads disputants away from repetition of a "party line" and toward a point where habitual positions are broken into more specific elements for discussion. In fact, the Project founders speak of their aim of developing more "complexity" and "differentiation" in positions "than can be conveyed through slogans" (Becker et al., 155, 157, 158). Increased complexity will in turn lead, they hope, to the "co-creation of a new conversation" (Becker et al., 155). Participants go from a situation in which "differences within 'sides' are denied or minimized" to one in which "differences among participants on the same side are revealed" (Chasin et al., 326).

Complexity and increased differentiation are introduced into dialogue as participants share relevant personal histories and question one another out of genuine curiosity while refraining from rhetorical questions and challenges (both of which are indulged in freely by Ciceronian debaters). Although the founders of the Project do not report whole dialogues, samples reveal points where positions are broken into more specific parts, complexity is increased, and more and newer subject matters are suggested. For instance, when a pro-Choice leader asked a pro-Life leader if he could make any argument for keeping abortion legal, the pro-Life leader replied "that he could: women would not die from illegal abortions" (Becker et al., 158). Such statements have the potential to enrich subsequent subject matters by making more complex a position that began, within the particular dialogue, as solidly pro-Life.

There has been little systematic evaluation of the work of groups like the Public Conversations Project. Whatever the outcomes of the dialogues these groups promote, it is interesting that they avoid descriptions suggesting that they search for compromises: The Public Conversations Project "avoids the term *common ground* because it is often understood to denote a static middle, a new position, or even a traitorous compromise" (Pearce and Littlejohn, 1997, 183–85). Participants report moving from static, secure positions into less comfortable ones. According to Laura Chasin, one of the founders of the Project, new subject matters emerge from new-found similarities and differences, and these tend to be questions of action: "Why are there so many abortions? What would be a way to reduce the number of abortions?" ("Conversation Therapy"). In a comparable project, "Searching for Common Ground," various action initiatives, like the prevention of teenage pregnancy, have emerged as material for discussion.

It is worth emphasizing that these contemporary initiatives do not mimic Ciceronian debate, nor could they be expected to. Nevertheless, they suggest an important point to be drawn from Cicero: finding paths to productive discussion of incommensurate public issues relies on the judgment of the responsive and engaged interlocutor, not on the justifications offered by a single conceptual system.

Stasis Points as Moments of Invention

We need to avoid medicinal models of solutions to the problems of incommensurability. There are no magic bullets to eliminate these most divisive issues. These issues are not the result of misunderstandings; they are material differences that cannot be eliminated. Differences, however, *are* the material of debate. They can be used to generate subject matters that may take their places as nodes on the intellectual matrix or the matrix of public conversation, points of rest and beginning points of further debate.

In issues of epistemology, it has been argued that the concept of *stasis* has suffered from underuse (Carter, 97). John T. Gage has noted that the recognition and use of *stasis* methods in epistemological disputes change our conception of rhetoric itself, which becomes not "'an act of persuasion in a manipulative sense . . . [but] the model for exploring the possibility of assent in the symbolic exchange of what one knows in the context of what others know'" (quoted in Carter, 97).[8]

Gage's position would certainly seem to be a sound description of Cicero's view of the usefulness of *stasis* methods. Ciceronian method is directed to locating the possibility of assent where there had been nothing but impossibility. It is precisely in situations of impossible decision making that we need inventiveness; those situations present themselves in contemporary circumstances as competitions between incommensurate frames.

Often, however, a sensed impossibility stymies discourse instead of promoting it. At these moments, there would seem to be no way in which judgment could help us produce anything worthwhile to say. But on the contrary, moments of *stasis* and dialogical methods like Cicero's can occasion a *kairotic* force that promotes inventiveness. A method of antithesis goes beyond bringing adversaries face to face. It forces the responsiveness of dialogic improvisation and at the same time allows disputants to explore and develop the implications of newly found similarities and differences.

Acting on Incommensurability
Rhetorical Judgment as Weaving

In the beginning pages of this work, I posed several questions: In an age of uncertainty, how are we to act? How can we take a position, say something worthwhile, and exercise judgment with respect to issues that confront us? By now I hope it is evident that although these questions can be posed in just this way, they do not have to be. In fact, by some reckonings, given the sort of uncertainty we do confront, my questions *should* be posed differently.

Posed as they are, these questions about action seem to conflate the notions of saying and choosing; in fact, saying is implicitly collapsed into choosing: exercising judgment leads to taking a position, which then provides worthwhile things to say. But the spirit of relativism that now characterizes Western epistemology has rendered the exercise of judgment problematic. With no consensus on ways of grounding knowledge claims, the judgments emerging from knowledge claims have limited authority and ultimately may yield nothing worthwhile for a person to say on a matter. Anything any of us might assert begs to be dismissed as a misguided attempt to utter some undefendable truth.

In the course of this study, I made a number of such "undefendable" assertions. At one point, for example, I echoed MacIntyre and Booth in condemning "emotivism." How can my condemnation, or theirs, have any influence when the emotivist (so-called) no doubt has a retort of equal and opposite weight? Considered as a problem of the relative weights of claims or counterclaims, saying something worthwhile is a matter of determining which side has or should be given more "weight." Determining the weight of an assertion would seem to be a challenge that ought to be met by epistemology: what mechanisms, what weights and measures are there for determining which claim can be uttered with more authority? If we could know that, then one side would have to yield to the other. But in the late twentieth century, epistemology has bowed out of this discussion, or at least has let us down; it will not provide us with that Archimedes' lever that fully authorizes us to say something because it is demonstrably right.

In 1962 William W. Bartley III, a Protestant theologian, described what

I have been calling the crisis in judgment and knowledge in terms of a *tu quoque* argument. The *tu quoque* reduces to three simple premises for Bartley: (1) rationality is limited, so "everyone has to make a dogmatic irrational commitment"; (2) therefore, one "has a right to make whatever commitment he pleases"; and (3) "therefore, no one has a right to criticize him for this" (90). The consequences for judgment are severe: if two people base their claims on different standards or frame them within different systems of rationality, then upon recognizing that difference, they both must admit that the question of standards is merely a matter of taste and the adoption of a system of rationality merely a choice. Furthermore, a person's position is to be judged, if at all, only relative to his own standard or frame. If common grounds for validation cannot be found, then both combatants must retire to their corners and say no more.

The results for practical and moral communication have been, by some accounts, assorted and devastating. One possible result, as we have seen, is that both combatants are rendered mute by a kind of existential crisis. How can we regard ourselves as rational if we cling to a position that we cannot defend against a refutation that is ultimately no less well grounded than our own? Christopher Johnstone suggests another version of muteness: an unwillingness to condemn. In the face of pluralism, "ethical relativism is attractive, of course. . . . But it is frightening because it leaves us with no final ground for making ethical judgments, and thus it leaves us with no satisfactory way of condemning acts" (178). Communication between incommensurate groups may just be rendered ineffective as it was for the humanists and Christians studied by Pearce, Littlejohn, and Alexander. The compelling reason for this ineffectiveness is that the form of rhetoric authorized by any one system of thought will be unpersuasive in an incommensurate system.

The problems resulting from the crisis in rationality are mitigated little when the word *communication* is invoked to cope with a logical incommensurability that philosophy cannot resolve. Often what is invoked is a simple call to tolerance and understanding that results, ironically, in the abandonment of actual productive discussion: if we share no common ground, we are reduced to showing rather than arguing or discussing: "All we can do is to show how the other side looks from our point of view. That is, all we can do is be hermeneutic about the opposition—trying to show how the odd or paradoxical or offensive things they say hang together with the rest of what they want to say, and how what they say looks when put in our own alternative idiom" (Rorty, *PMN*, 364–65). When "all we can do" is "show," then there is no ongoing conversation. Hence, relativism has the power to foreclose on discussion. Relativism and incommensurability, as forces assumed to dictate the course of rhetorical activity, are as devastating to the ongoing conversation as is the requirement for agreement.

Incommensurability, as the inevitable condition of a dominant Western epistemology, cannot be eliminated. Furthermore, judgment based exclusively on metaphors of weighing and measuring cannot be vindicated by rhetoric of any kind; Bartley's *tu quoque* and today's limited rhetorical activity should make that clear. One reason is that another legacy of the same epistemologically based rationality that yielded incommensurability is the assumption of *authorization* as the purpose of judgment and of rhetoric. Epistemology, by producing standards for judgment based on weighing, gave authority to some voices by filtering out others. In other words, it operated by authorizing from the outset what would be deemed rational talk and therefore what could be accepted as worthwhile talk. Voices that conformed to the dominant standard of discourse—those voices that appeared to meet the demands of the dominant portrait of rationality—had an easier time entering the conversation than those that did not. When eventually there emerged no agreed-upon set of argumentative standards that could compel universal adherence, the viability of standards and standard setting threatened to fall away altogether. With no other voice-giving mechanism available, rhetorics that rested on authorizing had to fall into silence themselves, and they threatened to yield only silence. This is the narrative about rhetoric implied by MacIntyre and Booth as they lament a slide into a progressive emotivism.[1]

Ironically, although there is a proliferation of new voices in a pluralistic world, that very proliferation can deafen us to the new kind of silencing rendered by relativism. A proliferation of new voices does little *by itself* to save discussion. Lyotard, for instance, supports the development of many language games, each with its own local rules, over Jurgen Habermas's attempt at a totalizing "regularization of the 'moves' permitted in all language games" (*Postmodern Condition,* 66). In other words, whereas Habermas had advocated a single standard for rational discourse, Lyotard wishes instead to salvage pluralism by endorsing many authorizing rhetorics. His is a move that helps to authorize a number of different rhetorics. However, without suggesting concretely ways in which these rhetorics might find points of contact in order to influence one another, Lyotard leaves the problem of incommensurability only partly addressed. Language games that mutually exclude one another cannot be collapsed together or subsumed any more than can competing paradigms or epistemological systems. When particular occasions bring games into conflict, under what rules should we be playing?

A concrete example of this difficulty comes from those feminist writers who are concerned with identifying, understanding, and legitimizing the "feminine style" in speaking. In their contribution to that effort, Jane Blankenship and Deborah C. Robson point out that the worlds of argument of American men and American women are sufficiently different to constitute different language games—and in fact, different cultures. As do some other scholars similarly engaged in the question of feminine style, Blankenship and Robson build from the idea that what is regarded as reasonable discourse by one group is not necessarily so regarded by the other. They suggest that female politicians may need to be "bicultural" and learn to move comfortably between the two worlds of discourse with their different language games if they are to be successful (355).

The idea of communicating biculturally is appealing, but it leaves problematic the position political women may really face. Biculturalism connotes a capacity to move between cultures comfortably. In the case of women political speakers, biculturalism conjures up a picture of women speaking in one language to women and in another to the dominant group of decision makers, who are men. But if the authorizing epistemologies of each are different, women speaking "like men" in the dominant public forum risk a loss of the feminine voice—not to mention a loss of culture—in decision making. Radical feminists have observed that women's interests cannot be fully served if their style of talk is co-opted by, or absorbed into, the traditional masculinity of the traditional public sphere. For women to adopt a so-called masculine style of talk is to risk eliminating from public recognition the feminine and perpetuating a public sphere constituted of and through talk that valorizes male experience. Endorsement, even tacitly, of this sense of public talk means putting women at risk of failure simply for talking like women, because a willingness to speak biculturally leaves intact and dominant the rules of a single language game. Hence, the original problem of incommensurability asserts itself, though in a particularly troubling way: whose rules of discourse will be followed when the two language communities are to be addressed as one public? Biculturalism does not overcome the deficiencies of authorizing rhetorics; rather it validates the presence of more than one authorizing rhetoric.

But as Blankenship and Robson themselves uncover as they look at women political speakers, most do not speak biculturally, at least in the sense I have described. Forced to make decisions about how to adapt, women struggle to find ways of risking neither pluralism nor influence. In struggling, they provoke and test their inventiveness in negotiating the constraints of two authorizing language games. Blankenship and Robson say that female political speakers have responded to these dilemmas by speaking in such a way as to influence not just the audience but the dominant language; they "change the lexicon or redefine the existing [dominant] lexicon" (355). Geraldine Ferraro influences the existing lexicon when she redefines "toughness" in feminine terms as the sort of difficulty faced particularly by women like her mother, who find themselves in an unresponsive social system (355). Other speakers, notably Ann Richards, resist the constraints of the dominant language game by introducing feminine standards of political and social truth, like personal experience and inductive reasoning, into political discussion. Her rhetoric, as Bonnie J. Dow and Marie Boor Tonn argue, functions "as a critique of traditional grounds for political judgment" (286–87) and thus helps to change the dominant lexicon.

In each case, the speaker goes beyond speaking biculturally to find ways—and places—for the two divergent communities to meet. In this respect, these are examples of rhetorics that are inventive, active, and artistic, rather than authorizing. They aim at creating new constructs, new linkages, new conceptualizations.

Foregrounding inventive rather than authorizing rhetorics suggests a restatement of the questions I asked earlier about finding ways of acting, saying, and judging. Specifically, *saying* no longer needs to be regarded as collapsed into *choosing*. Finding something worthwhile to say no longer needs to be dependent on judgments offered from inadequate or competing epistemologies, but it emerges from the sort of judgment that belongs to rhetoric when it is recognized to be an art.

The locations where inventiveness may take place are the locations of the impossible: times when incommensurate positions must be negotiated, even though they should not be negotiable, and points where a speaker feels pressured by the desire to secure a place from which to speak. Furthermore, in negotiating specific incommensurabilities, agents exercise active artistic judgment to find a variety of openings and ways to take advantage of those openings.

The idea of finding an opening and acting on it suggests a response to the more general problem approached in this study: recapturing useful discussion in the face of the crisis of judgment. If we cannot and do not want to eliminate incommensurability or pluralism, and if pluralism means different language games, how can active artistic judgment and the inventive rhetoric I have been discussing help promote discussion? In this case, the agent exercising rhetorical judgment begins with the opening presented in the difficulty itself and invents by virtue of discovering links generated by the particular oppositions and contrasts inherent in the difficulty. The "weighing and measuring" activities that we usually associate with spectator judgment and that are threatened by incommensurability are not activities useful to the rhetor; they are not inventive activities. The metaphors of weighing and measuring imply a discarding or elimination of the less adequate option, the less authorized voice. Active artistic judgment responds to incommensurability with a metaphor of creativity that acts as a complement to "weighing and measuring." I would suggest examining the implications of a "stitching or weaving" metaphor for judgment.

A similar metaphor is suggested implicitly by Nancy Fraser in an essay dealing with the problems feminism faces with respect to pluralism and public discourse. Like Lyotard, Fraser rejects as inherently hegemonic and historically inaccurate Habermas's vision of a single, dominant public sphere with a single language game. She points to the presence of "subaltern" publics that exist in stratified societies: "parallel discursive arenas where members of subordinated social groups invent and circulate counterdiscourses," through their own journals, alternative newspapers, and conferences (123). Similarly, in more egalitarian societies that have a level of multiculturalism, we need to "suppose a plurality of public arenas in which groups with diverse values and rhetorics participate. By definition, such a society must contain a multiplicity of publics" (126).

The problem then becomes, as Fraser points out, envisioning the way in which these publics can talk together about issues affecting them all. When needing to "talk across lines of cultural diversity," how can they do so? She asks, "Would participants in such debates share enough in the way of values, expressive norms, and therefore protocols of persuasion to lend their talk the quality of deliberations aimed at reaching agreement through giving reasons?" (126).

Her optimistic language in response to that question is striking. While admitting that understanding, thought of as "multicultural literacy," is one component of good discourse among pluralities of publics, she implies that more is required. It is really the recognition of a looseness in cultural identities that permits cross-discourse: "Cultural identities are woven of many different strands, and some of these strands may be common to people whose identities otherwise diverge, even when it is the divergences that are most salient" (Fraser, 127). Finding and making use of those common strands extends multicultural literacy into conversation.

The active artistic judgment necessary to inventive rhetoric looks for openings in the weaves and for connecting strands. Not coincidentally, weaving is one of the roots of the concept of *kairos:* it is "the 'critical time' when the weaver must draw the yarn through a gap that momentarily opens in the warp of the cloth being woven" (White, 13). Also not coincidentally, the actions of stitching or weaving have been used to characterize the "poetic creation" of oral poets (Ford, 301), and a stitching together activity seems to be characteristic of the fundamental commonplacing that takes place in oral composition.[2] Predictably, then, a weaving or stitching metaphor suggests how the thinker exercises active judgment in her attempts to enter, take part in, and even redirect the course of an ongoing conversation.

There may be a number of examples of the ways in which inventive thinking reweaves the fabric of an existing conversation in a culture. One concrete example from an epic singing is noted by Berkley Peabody, who analyzes Homer's singing of the Shield of Achilles passage from the *Iliad* to show how a simple but critical mistake compels the singer to make an imaginative correction. The generative moment for the correction is the point in the song at which Achilles says he is going to battle. The singer realizes, however, that he had mistakenly had Achilles lose his weapons earlier, so going to battle would be impossible. Homer "retrogresses to an earlier point in his composition, from which he then re-sings his song in a modified way so as to obviate the former trouble" (231). In essence, the singer works back, finds a new opening, and weaves in an element to the story that had not been there before. In seeking to create the performance, the singer, weaver-like, must be sensitive to openings—in this case openings suggested by echoes, themes, and formulas—to draw up the next element and weave it into the fabric of the song. Although ever mindful that the song is not uniquely his own and that some violations of myth are blasphemous, the singer nonetheless acts inventively within mythic constraints. And in this case, his contribution is itself influential to the myth, because as is typical of epic, the passage is retained in subsequent singings, even when there is no longer a similar mistake: "Like all traditional utterances, a passage once uttered becomes almost metaphysically real; and this passage despite its correction remains the principal peripeteia of the *Iliad*" (232).

"Weaving" captures with some aptness the judgment of the singer in such a circumstance, and in turn the circumstances that prompt such judgment. Ever alert to the opening—the caesura—the artistic weaver locates ways to work new patterns, new elements into the fabric. Thus, she moves through the work, responsive to the demands of the moment, with neither the patterns, the elements, nor the openings fully her own. The desire to work the fabric in a certain direction occasions the exercising of judgment. However, a clear mental picture of the completed work does not drive the judgment of the weaver so much as a loosely figured picture does. In other words, the weaver sees only that something, within some loosely describable bounds, must be produced. Consequently, the weaver concentrates on the moment and thus may find opportunity even in the problems created by dropped stitches or other errors. In a similar way, we exercise this sort of judgment when, out of alertness and an expectation to produce something, we find intellectual differences as opportunities from which we may develop new ideas.

Contemporary instances of moral and practical incommensurability may be regarded as such opportunities. Mixing some metaphors is necessary to clarify. Moments of incommensurability, recognized as problems, act as occasions for generating new responses, ideas, options, patterns, or constructs. Incommensurability, therefore, is not seen as logically intractable, with one hierarchical system unassailable by the terms of another; it is seen as a moment in an ongoing conversation—which is an active, intellectual "matrixing"—at which the weave has become too tight on each side for the fabric to continue to be made. Incommensurate frames, thought of in this way, are points of *stasis*, not unassailable justificatory systems. At a point of *stasis*—where each of us often begins by feeling very assured of the solidity, unassailability, and completeness of her position—the creative effort of the interlocutors must begin with the effort to disentangle, dismantle, or loosen the weaves on both sides as they exist at the particular time in the conversation. They must be loosened, not in order to bring down whole positions, but in order to allow the weaving to continue. With the looseness of weave recovered, the artist is encouraged to pick up and bring threads from her position together with threads from the other. Like Cicero's interlocutor, the rhetor does not see her options as limited to adoption of one position or the other, nor does she necessarily seek a neutral standpoint from which to adjudicate between them. She is, however, prepared to use what she has before her to suggest the beginnings of new positions (or new systems, new narratives).

But the weaving that continues from a recognition of a disruption is not without direction; new moves are not introduced "from whole cloth," or for the sake solely of novelty, or solely to shake expectations (although novelty and changed expectations may result). New moves are the results of alerted responsiveness. In the case of the rhetor, what guides her choices is that "what she has before her" is a problem to be solved. Choices are motivated and guided always with a particular problem in mind; this is what gives shape, direction, and a sense of community to the rhetor's effort.

In the case of modern incommensurability, the rhetor's choices are initiated and guided by anxiety over the threat to the judging self. The contemporary recognition of incommensurability causes discomfort to the rhetor over what has been a fairly routine acceptance of her capacity and the capacity of the intellectual community to decide on practices by using other accepted practices of weighing and measuring. The awakening from a "dogmatic slumber" that results is akin to the alertness brought about by the realization that stitches have been dropped, or by the mistake identified by Homer as he sang the Achilles shield narrative. The desire to proceed does not mean removing the abnormality in the weave but picking it up so as to act creatively on it.

Thus, active artistic judgment suggests a response to specific incommensurabilities as well as to a general anxiety attributable to the contemporary crisis in judgment. The judgment of the actor acts as a complement to the weighing and measuring of the spectator, especially at moments in time that are driven by problems that fall outside of decision-making norms. The three *technai* of commonplacing, topical thinking, and *stasis* all help to pull the self into a position of necessary responsiveness, and promote her active artistic judgment.

Adapted as it was to the inventional needs of the Sophists, commonplacing provided a means of invention consistent with their communicative goals and their beliefs about language and truth. Driven by the obligation to produce persuasion and by a *kairotic* belief that truth is generated out of the moment, the Sophists learned to be responsive to the potentialities in language to produce plausibilities. Commonplacing suggests a concrete alternative to spectator judgment.

Cicero's antithetical method, when put to work in philosophical debate, had the power to overcome moments of *stasis* that might have rendered such productive interaction impossible. Whereas the commonplacing of the Sophists and of the epic poets located links between moments in time, the antithetical method, coupled with a Ciceronian antidogmatism, encouraged responsiveness to potential similarities and differences among opposing schools of thought. Methods for overcoming *stases* and moving the debate in directions consequential to adherents of the rival positions are necessary for the actively judging self.

Perhaps most critical to the satisfactory conceptualization of active artistic judgment, however, was Aristotle's development of the rhetorical uses of topical thinking. In distinguishing rhetoric from dialectic, Aristotle also distinguished actual from hypothetical debate, real work from imagined work, and practical wisdom from contemplative wisdom. Furthermore, by transferring the method of dialectical topics to the circumstances of real work, he validated *both* the playfulness of sophistic commonplacing and the earnestness of the political work of the community. Topical thinking, with its grounding in the world of real problem solving and its prompting by the sound of conflicting voices, is a means of "turning a thing over in our mind" with respect to the specifics of a problem; generating a practical truth is its aim.

Judging actively requires nurturing a skill at responsiveness to problems and a willingness to continually rediscover and remake one's own place as part of a community. The rhetorical self accepts considerable temporal instability. Alerted responsiveness means recognizing that problems are not solved forever. New positions, systems, patterns, and options that are responses to one problem will not provide responses for the next; they are places of *stasis*, in place until the next recognizable challenge. Acting rhetorically, therefore, means constantly guarding against the tyranny of complacent self-acceptance. The rhetorical self must be able to shift position in the world of ideas in order to find the uniqueness of the next problem. By the same token, active artistic judgment exists only in its exercise in actual practice. The rhetorical self, therefore, must be immersed in the public world, reacting to its instabilities through performance and productivity—acting and inventing. She is of the world of public ideas, sufficiently engaged to know when a truth needs to be told. Her creativity may not be achievable from a Platonic method, which specifies meeting established norms, but it may be achievable through *technai* that allow her rhetorical self to emerge and develop, by forcing her constantly to orient herself with other rhetorical selves.

Notes

Chapter One

1. See, for instance, Jean-François Lyotard's treatment of Nazism in *The Differend*, especially 86–106. Lyotard sees Nazism as in part historical turning point, in part inevitable moment, in manifesting the triumph of the mythic narrative over the narrative of rational discourse that has been dominant since the Enlightenment.

2. See Jacobson, *Pride and Solace*, 18–19.

3. Sources in speech communication include a literature on rhetoric and epistemology. See, for instance, Richard A. Cherwitz and James W. Hikins, *Communication and Knowledge: An Investigation in Rhetorical Epistemology;* Thomas Farrell, "Knowledge, Consensus, and Rhetorical Theory"; Robert Francesconi and Charles W. Kneupper, "Invention and Epistemic Rhetoric: The Knowing/Knowledge Interaction"; E. Claire Jerry, "Rhetoric as Epistemic: Implications of a Theoretical Position"; and Robert L. Scott, "On Viewing Rhetoric as Epistemic." Of these, Scott's early article is considered to be the pioneering effort. Considerations of communication as it relates to the philosophy of science are summarized and analyzed effectively in Lawrence J. Prelli, *A Rhetoric of Science: Inventing Scientific Discourse.* Among the most striking occurrences of an interest in communication with respect to science is Kuhn's invocation in *The Structure of Scientific Revolutions* of persuasion as playing a part in scientific knowing (94). His concept of persuasion is, as Prelli points out, "conceptually underdeveloped" (87). See also John Ziman, *Public Knowledge: The Social Dimension of Science.* Attention to communication by other philosophers is abundant, and some of that literature is reviewed herein. Among the most influential treatments of some of the problems I attend to is in Gadamer's placement of rhetoric near the center of his complaint against method. See, for instance, *Truth and Method*, 19–29.

4. Hereafter, *Philosophy and the Mirror of Nature* will be abbreviated as *PMN*.

5. One version of the paradox is that in arguing against systematic philosophy, Rorty may nevertheless be arguing systematically. See *Contingency, Irony, and Solidarity,* 7–8. For a less sympathetic view, see Mark Migotti, "Peirce's First Rule of Reason and the Bad Faith of Rortian Post-Philosophy."

6. Throughout, where issues of pronoun gender present themselves, I have opted to alternate the uses of *he, him,* and *his* with uses of *she* and *her.* There are important exceptions, though. Where historically appropriate, I have used the masculine pronouns; for instance, where I refer to the Aristotelian rhetor, I use the masculine pronoun. Because of the dominance of men in this particular story of rhetoric, I often use feminine pronouns when present-day references are made.

7. Although Albert Lord's cautionary observation about relying too heavily on textual analysis is directed toward studying the epic poets, it applies here as well: methods must be examined "not only from outside in terms of textual analysis, but also from

within, that is, from the point of view of the singer of tales and of the tradition" (30). Not to do so may be to confuse the judgment of the later spectator with that of the actor doing the inventing and performing. This is a problem that can lead to an underrating or at least a misunderstanding of the artistry involved in the invention. This difficulty has plagued scholarship on epic poetry and sophistic commonplaces (See chapter 4 below).

Chapter Two

1. Kuhn himself reviews and tries to correct some of what he considers "total misunderstandings" in chapter 13 of *Essential Tension* (see especially p. 321).

2. Craig Dilworth, in 1988 still found what he called the "Gestalt Model" to be applicable and provocative for describing key differences in scientific metatheorizing.

3. The impact on Western philosophy of thinking in visual terms is dealt with most thoroughly, of course, in Rorty's *Philosophy and the Mirror of Nature*, but some works of Walter Ong, particularly *Orality and Literacy*, take up the subject of that impact. Carl Holmberg's essay "Dialectical Rhetoric and Rhetorical Rhetoric" is a lesser known source that deals provocatively with the force that visual-philosophical thought has exerted on even ancient rhetoric.

4. This totalizing effect of visual "systems" like paradigms is taken up in Chapter 6 in the discussion of the *stasis* method of invention.

5. It is worth noting that the original definition of commensurability, drawn from geometry, is visual, structural, and static; and it assumes inherently the importance of comparison. Kuhn's description of the geometric roots of the term is as follows: "The hypotenuse of an isosceles right triangle is incommensurable with its side or the circumference of a circle with its radius in the sense that there is no unit of length contained without residue an integral number of times in each member of the pair. There is thus no common measure." Kuhn goes on to point out, though, that "lack of a common measure does not make comparison impossible" ("Commensurability," 670). Describing and defending the possibility of comparison in those other situations is the point of his essay.

6. Davidson has expanded on this idea since this early publication and produced a line of thought that has had a strong influence on Rorty (see chapter 1 of his *Contingency, Irony and Solidarity*). For an early response by Davidson to Rorty, see Davidson's "Afterthoughts" to his "A Coherence Theory of Truth and Knowledge" in *Reading Rorty*, edited by Alan R. Malachowski.

7. Pearce, Freeman, Littlejohn and Alexander have, at several times subsequently to the 1987 article, examined the rhetoric of the "New Christian Right" as it relates to moral conflict. See Pearce, Littlejohn, and Alexander, "The Quixotic Quest for Civility: Patterns of Interaction Between the New Christian Right and Secular Humanists"; Freeman, Littlejohn, and Pearce, "Communication and Moral Conflict"; and Pearce and Littlejohn, *Moral Conflict*.

8. Kathleen Hall Jamieson, in *Eloquence in and Electronic Age*, complains that "contemporary political discourse tends to reduce the universe to two sides—one good,

one evil. . . . After drawing simplistic and often false dichotomies, contemporary speech tends to canonize one side and anathematize the other" (11).

9. For one dramatic example of the way Cartesianism muted voices, see Jacques Derrida's critique of Foucault's *Madness and Civilization*, "Cogito and the History of Madness," in *Writing and Difference.*

10. The fiction writer Salman Rushdie commented in his 1995 interview with Terry Gross that ours was the first generation in which a display of rage was seen to be sufficient warrant for a person to be given what he wants.

11. Arendt's "theory" of judgment had not actually been written at the time of her death. Beiner and others have divined it from what is strongly implicit in her other writings. See Beiner, "Interpretive Essay," in Arendt's *Lectures on Kant's Political Philosophy.*

12. I do not mean to imply here that there is no role for the listener in the development of meaning. Current thinking in rhetorical theory has been to break down the strictness of the traditional dichotomy of speaker/producer and listener/receiver. As a result, the study of rhetoric has been disabused of the notion that a listener has little to do with the development of meaning in a rhetorical transaction. In fact, the very idea that an individual truly originates meaning has come into question as well. I do make the point, however, that there is a type of judgment attributable to the person who *sees herself positioned* as speaker/producer and that serious study of that form of judgment has recently been overlooked. Barry Brummett, in his brief history of the study of popular culture as rhetoric, indicates that since the eighteenth century, interest in the judgment of "critics" or "consumers" of texts has grown, while interest in how people "originally produce" texts has diminished (50). I argue that the problem of incommensurability reintroduces a need to look at the judgment of the producer.

13. This insight was derived from remarks by Andrew Ford during a National Endowment for the Humanities Institute on the Greek Enlightenment, June 29, 1989.

14. This description of *apatê* as artful acting does not reflect a standard translation, which emphasizes the ideas of distortion and deception. I take up the question in more detail in Chapter 3.

Chapter Three

1. See, for instance, Russell H. Wagner's "The Meaning of Dispositio," 292–93. I believe my observation about the separation in time between invention and judgment holds even when an element of choice is introduced under the heading of invention, as it is when Cicero advises his son to scan all the topics for arguments and then use judgment to choose the stronger ones. See Clark, *Rhetoric in Greco-Roman Education*, 76–79, for a brief discussion of Cicero on this matter. Perhaps methods involving the *stasis* questions suggest more clearly that there is a component of judging that must be integrated with inventing. See Baldwin, *Ancient Rhetoric and Poetic*, 74–76.

2. Roberts translation; bracketed portions mine. All translations of Aristotle's *Rhetoric* are from Roberts, which I believe to be a particularly clear and pointed translation, unless otherwise noted. When appropriate, I have footnoted alternative transla-

tions, as well. Interestingly, Lawson-Tancred's translation of this passage also emphasizes the importance of system to Aristotle, while using the term "method": "Amongst the general public, then, some perform these tasks haphazardly, others by custom and out of habit, and since they admit of being carried out in both ways, it is apparent that it would also be possible to do them by a method. For it is possible to study the reason for success both by those who succeed by habituation and of those who do so by chance, and anything that is just of this kind everyone would agree to be the province of an art."

3. Perhaps it is a little unfair to Aristotle to suggest that he drew the boundary between rational and irrational so definitively, especially since, as Lawson-Tancred points out, Aristotle was at pains to include rhetoric among rational activities (14–17). Still, definitions of rationality were at the stake for Aristotle; and they came to be set in terms of systematization. Furthermore, at some subsequent points in history it was in terms of system that rhetoric was excluded from the rational, because it could not be reduced *only* to method. The narrowness of such a conception of rationality led Perelman and Olbrechts-Tyteca to ask, "Must we draw from this evolution of logic . . . the conclusion that reason is entirely incompetent in those areas which elude calculation and that, where neither experiment nor logical deduction is in a position to furnish the solution of a problem, we can but abandon ourselves to irrational forces, instincts, suggestion, or even violence?" (3).

4. I take this topic up again later in a discussion of Heidegger in the chapter on topics.

5. In "Creativity—A Dangerous Myth," Feyerabend provides a fascinating portrait of the dangers inherent in the contemporary mythology of creativity, which, he says, assumes erroneously that human beings *"start* causal chains, they are not just carried along by them" (707).

6. Although most of the time I will specify that I am discussing Gorgias or Protagoras, when I refer to the Sophists as a group, I refer to a "standard" list of fifth-century teachers referred to by Plato. This list includes Protagoras, Gorgias, Prodicus, Hippias, Thrasymachus, Critias, and Antiphon (Schiappa, "Oasis," 5–6). The list varies among writers according to their definitional criteria (see Schiappa, *Protagoras*, 3–12). In fact, there are accepted historical problems in defining the term *Sophist* (see Nehemas, "Eristic"), and problems in specifying a category of "sophistic rhetoric" at all (for Schiappa's summary of his ongoing debate with Poulakos on this latter topic, see *Protagoras,* 69–81). In accepting the "traditional" list, I bracket many of these issues in order to appropriate that fourth- and fifth-century thought that may help recapture a sense of active artistic judgment. To do so, I often respect the utility of contrasting Platonic or Aristotelian thought about language with "sophistic" thought.

7. Guthrie, mainly on evidence from Plato, notes that Protagoras, Gorgias, Thrasymachus, Prodicus, and Hippias all claimed to teach something like an art (*Sophists,* n.4, 44–45). Schiappa (*Protagoras*) delimits the definitional category "Sophist" in part as "those first professional educators who, more often than not, are associated with the *technê* (art or skill) of prose speech" (12).

8. I am indebted for this insight to Andrew Ford's lectures during the summer of 1989.

9. Plato's condemnation of those who could speak on either side of an issue accurately reflects his attitude toward the Sophists. However, some of his sharpest criticism of what he regarded as false philosophy was probably directed toward contemporaries who, he believed, did ruthless and careless battle based on word-play. Popular fascination with such "educators" needed to be reduced if the truth-seeking purpose of genuine philosophy was to survive and the proper education of the young was to be redeemed. See Plato's dialogue, *Euthydemus*.

10. Actually, Aristotle saw system more in terms of habit and practice than I give him credit for here. I deal with this question more fully in chapter 5 on topics.

11. See Richard Bett, "The Sophists and Relativism" and Schiappa, *Protagoras*, 126–30.

12. Gorgias, for instance, is reported to have studied with Empedocles (Untersteiner, 92; de Romilly, 14).

13. There is no extant version of Gorgias's treatise, but two reports of it exist, one by Sextus Empiricus and the other by the anonymous writer of *On Melissus, Xenophanes, and Gorgias*. A series of articles in *Philosophy and Rhetoric* (vol. 30, 1997) provides discussion of the virtues of each of these sources as well as the challenges of translating and interpreting the texts. References to Sextus's report of the text are to *The Older Sophists*, edited by Rosamund Kent Sprague.

14. Schiappa ("Interpreting Gorgias's 'Being'") identifies at least four serious "schools" of response.

15. The likelihood that Gorgias was responding to Parmenides is by no means universally accepted. Schiappa and Hoffman uphold the likelihood of that response while identifying and refuting arguments to the contrary.

16. Barnes, *The Presocratic Philosophers*.

17. See W. J. Verdenius, "Gorgias' Doctrine of Deception," for a counteropinion.

18. See Segal, "Gorgias and the Psychology of the Logos"; de Romilly, *Magic and Rhetoric in Ancient Greece;* Mourelatos, "Gorgias on the Function of Language"; and Adkins, "Form and Content in Gorgias' *Helen* and *Palamedes.*"

19. The same story is told of the still more ancient teachers of speech, Corax and Tisias, and may be a fiction. See Schiappa, *Protagoras*, 215.

20. There is some controversy about this point. G. B. Kerferd (45) reports that Gorgias was likely to have produced a treatise on rhetoric, *On the Right Moment in Time*, but White, without taking up Kerferd's assertion per se, argues the logical inconsistency of reducing the Gorgian *kairos* to principle (pt. 1, esp. 17). Probably Gorgias's work consisted of collections of model speeches (Untersteiner 96 and Guthrie, *Sophists*, 270).

21. I take all quoted material from "The Funeral Address" from Untersteiner who, I acknowledge, provides a rather liberal interpretation.

22. In fact, Dale L. Sullivan sees the Gorgian *kairos* as sufficiently disconnected from systematic procedure that Sullivan prefers to associate the Gorgian *kairos* with

"inspiration" rather than with "invention," although he acknowledges in a note that the place of *technê* in Gorgias's thought (that is, whether or not his *kairos* can even be called art or method) is controversial (319).

23. Again, Aristotle's rhetoric may be read as an example of a rhetoric that seeks to remove dissonance. I claim, however, that in Aristotelian rhetoric there is also a principle of *kairos* at work. See chapter 5 on topics.

Chapter Four

1. See Kennedy 102, and Ong, *Presence* 79–87.

2. A fuller exposition and examination of Protagoras's "two *logoi*" idea may be found in Schiappa, *Protagoras*, especially ch. 5.

3. See Schiappa, *Protagoras* 146–48.

4. See, for instance, Friedrich Solmsen's and Michael Gagarin's reviews of Havelock's *The Greek Concept of Justice* and Jack Goody and Ian Watt's "The Consequences of Literacy." Solmsen and Gagarin both dispute aspects of Havelock's literacy thesis long after it was originally published. Goody and Watt support and extend what has come to be called Havelock's "Great Leap" or the "Great Divide" theory of revolutionary cultural change in Havelock's in more recently observed cultures. On a related front, see a special edition of *Pre/Text* 7 (1986), entitled "The Literacy/Orality Wars," edited by C. Jan Swearingen, which takes up questions of the relevance of any cognitive differences in literacy and orality to our contemporary understandings of literacy. Of special interest to the present discussion are Swearingen's "Literate Rhetors and Their Illiterate Audiences: The Orality of Early Literacy," 145–64; Beth Daniell's "Against the Great Leap Theory of Literacy," 181–94; and Eric Havelock's "After Words: A Post Script," 201–8.

5. There is, of course, a limit to what may be inferred from Parry and Lord's observations. For instance, the Yugoslav poets, although illiterate themselves, did not live in a culture in which literacy had not been invented, as did Homeric bards. Still, it is helpful to remember that Parry and Lord, as classicists, were interested less in the Yugoslav poets than in finding evidence to confirm or disconfirm what their less direct study of the art of Homer had already led them to believe was the case of the ancient poets. Their work continues to have its defenders and detractors. For a sense of the debate, see J. A. Russo, "Is Oral or Aural Composition the Cause of Homer's Formulaic Style?"; Ian Morris, "The Use and Abuse of Homer"; and William F. Wyatt Jr., "Homer in Performance: *Iliad* I.348–427."

6. This habit is apparent as well in the frequent use of simile and conspicuous absence of metaphor in the Homeric epics. Versenyi writes that "the poetic device that contributes most to making even the ever-recurring moment varied and vivid is in its nature as paratactic, atomistic, and present-oriented as is Homeric time. Unlike the metaphor that fuses the dissimilar, the Homeric simile keeps the compared terms strictly separate and lets them touch at one or more points of similarity without merging" (*Man's Measure*, 9).

7. Whether or not the epic age was as uncritical as Versenyi and Havelock suppose

has been questioned. See, for example, Adkins, "Orality and Philosophy"; Jarratt, *Rereading the Sophists;* and Dallas Willard, "Concerning the 'Knowledge' of the Pre-Platonic Greeks."

8. The relationship between poetic and archaic philosophical prose is by no means clear. Havelock wrote, in 1983, "that what we call Greek literature from Hesiod down through the classical period is composed in a condition of increasing tension between the demands of the ear and the new possibilities afforded by the eye" ("Linguistic Task of the Presocratics," in Kevin Robb, ed., *Language and Thought in Early Greek Philosophy,* 9). The particulars of that tension are dealt with in the essays in Robb.

9. Cole sees what I am calling elaborations in the *Palamedes* to be "appropriate grounds for dismissing such cases in almost any situation" (76). In other words, rather than being a series of arguments generated through balances, the *Palamedes*, according to Cole, was written to be a pedagogical tool, a sort of mnemonic device that would allow students to remember and call up various arguments to suit the demands of a particular case.

Chapter Five

1. De Romilly provides a fuller description of this similarity in *Magic and Rhetoric in Ancient Greece.*

2. See Brian McHale, *Postmodernist Fiction,* 44–45.

3. These two statements of justice themselves provide a good example of incommensurability.

4. Although both Plato and Aristotle saw truth as prior, they saw truth as being grounded in different ways. Kennedy, in his translation of the *Rhetoric,* renders a phrase in this passage as follows: "because the true and the just are by nature stronger than their opposites" (1354b.12), and adds in a note that "Aristotle believed that truth was grounded in nature (*physis*) and capable of apprehension by reason. In this he differs both from Plato (for whom truth is grounded in the divine origin of the soul) and from the sophists (for whom judgments were based on *nomos* [convention], which in turn results from the ambivalent nature of language as the basis of human society)" (34).

5. Kathy Eden in *Poetic and Legal Fiction in the Aristotelian Tradition* has effectively described the role of image and imagination in legal judgment for Aristotle and for later rhetoricians. Legal judging and imagining are linked together and enriched by one another in Aristotle's thought. The capacity for what later would be called *similitudo* is linked to judging. Eden notes that the capacity for legal judging "is linked in the human soul to the act of imagining, so crucial to both rhetoric and poetry" (63).

6. This interpretation is based on the analysis by Lawrence W. Rosenfield in *Aristotle and Information Theory.*

7. For further perspectives on this distinction, see Bernard A. Miller, "Heidegger and the Gorgian *Kairos";* James S. Baumlin, "Decorum, Kairos, and the 'New' Rhetoric"; and Poulakos, "Toward a Sophistic Definition of Rhetoric."

8. John Wilson and Carroll C. Arnold developed a set of contemporary topics for the contemporary speaker drawn from an analysis of a thesaurus widely in use at the

time (the 1970s). In a discussion of these topics, Arnold stated that "a rhetorical topos must point a rhetor's mind to specific ways in which *both* speaker *and* audiences are *used* to thinking about and saying things" (in-class communication, 1976).

9. Interestingly, Freese translates "at short notice" as "on the spur of the moment."

10. It must be noted that Pirsig's protagonist failed to find such a method, a failure which precipitated his nervous breakdown.

11. Roberts translates: "The true and the approximately true are apprehended by the same faculty." Lawson-Tancred translates: "For it lies within the province of the same capacity to discern both truth and verisimilitude."

12. The essay referred to here, "Dialectic and Aristotle's *Topics*," was first published in 1978 in *Boethius's De Topicis Differentiis*, and was reprinted in Stump's later work, *Dialectic and Its Place in the Development of Medieval Logic*. References here are all to the 1978 work.

13. The final element in this series was suggested in correspondence from Carroll C. Arnold.

14. Beiner adds, by implication, that a false clarity in the *polis*, a complacency that requires correcting, also calls out rhetoric. He suggests the need, sometimes, for "provoking, perhaps even shocking, those whom I address" (*Political Judgment*, 96).

15. Each listing of the strategies included under the Possible, for instance, begins, in Ross's translation with "It may plausibly be argued" (1392a 8–9).

16. It needs to be stressed that Price himself is opposed to such a derogation of the enthymeme.

17. See Heidegger's essays "The Question Concerning Technology" and "The Origin of the Work of Art." For further consideration of Heidegger's need to respond to accusations of humanism, see Versenyi, *Heidegger, Being, and Truth*, chs. 2 and 3. For an interesting summary of Heidegger's ongoing difficulties with "placing" human beings within his scheme, see Michael E. Zimmerman, *Heidegger's Confrontation with Modernity*, ch. 11.

18. Actually, despite the changes to the notion of *technê* that Heidegger sees as attributable to Plato, Heidegger links Aristotle's notion of *technê* both to occasioning and to bringing forth. See "Question Concerning Technology," 12–13.

19. Worsham is citing Cyril Welch, "An Introduction to Writing." She quotes, specifically, from pages 79 and 78.

20. Nothstine acknowledges that he draws this insight from Robert L. Scott and James F. Klumpp's essay, "A Dear Searcher into Comparisons: The Rhetoric of Ellen Goodman."

Chapter Six

1. Later in the chapter, I treat as identifiable terms that should, in most cases, be distinguished; I intentionally use terms as diverse as "frame of reference," "philosophical position," or "paradigm" as virtually interchangeable with "conceptual system" as I use it here. I do so in order to identify these terms as similarly understandable as structured, hierarchical, and visual. For a thorough treatment of the ways in which such con-

cepts can be distinguished as well as identified, see Schiappa, "Burkean Tropes and Kuhnian Science."

2. It is interesting to consider the visual bias of a number of popular definitions of "argument." Featured regularly are definitions like this first one from the *Oxford English Dictionary:* "Proof, evidence, manifestation, token." The first definition in the 1993 Merriam Webster *Collegiate Dictionary* provides an even more dramatic example: "an outward sign." The association between argument, proving, and showing is striking. The implication is that argument consists of proving, which consists of a movement of mind from sign back to nature. This is consistent with Aristotle's equation, in the *Posterior Analytics,* of knowing with demonstration.

3. Cicero used two words for the questions or issues: *constitutiones* was used to refer to the questions in their rhetorical use, and *quaestiones* to refer to the questions used for philosophical debate. Primarily for simplicity's sake, I have used *constitutiones* throughout for both uses. Similarly, I have used *quaestio* to refer to the subject matter of a debate, regardless of whether or not the debate was forensic or philosophical. Cicero would have reserved *quaestio* for rhetorical matters and used the word *causa* for philosophical ones. See Buckley, 149 and 150.

4. None of this, of course, prevents Cicero from identifying himself with the New Academics for most of his career.

5. Lucullus himself identified the belief that accurate perception was impossible as a cornerstone of the New Academic position, but without setting the assertion up in its relationship to the opposing school. Cicero, however, indicated that the assertion gained its significance *as* the key point of difference between the rivals. The debate itself, and the relationships of difference between the schools that emerge from it and shape it, are of preeminent importance to Cicero.

6. See chapter 2 above on "Normal Rhetoric."

7. The original Public Conversations team included Richard Chasin, Margaret Herzig, Sallyann Roth, Laura Chasin, and Carol Becker (Chasin et al., 323).

8. See John T. Gage, "Towards an Epistemology of Composition."

Chapter Seven

1. I should add that the displays that Booth and MacIntyre might attribute to emotivism would not be so attributed by everyone, nor would they be considered evidences of a degraded rhetoric. Lyotard, for instance, might see them as "paralogisms."

2. Although I am using stitching and weaving as variations on the same theme, Ford's analysis is persuasive in showing that the stitching metaphor was distinct from the weaving metaphor in ancient references to ancient singing. Each metaphor had its own important significance in these references.

Works Cited

Adkins, Arthur W. H. "Form and Content in Gorgias' *Helen* and *Palamedes:* Rhetoric, Philosophy, Inconsistency and Invalid Argument in Some Greek Thinkers." *Essays in Ancient Greek Philosophy.* Ed. John P. Anton and Anthony Preus. Albany: State U of New York P, 1983. 107–28.

———. "Orality and Philosophy." *Language and Thought in Early Greek Philosophy.* Ed. Kevin Robb. La Salle, Ill.: Monist, 1983. 207–27.

Arendt, Hannah. *Between Past and Future: Six Exercises in Political Thought.* New York: Viking, 1961.

Arnold, Carroll C. "Oral Rhetoric, Rhetoric, and Literature." *Philosophy and Rhetoric* 1 (1968): 191–210.

———. "Rhetorical Topoi." Paper delivered at the annual convention of the Speech Communication Association, Houston, Texas, 1975.

Baldwin, Charles Sears. *Ancient Rhetoric and Poetic.* Gloucester, Mass: Peter Smith, 1959.

Barnes, Jonathan. *The Presocratic Philosophers.* Rev. ed. London: Routledge and Kegan Paul, 1982.

Bartley, William W. III. *The Retreat to Commitment.* New York: Knopf, 1962.

Baumlin, James S. "Decorum, Kairos, and the 'New' Rhetoric." *Pre/Text* 5 (1984): 171–83.

Becker, Carol, and Laura Chasin, Richard Chasin, Margaret Herzig, and Sallyann Roth. "From Stuck Debate to New Conversation on Controversial Issues: A Report from the Public Conversations Project." *Journal of Feminist Family Therapy* 7, 1/2 (1995): 143–63.

Beiner, Ronald. Interpretive essay. *Lectures on Kant's Political Philosophy.* By Hannah Arendt. Ed. Ronald Beiner. Chicago: U of Chicago P, 1984. 89–156.

———. *Political Judgment.* Chicago: U of Chicago P, 1983.

Bernstein, Richard J. *Beyond Objectivism and Relativism: Science, Hermeneutics, and Praxis.* Philadelphia: U of Pennsylvania P, 1983.

Bett, Richard. "The Sophists and Relativism." *Phronêsis* 34 (1989): 139–69.

Beye, Charles Rowan. *Ancient Greek Literature and Society.* 2nd. ed. rev. Ithaca: Cornell UP, 1987.

Bitzer, Lloyd F. "The Rhetorical Situation." *Philosophy and Rhetoric* 1 (1968): 1–14.

Blankenship, Jane, and Deborah C. Robson. "A 'Feminine Style' in Women's Political Discourse: An Exploratory Essay." *Communication Quarterly* 43 (1995): 353–66.

Booth, Wayne C. *Modern Dogma and the Rhetoric of Assent.* University of Notre Dame Ward-Phillips Lectures in English Language and Literature, vol. 5. Chicago: U of Chicago P, 1974.

Brummett, Barry. *Rhetoric in Popular Culture.* New York: St. Martin's, 1994.

Buchan, D. *The Ballad and the Folk.* London: Routledge and Kegan Paul, 1972.

Buckley, Michael J. "Philosophical Method in Cicero." *Journal of the History of Philosophy* 8 (1970): 143–54.

Burke, Kenneth. "Poetics and Communication." *Perspectives in Education, Religion, and the Arts.* Ed. Howard E. Kiefer and Milton K. Munitz. Albany: State U of New York P, 1970.

Burnet, J. *Early Greek Philosophy.* 4th ed. London: Adam and Charles Black, 1930.

Carter, Michael. "*Stasis* and *Kairos:* Principles of Social Construction in Classical Rhetoric." *Rhetoric Review* 7 (1988): 97–112.

Chasin, Richard, Margaret Herzig, Sallyann Roth, Laura Chasin, Carol Becker, and Robert R. Stains Jr. "From Diatribe to Dialogue on Divisive Public Issues: Approaches Drawn from Family Therapy." *Mediation Quarterly* 13 (1996): 323–44.

Cherwitz, Richard A., and James W. Hikins. *Communication and Knowledge: An Investigation in Rhetorical Epistemology.* Columbia: U of South Carolina P, 1986.

Clark, Donald Lemen. *Rhetoric in Greco-Roman Education.* New York: Columbia UP, 1957.

Cole, Thomas. *The Origins of Rhetoric in Ancient Greece.* Baltimore: Johns Hopkins UP, 1991.

Condit, Celeste Michelle. *Decoding Abortion Rhetoric: Communicating Social Change.* Urbana: U of Illinois P, 1990.

"Conversation Therapy for Abortion Foes." Narr. Noah Adams, Rept. Tovia Smith. *All Things Considered.* Natl. Public Radio. WRVO, Oswego, New York, 3 July 1992.

Copleston, Frederick. *A History of Philosophy: Greek and Rome.* New rev. ed. A History of Philosophy 1, parts 1 and 2. Garden City, N.Y.: Image Books, 1962.

Daniell, Beth. "Against the Great Leap Theory of Literacy." *Pre/Text* 7 (1986): 181–93.

Davidson, Donald. "A Coherence Theory of Truth and Knowledge." *Reading Rorty: Critical Responses to Philosophy and the Mirror of Nature (and Beyond).* Ed. Alan R. Malachowski. Oxford: Basil Blackwell, 1990. 120–38.

————. "On the Very Idea of a Conceptual Scheme." *Proceedings of the American Philosophical Association* 47 (1973–74): 5–20. Rpt. in *Relativism.* Ed. Jack W. Meiland and Michael Krausz. Notre Dame: U of Notre Dame P, 1982. 66–80.

De Romilly, Jacqueline. *Magic and Rhetoric in Ancient Greece.* Cambridge: Harvard UP, 1975.

Derrida, Jacques. *Writing and Difference.* Trans. Alan Bass. Chicago: U of Chicago P, 1978.

Dilworth, Craig. "The Gestalt Model of Scientific Progress." In *Scientific Knowledge: Selected Proceedings of the Joint International Conference on the History and Philosophy of Science Organized by the IUHPS.* Ed. Imre Hronszky, Márta Fehér, Balázs Dajka. Dordrecht: Kluwer, 1988.

Dieter, Otto Loeb. "Stasis." *Speech Monographs* 17 (1950): 345–69.

Dow, Bonnie J., and Marie Boor Tonn. " 'Feminine Style' and Political Judgment in the Rhetoric of Ann Richards." *Quarterly Journal of Speech* 79 (1993): 286–302.

Duncan, Thomas Shearer. "Gorgias' Theories of Art." *Classical Journal* 33 (1938): 402–15.

Eden, Kathy. *Poetic and Legal Fiction in the Aristotelian Tradition.* Princeton: Princeton UP, 1986.

Enos, Richard Leo. *Greek Rhetoric before Aristotle.* Prospect Heights, Ill.: Waveland, 1993.

Farrell, Thomas. "Knowledge, Consensus, and Rhetorical Theory." *Quarterly Journal of Speech* 62 (1976): 1–14.

Feyerabend, Paul. *Against Method: Outline of an Anarchistic Theory of Knowledge.* London: Verso, 1978.

———. "Creativity: A Dangerous Myth." *Critical Inquiry* 13 (1987): 700–711.

Finnegan, Ruth. *Oral Poetry.* Cambridge: Cambridge UP, 1977.

Ford, Andrew. "The Classical Definition of ΡΑΨΩΙΔΙΑ." *Classical Philology* 83 (1988): 300–307.

Foss, Sonja K. "Equal Rights Amendment Controversy: Two Worlds in Conflict." *Quarterly Journal of Speech* 65 (1979): 275–88.

Francesconi, Robert, and Charles W. Kneupper. "Invention and Epistemic Rhetoric: The Knowing/Knowledge Interaction." *Visions of Rhetoric: History, Theory and Criticism.* Ed. Charles W. Kneupper. Arlington, Texas: Rhetoric Society of America, 1987. 106–15.

Fraser, Nancy. "Rethinking the Public Sphere: A Contribution to the Critique of Actually Existing Democracy." *Habermas and the Public Sphere.* Ed. Craig Calhoun. Cambridge: MIT P, 1992. 109–42.

Freeman, Sally A., Stephen W. Littlejohn, and Barnett Pearce. "Communication and Moral Conflict." *Western Journal of Communication* 56 (1992): 311–29.

Gadamer, Hans-Georg. *Truth and Method.* Trans. and ed. Garrett Barden and John Cumming. New York: Seabury, 1975.

Gagarin, Michael. Rev. of *The Greek Concept of Justice: From Its Shadow in Homer to Its Substance in Plato*, by Eric Alfred Havelock. *American Journal of Philology* 101 (1980): 128–31.

Gage, John T. "Towards an Epistemology of Composition." *Journal of Advanced Composition* 2 (1981): 1–9.

Ginsburg, Faye D. *Contested Lives: The Abortion Debate in an American Community.* Berkeley: U of California P, 1989.

Goody, Jack, and Ian Watt. "The Consequences of Literacy." *Literacy in Traditional Societies.* Ed. Jack Goody. Cambridge: Cambridge UP, 1968. 27–68.

Grassi, Ernesto. *Rhetoric as Philosophy.* University Park: Pennsylvania State UP, 1980.

Gregg, Richard B. *Symbolic Inducement and Knowing: A Study in the Foundations of Rhetoric.* Columbia: U of South Carolina P, 1984.

Guthrie, W. K. C. *The Presocratic Tradition from Parmenides to Democritus.* Vol. 2 of *A History of Greek Philosophy.* Cambridge: Cambridge UP, 1965.

———. *The Sophists.* Cambridge: Cambridge UP, 1971.

Habermas, Jürgen. *Legitimation Crisis.* Trans. Thomas McCarthy. Boston: Beacon, 1975.

Harvey, David. *The Condition of Postmodernity: An Enquiry into the Origins of Cultural Change.* Oxford: Basil Blackwell. 1989.

Hauser, Gerard A. "Searching for a Bright Tomorrow: Graduate Education in Rhetoric During the 1980's." *Communication Education* 28 (1979): 259–70.

Havelock, Eric A. "After Words: A Post Script." *Pre/Text* 7 (1986): 201–8.

———. "The Linguistic Task of the Presocratics." *Language and Thought in Early Greek Philosophy.* Ed. Kevin Robb. La Salle, Ill.: Monist, 1983. 7–82.

———. *The Literate Revolution in Greece and Its Cultural Consequences.* Princeton: Princeton UP, 1982.

———. *Preface to Plato.* Cambridge: Belknap Press of Harvard UP, 1963.

Heidegger, Martin. *An Introduction to Metaphysics.* Trans. Ralph Manheim. New Haven: Yale UP, 1959.

———. "The Origin of the Work of Art." Trans. Albert Hofstadter. *Basic Writings.* Ed. David Farrell Krell. New York: Harper, 1977. 143–88.

———. "The Question Concerning Technology." Trans. William Lovitt. *"The Question Concerning Technology" and Other Essays.* New York: Harper, 1977. 3–35.

Holmberg, Carl. "Dialectical Rhetoric and Rhetorical Rhetoric." *Philosophy and Rhetoric* 10 (1977): 232–43.

Irwin, Terence. Introduction. *Gorgias* by Plato. Trans. Terence Irwin. Clarendon Plato Series. Oxford: Clarendon, 1979.

Jacobson, Norman. *Pride and Solace.* Berkeley: U of California P, 1978.

Jameson, Fredric. Foreword. *The Postmodern Condition: A Report on Knowledge* by Jean-François Lyotard. Trans. Geoff Bennington and Brian Massumi. Minneapolis: U of Minnesota UP, 1979.

Jamieson, Kathleen Hall. *Beyond the Double Bind: Women and Leadership.* New York: Oxford UP, 1995.

———. *Eloquence in an Electronic Age: The Transformation of Political Speechmaking.* New York: Oxford UP, 1988.

Jarratt, Susan C. *Rereading the Sophists: Classical Rhetoric Refigured.* Carbondale: Southern Illinois UP, 1991.

Jerry, E. Claire. "Rhetoric as Epistemic: Implications of a Theoretical Position." *Visions of Rhetoric: History, Theory and Criticism.* Ed. Charles W. Kneupper. Arlington, Texas: Rhetoric Society of America, 1987. 119–134.

Johnstone, Christopher Lyle. "Ethics, Wisdom, and the Mission of Contemporary Rhetoric: The Realization of Human Being." *Central States Speech Journal* 32 (1981): 177–88.

Kant, Immanuel. *The Critique of Pure Reason.* Trans. Norman Kemp Smith. New York: St. Martin's, 1987.

Kennedy, George A. *The Art of Persuasion in Greece.* Princeton: Princeton UP, 1963.

Kerferd, G. B. *The Sophistic Movement.* Cambridge: Cambridge UP, 1981.

Kuhn, Thomas S. "Commensurability, Comparability, Communicability." *Proceedings of the Biennial Meeting of the Philosophy of Science Association.* Ed. P. D. Asquith and T. Nickles. East Lansing: Philosophy of Science Association, 1983. 669–88.

———. *The Essential Tension: Selected Studies in Scientific Tradition and Change.* Chicago: U of Chicago P, 1977.

————. "Rationality and Theory Choice." *Journal of Philosophy* 80 (1983): 563–70.

————. *The Structure of Scientific Revolutions.* 2nd ed. enlarged. Foundations of the Unity of Science Vol. 2, No. 2. Chicago: U of Chicago P, 1970.

Levy, Jeffrey J. "The Influence of Cicero on the Rhetorical Perspective of Richard McKeon." Master's thesis, Pennsylvania State U, 1974.

Littlejohn, Stephen W. *Theories of Human Communication.* 4th ed. Belmont, Calif.: Wadsworth, 1992.

Lord, Albert B. *The Singer of Tales.* New York: Athenaeum, 1976.

Lyotard, Jean-François. *The Differend: Phrases in Dispute.* Minneapolis: U of Minnesota P, 1988.

————. *The Postmodern Condition: A Report on Knowledge.* Trans. Geoff Bennington and Brian Massumi. Minneapolis: U of Minnesota P, 1979.

MacIntyre, Alasdair. *After Virtue.* 2nd ed. Notre Dame: Notre Dame UP, 1984.

Makin, Stephen. "How Can We Find Out What the Ancient Philosophers Said?" *Phronêsis* 33 (1988).

Malachowski, Alan R., ed. *Reading Rorty: Critical Responses to Philosophy and the Mirror of Nature (and Beyond).* Oxford: Basil Blackwell, 1990.

Matteo, Anthony M. "Grounding the Human Conversation." *Thomist* 53 (1989): 235–58.

McHale, Brian. *Postmodernist Fiction.* New York: Methuen. 1987.

McKeon, Richard. "Rhetoric and Poetic in the Philosophy of Aristotle." *Aristotle's "Poetics" and English Literature.* Ed. Elder Olson. Chicago: U of Chicago P, 1965. 201–36.

Migotti, Mark. "Peirce's First Rule of Reason and the Bad Faith of Rortian Post-Philosophy." *Transactions of the Charles S. Peirce Society* 31 (1995): 89–136.

Miller, Bernard A. "Heidegger and the Gorgian *Kairos.*" *Visions of Rhetoric: History, Theory and Criticism.* Ed. Charles W. Kneupper. Selected Proceedings of the Rhetoric Society of America, May 29–June 1 1986, Arlington, Texas. Arlington: Rhetoric Society of America, 1987. 169–84.

Milo, Ronald D. *Aristotle on Practical Knowledge and Weakness of Will.* Studies in Philosophy 6. The Hague: Mouton, 1966.

Morris, Ian. "The Use and Abuse of Homer." *Classical Antiquity* 17 (1986): 81–138.

Mourelatos, Alexander P. D. "Gorgias on the Function of Language." *Philosophical Topics* 15 (1987): 135–70.

Nehemas, Alexander. "Eristic, Antilogic, Sophistic, Dialectic: Plato's Demarcation of Philosophy from Sophistry." *History of Philosophy Quarterly* 7 (1990): 3-16.

Nothstine, William L. " 'Topics' as Ontological Metaphor in Contemporary Rhetorical Theory and Criticism." *Quarterly Journal of Speech* 74 (1988): 151–63.

Notopoulos, James A. "Parataxis in Homer: A New Approach to Homeric Literary Criticism." *Transactions of the American Philological Association* 80 (1949): 1–23.

Ochs, Donovan J. "Aristotle's Concept of Formal Topics." *Speech Monographs* 36 (1969): 419–25.

Ong, Walter J. *Orality and Literacy: The Technologizing of the Word.* New Accents. London: Methuen, 1982.

————. *The Presence of the Word: Some Prolegomena for Cultural and Religious History.* New York: Simon, 1967.

————. "Ramist Rhetoric." Ong. *Ramus—Method and Decay of Dialogue.* Cambridge: Harvard UP, 1958. Rpt. in *The Province of Rhetoric.* Ed. Joseph Schwartz and John A. Rycenga. N.Y.: Ronald, 1965. 226–55.

Peabody, Berkley. *The Winged Word: A Study in the Technique of Ancient Greek Oral Composition as Seen Principally through Hesiod's* Works and Days. Albany: State U of New York P, 1975.

Pearce, W. Barnett, and Stephen W. Littlejohn. *Moral Conflict: When Social Worlds Collide.* Thousand Oaks, Calif.: Sage, 1997.

Pearce, W. Barnett, Alison Alexander, and Stephen W. Littlejohn. "The New Christian Right and the Humanist Response: Reciprocated Diatribe." *Communication Quarterly* 35 (1987): 171–92.

Pearce, W. Barnett, S. W. Littlejohn, and Alison Alexander. "The Quixotic Quest for Civility: Patterns of Interaction Between the New Christian Right and Secular Humanists." *Secularism and Fundamentalism Reconsidered: Religion and the Political Order.* Vol. 3. Ed. J. K. Hadden and A. Shupe. New York: Paragon House. 152–77.

Perelman, Ch., and L. Olbrechts-Tyteca. *The New Rhetoric: A Treatise on Argumentation.* Trans. John Wilkinson and Purcell Weaver. Notre Dame: U of Notre Dame P, 1969.

Perry, B. E. "The Early Greek Capacity for Viewing Things Separately." *Transactions of the American Philological Association* 68 (1937): 410-12.

Pirsig, Robert M. *Zen and the Art of Motorcycle Maintenance.* New York: William Morrow & Co., 1974.

Porus, N. L. "Incommensurability, Scientific Realism and Rationalism." *Scientific Knowledge Socialized: Selected Proceedings of the 5th Joint International Conference on the History and Philosophy of Science Organized by the IUHPS, Vezprem, 1984.* Ed. Imre Hronszky, Márta Fehér, Balázs Dajka. Dordrecht: Kluwer, 1988. 375–83.

Poulakos, John. "Rhetoric, the Sophists, and the Possible." *Communication Monographs* 51 (1984): 215–26.

————."Toward a Sophistic Definition of Rhetoric." *Philosophy and Rhetoric* 16 (1983): 35–48.

Prelli, Lawrence J. *A Rhetoric of Science: Inventing Scientific Discourse.* Columbia: U of South Carolina P, 1989.

Price, Robert. "Some Antistrophes to the Rhetoric." *Philosophy and Rhetoric* 1 (1968): 145–64.

Putnam, H. "Philosophers and Human Understanding." *Scientific Explanation: Papers Based on Herbert Spencer Lectures Given in the University of Oxford.* Ed. A. F. Heath. Oxford: Clarendon, 1981. 99–120.

Robb, Kevin, ed. *Language and Thought in Early Greek Philosophy.* La Salle, Ill.: Monist, 1983.

Rorty, Richard. *Contingency, Irony and Solidarity.* Cambridge: Cambridge UP, 1989.

———. "The Historiography of Philosophy: Four Genres." *Philosophy in History: Essays on the Historiography of Philosophy.* Ed. Richard Rorty, John B. Schneewind, and Quentin Skinner. Cambridge: Cambridge UP, 1984. 49–75.

———. *Philosophy and the Mirror of Nature.* Princeton: Princeton UP, 1979.

———. "Science as Solidarity." *The Rhetoric of the Human Sciences: Language and Argument in Scholarship and Public Affairs.* Ed. John S. Nelson, Allan Megill, and Donald N. McCloskey. Madison: U of Wisconsin P, 1987. 38–52.

Rosenfield, Lawrence W. *Aristotle and Information Theory: A Comparison of the Influence of Causal Assumptions on Two Theories of Communication.* The Hague: Mouton, 1971.

Rosenmeyer, Thomas G. "Gorgias, Aeschylus, and *Apatê.*" *American Journal of Philology* 76 (1955): 225–60.

Rushdie, Salman. Inter. Terry Gross. *Fresh Air.* National Public Radio. WRVO, Oswego, New York. 25 Jan. 1995.

Rushing, Janice Hocker. "*E.T.* as Rhetorical Transcendence." *Quarterly Journal of Speech* 71 (1985) 188–203.

Russo, J. A. "Is Oral or Aural Composition the Cause of Homer's Formulaic Style?" *Oral Literature and the Formula.* Ed. B. A. Stolz and R. S. Shannon. Ann Arbor: Center for the Coordination of Ancient and Modern Studies, University of Michigan, 1976. 31–71.

Schiappa, Edward. "Burkean Tropes and Kuhnian Science: A Social Constructionist Perspective on Language and Reality." *Journal of Advanced Composition* 13 (1993): 401–22.

——— "Interpreting Gorgias's 'Being' in *On Not Being or On Nature.*" *Philosophy and Rhetoric* 30 (1997): 13–30.

———*Protagoras and Logos: A Study in Greek Philosophy and Rhetoric.* Columbia: U of South Carolina P, 1991.

———"Sophistic Rhetoric: Oasis or Mirage?" *Rhetoric Review* 10 (1991): 5–18.

Schiappa, Edward, and Stacey Hoffman. "Intertextual Argument in Gorgias's *On What Is Not:* A Formalization of Sextus. *adv Math 7.77–80.*" *Philosophy and Rhetoric* 27 (1994): 156–61.

Schiappa, Edward, and Omar Swartz. Introduction. *Landmark Essays on Classical Greek Rhetoric.* Ed. Edward Schiappa. Davis, Calif.: Hermagoras, 1994.

Scott, Robert L. "On Viewing Rhetoric as Epistemic." *Central States Speech Journal* 18 (1967): 9–17.

Scott, Robert L., and James F. Klumpp. "A Dear Searcher into Comparisons: The Rhetoric of Ellen Goodman." *Quarterly Journal of Speech* 70 (1984): 69–79.

Segal, Charles P. "Gorgias and the Psychology of the Logos." *Harvard Studies in Classical Philology* 66 (1962): 99–155.

Solmsen, Friedrich. Rev. of *The Greek Concept of Justice: From its Shadow in Homer to Its Substance in Plato,* by Eric A. Havelock. *Classical World* 72 (1979): 430–31.

Stump, Eleonore. "Dialectic and Aristotle's *Topics.*" In *Boethius's De Topicis Differentiis.* Trans. Eleonore Stump. Ithaca: Cornell UP, 1978. 159–78.

————. *Dialectic and Its Place in the Development of Medieval Logic.* Ithaca: Cornell UP, 1989. 10–30.

Sullivan, Dale L. "*Kairos* and the Rhetoric of Belief." *Quarterly Journal of Speech* 78 (1992): 317–32.

Swearingen, C. Jan. "Literate Rhetors and Their Illiterate Audiences: The Orality of Early Literacy." *Pre/Text* 7 (1986): 145–62.

Untersteiner, Mario. *The Sophists.* Trans. Kathleen Freeman. New York: Philosophical Library, 1954.

Verdenius, W. J. "Gorgias' Doctrine of Deception." *The Sophists and Their Legacy.* Ed. G. B. Kerferd. Proceedings of the Fourth International Colloquium on Ancient Philosophy with Projektgruppe Altertumswissenschaften der Thyssenstifting at Bod Homberg, Aug. 29–Sept. 1, 1979. Wiesbaden: Steiner, 1987. 116–28.

Verene, Donald Phillip. *Vico's Science of Imagination.* Ithaca: Cornell UP, 1981.

Versenyi, Laszlo. *Heidegger, Being, and Truth.* New Haven: Yale UP, 1965.

————. *Man's Measure: A Study of the Greek Image of Man from Homer to Sophocles.* Albany: State U of New York P, 1974.

Wagner, Russell H. "The Meaning of Dispositio." *Studies in Speech and Drama in Honor of Alexander M. Drummond.* Ithaca: Cornell UP, 1944. 285–94.

Weimer, Walter B. "Science as a Rhetorical Transaction: Toward a Nonjustificationist Conception of Rhetoric." *Philosophy and Rhetoric* 10 (1977): 1–29.

Weinsheimer, Joel C. *Gadamer's Hermeneutics: A Reading of Truth and* Method. New Haven: Yale UP, 1985.

Welch, Cyril. "An Introduction to Writing." *Philosophy and Rhetoric* 17 (1984): 73–97.

White, Eric Charles. *Kaironomia: On the Will to Invent.* Ithaca: Cornell UP, 1987.

Willard, Dallas. "Concerning the 'Knowledge' of the Pre-Platonic Greeks." *Language and Thought in Early Greek Philosophy.* Ed. Kevin Robb. La Salle, Ill.: Monist, 1983. 244–54.

Wilson, John F., and Carroll C. Arnold. *Public Speaking as a Liberal Art.* 4th ed. Boston: Allyn and Bacon, 1978.

Worsham, Lynn. "The Question Concerning Invention: Hermeneutics and the Genesis of Writing." *Pre/Text* 8 (1987): 197–246.

Wyatt, William F., Jr. "Homer in Performance: *Iliad* I.348–427." *Classical Journal* 83 (1988): 289–97.

Ziman, John. *Public Knowledge: The Social Dimension of Science.* Cambridge: Cambridge UP, 1968.

Zimmerman, Michael E. *Heidegger's Confrontation with Modernity: Technology, Politics, and Art.* Bloomington: Indiana UP, 1990.

Zyskind, Harold. "Some Philosophical Strands in Popular Rhetoric." *Perspectives in Education, Religion, and the Arts.* Ed. Howard E. Kiefer and Milton K. Munitz. Albany: State U of New York P, 1970.

Translations of Classical Works

Unless otherwise noted, translations of Aristotelian works are from the following sources:

Aristotle. *Categories*. Trans. E. M. Edghill. *The Basic Works of Aristotle*. Ed. Richard McKeon. New York: Random House, 1941.

———. *On Interpretation*. Trans. E. M. Edghill. In McKeon.

———. *Nichomachean Ethics*. Trans. W. D. Ross. In McKeon.

———. *Politics*. Trans. Benjamin Jowett. In McKeon.

———. *Posterior Analytics*. Trans. G. R. G. Mure. In McKeon.

———. *Rhetoric*. Trans. W. Rhys Roberts. In McKeon.

———. *Topics*. Trans. W. A. Pickard-Cambridge. In McKeon.

Other translations of *The Rhetoric* are the following:

Aristotle's "Art" of Rhetoric. Trans. Henry Freese. Loeb Classical Library. Cambridge: Harvard UP, 1982.

Aristotle, *On Rhetoric: A Theory of Civic Discourse*. Trans. with Introduction, Notes, and Appendices by George A. Kennedy. New York: Oxford UP, 1991.

Aristotle, *The Art of Rhetoric*. Trans. H. C. Lawson-Tancred. London: Penguin, 1991.

Works by Cicero are all from Loeb Classical Library editions:

Cicero. *De Inventione*. Trans. H. M. Hubbell. Loeb. Cambridge: Harvard UP, 1976.

———. *De Natura Deorum* and *Academica*. Trans. H. Rackham. Loeb: Harvard UP, 1961.

———. *De Oratore*. Trans. E. W. Sutton and H Rackham. Vols. 3–4. Loeb. Cambridge: Harvard UP, 1976 and 1977.

———. *Tusculan Disputations*. Trans. J. E. King. Loeb. Cambridge: Harvard UP, 1960.

Unless otherwise noted, translations of works of the Sophists and of ancient commentators on the Sophists are taken from the following:

The Older Sophists: A Complete Translation by Several Hands of the Fragments in Die Fragmente Der Vorsokratiker by Diels-Kranz. Ed. Rosamond Kent Sprague. Columbia: U of South Carolina P, 1972.

Index